Institutional Development

þ12

A World Bank Publication

Institutional Development
Incentives to Performance

Arturo Israel

Published for The World Bank
THE JOHNS HOPKINS UNIVERSITY PRESS
Baltimore and London

The Johns Hopkins University Press
Baltimore, Maryland 21211
First printing October 1987
First paperback printing January 1989
Second paperback printing July 1990

The findings, interpretations, and conclusions
expressed in this study are the results of research
supported by the World Bank, but they are entirely
those of the author and should not be attributed
in any manner to the World Bank, to its affiliated
organizations, or to members of its Board of
Executive Directors or the countries they represent.

Library of Congress Cataloging-in-Publication Data

Israel, Arturo.
  Institutional development.

  "Published for the World Bank."
  Includes bibliographies and index.
  1. Economic development projects—Developing
countries. I. International Bank for Reconstruction
and Development. II. Title.
HC59.72.E44177   1987   338.9′009172′4   87-45494
ISBN 0-8018-3873-8

Contents

Preface   ix

1. *Institutional Weakness: A Roadblock to Development   1*

   Experience with Institutional Development   1
   Overview   4
   Note   7

Part I. Patterns of Institutional Development

2. *Methodology   11*

   Definitions   11
   Efficiency and Effectiveness   12
   Data Base   14
   Notes   17

3. *The World Bank's Experience   18*

   General Results   19
   Sectoral and Subsectoral Patterns   20
   Country Patterns   22
   Patterns by Activity   23
   Results by Type of Investment   24
   Notes   26

4. *The Standard Explanations   28*

   The State of the Art   28
   The Explanations   31
   Notes   41

Part II. Alternative Explanations

5. *Specificity   47*

   The Concept of Specificity   48
   Potential for Specification   52

Nature of Effects   57
How the Actors Are Affected   61
Reactions of the Actors   64
Toward a Specificity Index   68
Notes   72

6. *Technology and the Degree of Specificity*   74

Industry, Modernity, and Organization Theory   75
Characteristics of Technology   77
Special Cases   81
The World Bank's Experience   85
Notes   87

7. *Competition and Competition Surrogates*   89

Definitions   89
Mechanisms   92
Limitations of Competition   96
The World Bank's Experience   101
Interactions   104
Notes   106

Part III. Operational Conclusions

8. *National Strategies to Increase Institutional Capacity*   111

Elements of a Countrywide Operational Strategy   113
Macro Implications of Specificity and Competition   120
Wages and Salaries   126
Commitment   132
Notes   142

9. *The Performance of Individual Institutions*   145

General Strategies   146
Mechanisms to Compensate for Lack of Specificity   150
Mechanisms to Compensate for Lack of Competition   165
Notes   176

10. *A Successful Managerial Approach: The Training and Visit System of Agricultural Extension*   178

Basic Principles of Organization and Management   179
Prerequisites of Success   183
Criticisms of T&V   185
Application of T&V Principles to Other Activities   187
Further Improvements in T&V   191

Notes *192*

11. *Conclusions for Program and Project Design* *193*

The Problem of Complexity *195*
Recommendations *197*
Note *200*

Appendix *202*

Index *208*

Development depends not so much on finding optimal combinations for given resources and factors of production as on calling forth and enlisting for development purposes resources and abilities that are hidden, scattered or badly utilized.
                —Albert O. Hirschman, *Strategy for Economic Development*

Preface

This book has had a long gestation period and has been a personal project on the side, mostly weekends and holidays, for several years. The idea emerged in the late 1970s, during my tenure as project policy adviser at the World Bank. From the broad perspective of that position, it quickly became clear that many of the real problems with development programs and projects lay not so much in their design and planning as in their implementation. Moreover, the real implementation problems were mostly institutional and managerial—in other words, rooted in the difficulties countries have in getting things done. Although this obviously was not a new or startling discovery, I was surprised that relatively little attention was being given to these problems—except for a string of general statements about their importance—and that it was implicitly accepted that anybody, from any profession, could deal with institutional issues. As discussed in the book, the main reason for this attitude is that institutional development is considered a "soft" subject, one which can be handled in the course of normal operations by engineers, economists, financial analysts, or whoever happens to be involved. Since institutional development is everybody's business, it often becomes, in practice, nobody's business.

While continuing to work as project policy adviser, I began to spend an increasing proportion of my time on matters of institutional development, getting to know and understand the Bank's experience and participating in operational work. The initial opportunity to review the Bank's experience more systematically and acquaint myself with the literature came during a five-month period in 1979 at Queen Elizabeth House in Oxford, as part of a sabbatical year. Upon my return to the Bank, work pressures and the expanding activities in institutional development left little time for research and writing. Still, snatching time here and there, I was able to have a first draft ready early in 1983. But then, paradoxically, success conspired against making further progress. The establishment of the Public Sector Management Unit at the Bank and the launching of a large program in this area, under my direction, made it impossible to continue with the project. The manuscript languished for two and a half years until Warren Baum gave me the idea that eventually saved the effort. I became a visiting scholar at the Rockefeller Foundation's Center in Bellagio, Italy, where I spent the month of October 1985 updating and completing the manuscript. After that, the timing has been the normal one to be expected of a sideline such as this.

During this long period many people have helped in many ways, and it would be very difficult to give full credit to all of them. I wish to highlight a few: Herman van der Tak, who supported the original efforts and the sabbatical leave, and Visvanathan Rajagopalan, who quietly encouraged me to continue with the project and supported the Bellagio stint. Warren Baum, Richard Heaver, James Kearns, Francis Lethem, Linda Muller, Samuel Paul, Nimrod Raphaeli, and Peter Wright, from the Bank, read the initial draft and made important comments that helped me recast the paper. Very useful suggestions were made by Robert Chambers, from the Institute of Development Studies at the University of Sussex, John Montgomery, of Harvard University, and two anonymous reviewers.

David Leonard, from the University of California, Berkeley, and his colleagues Paula Consolini and Julia Strauss deserve a special mention. They undertook an in-depth review of the manuscript and, among other things, advised me on the literature to support the arguments made in the book and suggested approaches and perspectives to consider.

Dorothy Aaby and Zenaida Kranzer also deserve a special mention, because they were kind enough to type and retype the manuscript in addition to their normal work at the Bank, all the while having to contend with a computer illiterate like me, who still insists on using yellow pads.

And, last but not least, my family, and especially my wife, Miriam, deserve special mention for their support and patience during the long periods when this sideline claimed much of my free time. In fact, Miriam acted for a long time as an unpaid and willing research assistant. She deserves much credit, and this book is dedicated to her in more than one way.

July 1987

1 Institutional Weakness: A Roadblock to Development

Institutional development refers to the process of improving the ability of institutions to make effective use of the human and financial resources available. The field has been defined in many different ways and sometimes goes under other names, which refer to all or parts of it: institution building, public sector management, public administration, and so on. No matter which label is used, the main objective is to make effective use of a country's resources, an objective that is central to the development effort and has acquired special urgency in the recent economic crisis.

The interest in institutional development is by no means new. It has always been part of development strategies, with high points closely related to impulses from development agencies or foundations. The Rockefeller and Ford Foundations, for example, had programs to establish public administration and management institutes in the 1950s and 1960s, and the U.S. Agency for International Development undertook institution building in the 1960s and early 1970s. Each cycle has had its pluses and minuses, and all have left a sizable positive legacy. At present, we seem to be on the upswing of another cycle, with new sponsors and approaches, in which the World Bank has played a central role.

Experience with Institutional Development

Institutional development, in one form or another, has been part of the World Bank operations almost since its inception. Most programs financed by the Bank contain not only "hard" investments—in physical components such as railway rolling stock, roads, power plants, and irrigation systems—but also a component usually called institutional development. A highway program may include, in addition to construction, several measures to improve the effectiveness of the highway agency. These measures would provide the necessary funds for technical assistance and could range from a general reorganization to the strengthening of specific functions, such as planning, accounting, maintenance, or staff training. In cases where most of the investment is in the provision

1

of services, such as agricultural extension, education, or health care, institutional development might be the main objective.

By the mid-1970s, many of the original institutional development programs were completed and had been in operation for a while, and the Bank had begun systematic ex post evaluations of them. It then became more apparent that the physical components of programs had generally been more successful than the institutional development components. Building a highway seems to be easier than maintaining it or improving the financial management of a highway department. It is easier to build irrigation canals than to put a workable water management system in place, and so on. In fact, general Bank reviews of past activities have consistently arrived at the conclusion that the physical components of programs have been successful about twice as often as have institutional development components. And in reviews of difficulties and delays in implementation, managerial or institutional problems emerge as the most important causes, although their exact nature is seldom defined or analyzed in detail.

During the same period, the Bank increased its emphasis on poverty alleviation and launched massive efforts in integrated rural and urban development programs, population and health services, and primary education. It therefore had to work with some of the weakest and more difficult institutions in a country. The difficulties intrinsic to these institutions make success even more problematic and highlight the need to improve the effectiveness of institutional development programs. In the early 1980s, to help countries deal with the worldwide recession and the depression in many of their economies, the Bank broadened its activities to include so-called structural adjustment and sectoral adjustment loans. These programs have presented new challenges for central government agencies, with such functions as the management of economic policies, and for the institutional structure of sectors.

As a result, the interest and activities in institutional development have increased, not only at the World Bank but among other development agencies, the academic community, and the countries themselves. At the Bank, several activities have been completed or are under way: the *World Development Report 1983*[1] on the topic of management in development is especially noteworthy, as is the ongoing review of the Bank's experience, to which this volume contributes.

Within the development community, however, in spite of strong statements about the essential role of institutional development, there is a sort of fatalism about its potential contribution to the development effort. Institutional weakness is considered to be one of those problems about which not much can be done. Until recently, many practitioners had given up trying. Instead, they suggested intensifying other factors—

investments, education, even cultural change—to see whether these troublesome institutional weaknesses could be overcome or bypassed, or whether institutions might solve the problem by themselves. Other specialists have adopted an intellectually elegant form of escapism; they ignore those aspects of the development process, such as institutional issues, that cannot be nicely quantified and concentrate on those that can be analyzed through equations.

Why? There seem to be two main reasons. One is that development theory and practice have been for a long time in the hands of economists, who have a long tradition of focusing on resource allocation and allocative efficiency, not on the most effective ways of *using* the allocated resources. In most development strategies the emphasis is still on planning and appraisal but not on implementation, on investments and policies but not on operations. Moreover, the quantitative bias of economics and economic development in recent decades favors the analysis of resource allocation issues, such as planning and forecasting, rather than issues of implementation, which are less quantifiable.

To be sure, economists dealing with development have been aware of this problem for a long time, beginning with Schumpeter and especially with Hirschman. The "unexplained residual factor" has been closely linked to management and organization and, through them, to the culture and politics of a particular society. Leibenstein talks about X efficiency, Bauer about the aptitudes and attitudes of the population and the nature of the social institutions and political arrangements. These "unexplained" factors deal with how things work; it is a question not only of allocating resources well but also of using them well. Aside from acknowledging the existence of these factors, however, most economists still happily return to their equations.

The second reason for the neglect of institutional issues is that it is indeed a messy area. The disciplines such as management science and development administration have not been particularly successful in tackling the problems of developing countries. The main thrust of management science has been toward private sector issues in developed countries, and there have been difficulties in adapting it to public or mixed activities in poorer and more politicized environments. Development administration has emerged only recently from an excessive emphasis on the formal aspects of organization. Many attempts have been made to improve the effectiveness of institutions in developing countries, but without much success.

Thus, the dialogue between the administrators and managers and the specialists from other disciplines involved in development has not been very productive. There is an impatience to do things that are tangible: when in doubt, build another road, or rebuild one; don't get lost in the intricacies of attempting to improve the maintenance organization. Moreover, the application of organizational or managerial approaches has often been ill-adapted to a specific cultural and political milieu and may have been more damaging than if the solution had been left to local traditions and common sense.

Policymakers shy away from areas that they cannot grasp or that experts do not seem to understand well. Although many policymakers are aware of the importance of institutions in a development strategy, they still do not give it the necessary priority, in part because they believe that there is no clear way of going about it. And of course building and inaugurating are politically more attractive than maintaining or operating. This is a pity, because the waste implicit in the ineffective use of resources is undoubtedly at the core of underdevelopment.

Overview

This volume explores a couple of avenues that look promising in helping to increase the effectiveness of institutional development programs. Part I explores the patterns of success or failure found in ex post evaluations of programs undertaken by the World Bank, and attempts to define the causes. Contrary to expectations, the pattern of results of institutional development programs was stronger by sector, subsector, and activity than by country. The most successful were found in industry, telecommunications, utilities, and finance; the least successful in agriculture, education, and services. Within institutions, technical and financial activities fared the best, while maintenance, personnel issues, and coordination were the least successful.

In trying to explain the success of institutional development, the World Bank's evaluations focus on the local commitment to the institutional development program, the absence of price distortions, the successful application of management techniques, good planning and careful preparation of the programs, outstanding managers, and exogenous factors. These explanations, however, do not provide a sufficiently satisfactory conceptual framework or an adequate explanation of the pattern of results found by the evaluations.

Part II then concentrates on two other factors, labeled "specificity" and "competition," which seem to provide a more coherent explanation of institutional performance and which offer incentives to improve that performance.

Specificity is defined in terms of two groups of elements: (1) the extent to which it is possible to specify for a particular activity the objectives to be attained, the methods of achieving those objectives, and the ways of controlling achievement and rewarding staff; and (2) the effects of the activity—their intensity, how long it takes for them to become apparent, the number of people and other activities affected, and the practical possibilities of tracing the effects. The hypothesis developed here is that the higher the degree of specificity, the more intense, immediate, identifiable, and focused will be the effects of an activity. Conversely, the lower the degree of specificity, the weaker, less identifiable, and more delayed and diffuse will be those effects.

To illustrate this concept, a spectrum of activities is discussed that ranges from those with high specificity, mainly high-technology, financial, or industrial activities, to those with low specificity, mainly low-technology, social activities related to human behavior (people-oriented), such as rural development programs and health care. The extent of specificity will affect the operations of the institution and the behavior of its staff. Low-specificity activities are shown to offer very weak incentives and to permit a wide latitude in the definition of jobs and in the degree of freedom left to the staff. Conversely, high specificity imposes a stricter definition of jobs, fewer degrees of freedom, and less latitude in the organizational structure. In general, lack of specificity makes the management of an activity far more complex and difficult.

Competition is defined much more broadly than in the traditional economic concept. In addition to external competition from others attempting to provide the same or similar goods or services, three other kinds of competitive pressures may possibly be exerted on an organization. They are referred to here as competition, or market, surrogates because they are capable of influencing institutional performance when market competition is not possible or desirable. These pressures could be brought to bear by clients, beneficiaries, or suppliers; by the political establishment and controlling and regulatory agencies (acting as clients and shareholders); and by managerial and organizational measures that create a competitive atmosphere among units and individuals within the institution.

The detailed analysis and development of these concepts of specificity and competition reveal the enormous handicap under which the low-specificity, noncompetitive activities operate. They simply do not have these two powerful incentives to performance. This conclusion is important for a country's development strategy, since the activities at the nonspecificity, noncompetitive end of the spectrum are the very ones that are crucial to the alleviation of poverty and to progress in rural areas.

Part III then develops the operational implications of specificity and competition for the country as a whole and for individual entities or groups of them.

The experience to date and the analysis in this book suggest that countries need to become more aware of the importance of improving institutional performance and of reducing the demands on institutions and managers made by development programs. They need to give higher priority to the plight of low-specificity and noncompetitive activities and design institutional solutions especially for them; they simply cannot use the techniques and approaches that have worked in high-specificity, competitive activities. Despite the lure and prestige of technology, developing countries will break out of poverty mainly through activities at the other end of the spectrum. The study concludes that in addition to improving the performance of individual entities countries can raise the level of performance of all the institutions in a given sector or in the economy as a whole by adopting policy measures that derive directly from the concepts of specificity and competition.

Other conclusions have to do with the choice of technologies that are appropriate to the managerial capacity available; the remuneration and general incentives for managers and highly skilled personnel, which will enable the country to retain those skills; and the ways of assessing and building up a country's commitment to an institutional development program.

Operational conclusions pertaining to the performance of individual institutions suggest managerial and organizational measures to simulate the incentives provided by specificity and competition when they are weak or nonexistent. Because the intrinsic characteristics of low-specificity activities make the design and implementation of strong incentives almost impossible, modifications of such standard management tools as recruitment, incentives to personnel, and training are proposed in order to introduce specificity surrogates. Emphasis is placed on such nonpecuniary approaches as professionalization (the introduction of professional values and standards) at all levels of the hierarchy. Ways of changing the role of managers themselves are also considered, which would strengthen their professional and operational support of their subordinates and increase their involvement in the external political environment affecting their institution.

The competitive atmosphere faced by an institution is partly defined by government policies regarding foreign trade, monopolies, regulations, and so on. In addition, a government could adopt a "competition policy" that would establish the extent to which it is willing to promote some of the competition surrogates that are discussed in this book. They include increasing the external competition faced by public entities by allowing private concerns to compete with all or part of their activities; making the rules under which some public entities operate closer to those prevailing in competitive environments; organizing clients, beneficiaries, and suppliers to exert pressure on public institutions; and using the pressure from politicians and regulators to help an agency achieve its objectives. Competition surrogates internal to an organization are also explored. They include ways that managers can encourage competition among individuals or groups and organizational changes to promote better performance.

Chapter 10 then reviews one managerial approach that so far seems to be the most successful attempt at combining many of the operational conclusions arrived at in this analysis. This is the training and visit system of agricultural extension. Its principles could easily be applied to the provision of other services such as health care, family planning, and nutrition. They may even have some general application to less obvious areas such as primary education, industry, and the management of large agencies.

The last set of conclusions relates to program design and complexity. Chapter 11 concludes that some programs are excessively complex because their design does not take account of institutional weaknesses. Programs often try to attack several development constraints simultaneously. They therefore require so many components and place so many demands on the institutional structure of the country that they are doomed to failure. This final chapter reviews various ways of avoiding this mistake and of balancing the economic, technical, and institutional factors in the design of a program. In particular, the simplification of objectives and the reduction in the number of programs, especially in low-specificity and noncompetitive activities, will greatly increase the chances of success of those programs. Most developing countries can successfully undertake only a few development programs at a time.

Note

1. New York: Oxford University Press, 1983.

Part I

*Patterns
of Institutional
Development*

2 Methodology

Why is the performance of one institution better than that of another in a similar environment? There is little in the literature that deals directly with this central question, and there is no accepted theory in this field. But that is no reason not to look for answers. After all, there are many levels and kinds of knowledge. Although a full theory of institutional effectiveness is not possible at this stage, the purpose of this book is to seek partial explanations, analytical frameworks in which parameters are not clearly specified, and even a few models—that is, educated insights with practical implications. This exploratory purpose determines the methodology. The data on which the study is based are of uneven quality and are used mainly to trigger the formulation of hypotheses. Thus, I have followed the time-honored approach of finding a few facts and then trying to explain them.

Definitions

The terms "institution" and "institutional development," or "institution building," mean different things to different people. Here institutional development is synonymous with institution building and is defined as the process of improving an institution's ability to make effective use of the human and financial resources available. This process can be internally generated by the managers of an institution or induced and promoted by the government or by development agencies.[1]

The broad concept of institution encompasses entities at the local or community level, project management units, parastatals, line agencies in the central government, and so on. An institution can belong to the public or the private sector and may also refer to governmentwide administrative functions. This study focuses on individual institutions or groups of institutions: a ministry of education, a railway company, an industrial plant, an agricultural development bank, a power agency, a rural extension service, a farmers' cooperative, or the local branch of a central government agency.

Typically, institutional development (or institutional analysis) is concerned with management systems, including monitoring and evaluation; organizational structure and changes; planning, including planning for an efficient investment process; staffing and personnel policies; staff training; financial performance, including financial management and planning, budgeting, accounting, and auditing; maintenance; and procurement. Other issues, especially under a sectoral or subsectoral focus, are interagency coordination and sectoral policies regarding institutions.

Efficiency and Effectiveness

Institutional effectiveness is relative to the location, activity, and technology of the institution. Assessing effectiveness and making comparisons across countries, sectors, and technologies therefore raises formidable methodological problems. How does one compare, for example, similar activities in different regions or countries (is the telecommunications agency in Burkina Faso more effective than that in Colombia?), or different types of institutions within the same country (is the pipeline company in Bolivia more effective than the agricultural development bank?), or even different types of institutions in different countries (is the industrial plant in Turkey more effective than the highway department in Thailand?).

To what extent are such comparisons possible? Several clarifications are in order. First, it is important to keep in mind the distinction between efficiency and effectiveness. The concept of effectiveness is broader and should include the capacity of an institution to define and agree on its appropriate operational objectives. In this context the criterion for effectiveness is how well an organization is doing relative to its own set of standards. But effectiveness can also be measured with regard to standards that are external to the institution. There is, however, no consensus in the literature on which external standards to use. For example, some analysts emphasize the impact of the institution on individual participants (the sociopsychological level of analysis).[2] Another group focuses on institutional contributions to societal systems.[3]

The concept of efficiency refers only to the way in which the resources available are used to achieve the objectives established, without regard to whether those objectives or goals are the right ones. Technically, an efficient institution is one exhibiting a high ratio of output to input. In this sense, an inefficient organization can be relatively effective if it achieves the right objectives, even though at a high cost. Conversely, and often with more damaging results, an institution could be considered efficient from an input-output perspective, but be pursuing the wrong objectives. For example, a technical school could be very efficient in training a type of technician not required by the country, or a factory could be producing more fertilizer than is necessary.[4]

Another distinction is that between allocative and operational efficiency. Allocative efficiency has to do with the allocation of resources through prices, markets, and administrative interventions. Operational efficiency has to do with maximizing "the use of labor and capital through the sound management of enterprises, projects, and programs in both the public and private sectors."[5]

Second, a strict comparison of effectiveness among institutions is neither possible nor really necessary. Economists will understand that an attempt to compare effectiveness among institutions is similar to the attempts in economic theory to make interpersonal comparisons of utility: it is not possible but, more to the point, it is not necessary for a sound theory. All that is required is an ordinal measurement, a ranking, that can be defined in very general terms. It is sufficient for our purposes to establish whether institution A has been more effective *in its own field* (a sector or subsector) than institution B in its field. This ranking is helped by the possibility of making more precise comparisons of effectiveness among activities that are common to many institutions. For example, accounting has to be undertaken in some form in practically all cases, and there are objective standards to compare the effectiveness of accounting systems which would apply equally to a hospital or a steel mill. When several activities—such as personnel management, maintenance, and some types of training—are appraised in this way, the ranking of effectiveness among institutions becomes more accurate. In addition, comparisons have to take into account the environment in which the institutions operate: a telephone system in Mali could be very effective in relation to its environment, but still be much less effective than that in Sweden.

Third, comparisons of effectiveness become increasingly difficult as the subjects become broader. It is easy to compare the effectiveness of two identical pieces of equipment producing the same output, but the comparisons become more difficult if two or more types of output are produced with the same machines, different machines, or whole factories. Effectiveness is also affected by the resources devoted to an activity, as in the case of two identical offices—one with and the other without a photocopying machine.

The complexities described are merely the technical difficulties of the concept. Much more overwhelming are the cultural and technological ones. One consequence of the Industrial Revolution and the resulting mechanization and automation was that in the realm of industrial activities people were able to define objectives, determine a path for achieving them, and control their achievements with a degree of specificity that was previously available in only a very limited number of activities. The result was a higher level of discipline and a new set of attitudes among the individuals involved. These developments helped to define standards of institutional effectiveness that became implicitly accepted as valid for most activities in industrialized societies. But these standards, based on high specificity and the possibility of quantification, are directly applicable only to industrial or similar activities. They cannot be applied to people-oriented or pre-industrial activities for which that level of specificity is not possible. When attempts have been made to apply these standards to other activities, they have generated tensions that in the end have reduced the effectiveness of those activities and alienated the actors involved. This applies in all societies, but more clearly in developing ones, where the contrast between the activities with high specificity and those with low specificity is more acute. This point is developed in later chapters.

The standards of effectiveness should be more attuned to the culture in which they are applied. Industrialization has resulted in a fairly universal modernization that transcends the initial cultural environment. Within the industrial sector, concepts of effectiveness apply almost equally well in any country. The difficulties arise in activities which are much more influenced by local cultural patterns. Although standards of effectiveness for oil refineries are almost universal, those for ministries of education have to allow for the level and nature of political intervention in the society, the importance attached to education, social norms such as seniority, and the like. It may be that a ministry of education is not very effective when measured by industrial standards, but it could be performing reasonably well in its cultural context.

Overall, then, the rankings of institutional effectiveness or performance analyzed here have an important qualitative component. In addition, the analysis is based on a fairly large—but uneven—number of objective indicators of operational performance and on studies of specific aspects of operations described below. An important distinction that I tried to maintain in the course of the review was between the level (or ranking) of performance of an institution and the level of success or failure of the institutional development program as such.

Data Base

The study is based on two groups of information, both related to experience gained in development projects financed by the World Bank. The first group comprises 175 ex post evaluation studies of 222 projects, representing thirteen subsectors in sixty-six countries (see the Statistical Appendix). Ex post evaluations deal with completed projects, most of which were initiated in the late 1960s or early 1970s and in operation in the middle or late 1970s. Because of this time frame the sample contains a high proportion of institutions in the so-called traditional sectors—

transport, power, and industry—although it also includes a large number in agriculture and integrated rural development. In addition to the original sample, I reviewed several later operations, especially in agriculture, urban development, and population, health, and nutrition, which had enough implementation experience to contribute to the analysis.

In analyzing these projects I focused not on the investment component but on the institutions behind the investments and on the efforts to strengthen them. In many projects more than one institution is involved either in implementing the investment program or, more broadly, in strengthening sectoral or subsectoral institutional setups. I have taken for analysis only the principal institution in each program. The sample comprised 159 principal institutions—fewer than the number of projects, because in many cases the Bank dealt with a particular institution over the course of several loans.

These ex post evaluation studies vary considerably in depth, quality, and their coverage of institutional issues. Many are cursory reviews that did not go into much detail, perhaps because institutional development was not important in the operation being reviewed or the evaluator attached little importance to institutional issues. At the other extreme, a growing number of increasingly sophisticated evaluations focus almost exclusively on institutional issues.[6] In most cases, however, the evaluation of these issues is hampered by a poor definition of objectives and by the lack of baseline data and accepted methodologies for undertaking these evaluations.

This information was used in different forms as the basis for the analysis in this study. By far the most important use was as qualitative contributions to and illustrations for the conceptual framework. As expected, this is not a subject that lends itself well to quantitative treatment.

Nevertheless, I did try my hand at quantification, an exercise that proved to be quite useful in supporting the ideas developed in chapters 5, 6, and 7. After cataloging the causes for success or failure given by the evaluations, I drew up a list of potential explanatory variables that either were explicitly indicated by the evaluation or could be derived from the analysis. The degree of institutional effectiveness or performance was considered the dependent variable, and there were twelve independent or explanatory variables in the initial round:

1. Degree of specificity of the agency's activities
2. Degree of competition faced by the agency
3. Degree of geographical dispersion of the agency's activities
4. Degree of political support or commitment
5. Degree of overt political intervention
6. Presence of outstanding managers

7. Effectiveness in the application of management techniques
8. Exogenous factors
9. Results (rate of return) of the project investment
10. Degree of success of institutional development program
11. Deficit (or the absence of revenue) or surplus
12. Salary levels lower than average

These variables are explained in the appendix to this book. Each case was ranked with regard to the variables, for some variables on a scale of 1 to 5, for others on a scale of one to three; a few variables were used as dummies (yes or no). The rankings were made on the basis of information in the evaluation, often in consultation with the evaluators. The rankings were then used in simple forms of discriminant analysis (for example, to determine which cases have the highest or lowest ratings with regard to specificity or geographical dispersion and to identify the characteristics of the agencies with deficits) and in a number of attempts at simple and multiple regression analysis. Several of the variables were then discarded and others were added (see chapter 4). As a result of this initial analysis, I concentrated on developing two new concepts: specificity and competition.

This is the formal part of the data base. But most of the analysis is supported by evidence and impressions I gathered in the course of my work at the World Bank as project policy adviser, reviewing the general trends in project implementation and dealing with some of the most difficult cases from an institutional point of view. Since 1976 the Bank has had semi-annual implementation reviews of all its operations, which proved to be an invaluable source of information. In addition, since the mid-1970s several ex post evaluations of institutional development programs have gone deeper into the reasons for success or failure than the reviews of individual projects. I was directly involved in many of the evaluation studies in the sample and supervised a considerable proportion of them. More recently, the increased attention paid by the World Bank to institutional development has allowed me to work full time in this field and add considerably to the data and impressions on which this study relies.

Although the World Bank's experience has been used to trigger the analysis, it is certainly not the only development agency trying its hand at institutional development. The U.S. Agency for International Development (USAID) in particular has had a long history of efforts in this area.[7] The results of their experience have also been used as background in this study. The focus is on institutional development in developing countries, and I have tried to concentrate on issues that are relevant to policymakers and professionals in those countries. The World Bank's performance in this field has not been analyzed, but some of the operational conclusions in Part III are of direct relevance to the Bank.

Notes

1. The concept of institutional development or institution building has gone through several stages among donor agencies and through many definitions. One of the latest says that "institutional development is the process of creating a new pattern of activities and behaviors that persists over time because it is supported by indigenous norms, standards and values" (D. V. Brinkerhoff, "The Evaluation of Current Perspectives on Institutional Development: An Organizational Focus," Institutional Development Management Center, University of Maryland, March 1985).

2. See, for example, Larry L. Cummings, "Emergence of the Instrumental Organization," in *New Perspectives on Organizational Effectiveness*, Paul S. Goodman and Johannes M. Pennings, eds. (San Francisco, Calif.: Jossey-Bass, 1977), pp. 56–62.

3. Talcott Parsons' approach is an example of this type of criteria. See his *Structure and Process in Modern Societies* (Glencoe, Ill.: Free Press, 1960).

4. Many authors have defined efficiency and effectiveness. See, for example, Charles W. Hofer and Daniel Schendel, *Strategy Formulation: Analytical Concepts* (St. Paul, Minn.: West, 1978).

5. World Bank, *World Development Report 1983* (New York: Oxford University Press, 1983), p. 42.

6. Since the establishment of a special unit to undertake ex post evaluation of its activities in the early 1970s, the World Bank has accumulated a considerable number of studies of its experience in institutional development, with all the shortcomings just described. Most of these studies have been for internal use, in part because of their confidential nature. The *World Development Report 1983* is perhaps the most comprehensive attempt to distill that experience. Other, more specific studies, including the background papers to the *World Development Report 1983*, have been published as World Bank Staff Working Papers and Discussion Papers, most of which are referred to in this book.

7. See William J. Siffin, "Two Decades of Public Administration in Developing Countries," in *Education and Training for Public Sector Management in Developing Countries*, Laurence D. Stifel, James S. Coleman, and Joseph E. Black, eds. (New York: Rockefeller Foundation, 1977); and Dennis A. Rondinelli, "Development Administration and Management in U.S. Foreign Aid Policy" (Washington, D.C.: National Association of Schools of Public Affairs and Administration, 1984).

3 The World Bank's Experience

The efforts toward institutional development in World Bank–financed projects have changed considerably over time, with important sectoral and subsectoral variations. Most of the earlier operations concentrated on only one or two institutional issues at a time. For example, there was a heavy emphasis on maintenance and planning in the case of highway agencies, on staffing and training in agricultural agencies, and on management methods and financial matters in public utilities. As the Bank moved into institutionally more difficult projects in agriculture, education, and urban and rural development, it developed a broader view of the institutions involved. Concentrating on one or two aspects became less feasible, and several issues were tackled simultaneously.

For the uninitiated, a World Bank "project" perhaps needs to be defined.[1] It is a complex unit that contains two main components: physical development—such as a dam, a road, a power plant, or agricultural or industrial credit—and institutional development. The latter could be a relatively minor component, such as the financing of a small training program, or a major undertaking to create or overhaul an agency, in which case it could comprise practically all aspects listed in chapter 2 (under "Definitions"). In general, financing for institutional development programs comes from the country itself or from other bilateral and multilateral sources of finance. To strengthen an institution the Bank will typically help finance several technical assistance components (such as consultants or special studies), infrastructure and materials (such as the construction of buildings or the acquisition of motor vehicles), or, on special occasions, the salaries of key staff for a certain period. Of course, some important institutional development requires little or no financing and is undertaken directly by the agencies involved.

For the Bank, the main dilemma has been how to reconcile the twin objectives of physical development and institutional development. For example, if a railway urgently needs new track and the performance of the company is seriously deficient, it is more expeditious to get the track built by foreign contractors, consultants, and supervisors and completely bypass the railway organization. This approach, however, would have no effect on the railway's institutional development or would have a negative effect because of the resulting frustration and discouragement in the organization or the loss of its best people to the foreign contractors. If the railway is to be in charge and track rehabilitation is to be a tool for strengthening its capacity, the construction will probably be slower and less efficient.

Institutional development is a slow process; it certainly takes longer than for the implementation of a more traditional investment. For this reason, the most successful attempts have been those in which the Bank has promoted, and the country has accepted, institutional development over long periods, usually several decades, in the course of several investment projects.

Although traditionally the Bank has confined its institutional development activities to one or at most a few institutions in a project or series of projects, these activities have expanded considerably in recent years. In the management of public enterprises attention is no longer exclusively on the internal factors and now encompasses the relations between the central government and the enterprises, as well as the framework or rules of the game under which the enterprises operate. The rationale is that a large proportion of the factors determining the performance of public enterprises are under the control of central government agencies. This broader approach has resulted in a large number of technical assistance operations to reform public enterprises. Other new activities have to do with a country's management of its economic policies at the macro and sectoral level and are derived from the Bank's so-called structural adjustment loans. To strengthen the institutional setup for the management of economic policies, the Bank has again financed technical assistance. These newer types of operations, however, are not reviewed here.

General Results

The review of the Bank's experience in institutional development shows a pattern by sector, subsector, and activity but, except in a few cases, not by country. Although some sectors, subsectors, and activities have had consistently good or bad results over long periods in most countries, few countries have consistently had successes or failures in most sectors. The most successful institutional development programs were in industry, telecommunications, some utilities, development finance companies or industrial development banks, and "industrial" types of agriculture such as plantations. A mixed performance was found in other utilities (a rather large group), transport projects (ports and highways), and agricultural credit institutions. Poorer results were registered in most other types of agriculture, education, and railways. Additional cases of institutional development programs in integrated rural and urban development suggest that many will also fall into this last category.

Within institutions, the most successful institutional development programs were those related to technical and financial aspects; mixed results were obtained in planning, commercial activities, and extension services. Less satisfactory results were registered in training (although programs for technical and general training and the establishment of training centers were relatively more successful), maintenance, improvement in organizational structures and processes, personnel management, interagency coordination, and sectorwide reforms.

These results were indirectly confirmed by analyzing the implementation of different types of project components. In brief, equipment components were generally implemented more easily than civil works, and civil works more easily than the provision of services. These patterns appear more clearly in complex projects: in the case of railways, locomotives and wagons were acquired and in operation before the track was renewed or the workshops built, and the track was generally ready before an organization was in place for its maintenance. In integrated rural development projects, tractors, trucks, or machinery were available before the feeder roads were completed, and the roads were ready before an effective marketing or extension structure was operational.

Good progress in institutional development took place mainly in institutions or activities which already had a relatively high standard of performance. Similarly, in only a few cases were the institutional improvements satisfactory if the investment projects as a whole were not successful.

These results are discussed in more detail below and are further developed in later chapters, together with the possible reasons for the patterns.

Sectoral and Subsectoral Patterns

An unmistakable pattern of sectoral and subsectoral results suggests that, in agriculture, the least effective institutions were those dealing with livestock and certain aspects of integrated rural development. Institutions in agricultural credit and irrigation had mixed results, and those related to plantation-type projects (most of them in Africa) were the most successful.

Among agricultural activities in Africa, for example, one very successful institution dealt with smallholder tea development in Kenya. In about fifteen years, it developed considerable professional experience, established good relations with and had a good response from smallholders, and introduced more productive varieties of tea.[2] Similar successes were registered with the introduction of oil palm in Côte d'Ivoire and cocoa in Nigeria, in many cases through large plantations, not smallholder operations. In contrast, livestock projects and agencies dealing with livestock have been generally unsuccessful in Africa (Kenya, Madagascar, and Zambia) and have faced serious difficulties elsewhere, including some of the relatively advanced countries in Latin America.[3]

The success of institutions dealing with telecommunications is striking: most agencies in this field seem to show a level of effectiveness well above that of agencies in other sectors. This holds true in a wide range of countries from Burkina Faso and Ethiopia to Costa Rica, Fiji, India, and Indonesia. Telecommunications agencies made progress in spite of the negative effects of political turmoil or other difficulties in each country.

A similar pattern was found among many institutions related to industrial projects, including a few pipeline operations, and development finance companies. At a time when Pakistan was at war and facing major economic and political difficulties, an industrial project and a gas pipeline operation were separately begun by two efficient companies. They managed to overcome the general difficulties, implemented the projects and put them into operation, and considerably strengthened their internal organization and management. At the same time, implementation of an urban water supply project and a national highway project suffered serious difficulties. The agencies in charge did not improve in spite of expensive institutional development programs, but deteriorated considerably. Many of the difficulties could be traced to the general economic and political problems, which the agencies did not have the strength to overcome. Surely, it is not fair to blame an institution for failing during a period of war and political turmoil; the point here is that some of them were sufficiently strong to make progress in spite of those conditions.

In Bolivia, also during political turmoil and economic difficulties, a pipeline project was implemented, although with some delay, and began to operate normally in spite of the nationalization of the company itself after a long-drawn-out process. In the same period, a livestock project had serious difficulties and the institution in charge did not improve in any noticeable way during implementation. Perhaps those countrywide difficulties made institutional progress impossible, but this livestock project did not improve its performance even after those general problems had abated.

In the power sector there have been notable successes similar to those in industry. In Peru and Turkey general difficulties did not prevent institutional progress and high levels of performance, and the Tanzania Electric Supply Company Limited (TANESCO) has maintained a high level of effectiveness in spite of the general institutional deterioration of the country.[4] But elsewhere (in Sudan and Argentina) power companies seem to have been overwhelmed by countrywide difficulties, and their performance has been worse than that of power companies in other countries, although most probably still better than the average in the country. In more recent years, the overall effectiveness of power companies has deteriorated because many governments have been reluctant to raise tariffs sufficiently to compensate for increases in energy prices. Although this deterioration has affected mainly the financial aspects, in a few extreme cases technical operations have also suffered.

In the case of highways, the main difficulties have been with maintenance, a complex activity from a managerial point of view.[5] On the whole, highway departments have not been among the most effective institutions in any country, and the Bank's experience in this respect has been mixed. In a few countries, considerable institutional progress took place as a consequence of lengthy programs that continued through several projects, while elsewhere similar approaches have yielded meager results.

Railways are among the entities facing the gravest operational difficulties worldwide. There are exceptions (India, the Republic of Korea, Malaysia, Spain, and Taiwan), but the picture that emerges is one of many attempts to improve operational efficiency over decades, with little to show at the end. With regard to the technical aspects of operation, however, most railways would be considered above average in each country; in a narrow sense, they can be said to be technically "effective."[6]

Progress in institutional development is closely correlated with the level of institutional performance at the beginning of the program: institutions that were strong initially progress faster than weak ones. The sectoral patterns already described apply here as well: in telecommunications or development finance companies, institutional development programs have brought considerable improvements, much along the lines originally expected. Overall, institutions that were strong at the outset were, almost by definition, more aware of their shortcomings and participated more actively in the design and implementation of the institutional development programs. Conversely, improvement of many weak institutions in agriculture, education, or water supply has been slow, and the original institutional objectives have not been achieved. The agencies were not quite convinced of the need for the program and did not fully support it.[7]

Country Patterns

To say that no country patterns were found is to speak in relative, not absolute terms. It does not mean that there are no differences in the overall effectiveness of institutions from one country to the next: all activities in one country could be more effective than all activities in another. Glaring differences among countries in the availability of professional and technical skills, the consistency of policies, or cultural traits can cause wide variations in institutional performance. But the sectoral patterns within countries are stronger and more consistent than any pattern detected among countries. In a given developing country the telecommunications agency and the development finance company may be among the most effective institutions, but they will not necessarily work at the same level of effectiveness as those in a more institutionally advanced country. Some of these absolute differences are quite visible in the World Bank's experience. For example, the institutions dealing with livestock in Latin America perform better than those in Africa (including those staffed by expatriates), although in both regions livestock agencies might be among the less effective. Similar differences appear in other sectors. The comparisons also have to be qualified with regard to the complexity of the activities in the same sectors in countries at different levels of institutional development: a development finance company or agricultural bank in Brazil or Korea will undertake much more complex activities than similar institutions in Sub-Saharan Africa.

Patterns by Activity

The activities of an institution are the various functions it performs, such as production, planning, marketing, maintenance, and training. The patterns by type of activity are less clear than the sectoral and subsectoral patterns because it has been difficult to evaluate the performance of parts of an institution, but some conclusions are possible. In many cases where practically no other improvement was registered, there was some progress in technical or financial matters. For example, in a livestock project in Kenya it was found, in retrospect, that the institutional development program was badly conceived. Despite enormous problems in implementing the project there was some improvement in the technical aspects of the operation. A telecommunications project in Papua New Guinea contained an institutional development program that was successful in most technical and financial areas but experienced difficulties with the training component. And a development finance company in Morocco improved in financial and staffing areas but made less progress in coordination.

Planning and coordination have been among the most difficult areas in which to achieve an acceptable level of performance. Successful institutions that managed to improve in most areas have failed in planning or coordination functions (oil palm in Cameroon, telecommunications in Ethiopia, railways in India, highways in Malawi, an industrial bank in Nigeria, railways in Spain). Even relatively successful agencies, such as the power companies in Colombia, have had serious difficulties in arriving at a workable arrangement for their interconnections.

Other examples include a power agency in the Philippines that showed considerable progress in technical, financial, and managerial matters, but much less in training and coordination; a water supply agency in Malaysia that made good advances in financial and purely organizational aspects, but could not solve important staffing difficulties; a development bank in Morocco that moved ahead in several areas, including staffing, but could not solve its coordination problems; and an education agency in Guyana that could not make much progress in almost any activity, but did improve some technical aspects. The list could be extended by dozens of other cases. Several examples are exceptions to the pattern. For instance, in Mali the railways made progress faster in training and staffing matters than in financial management.

Results by Type of Investment

A high correlation was found between the initial level of institutional performance, the degree of progress in the institutional development component, and the success of the overall investment project. Conversely, the reasons for the failure of institutional development and of an investment are often similar, such as distorted prices or lack of adaptation to political or cultural realities. Most projects registered results in the physical component that were better than or similar to results in the institutional development component.[8] In three subsectors, however, institutional development programs seem to have been the more successful: plantation-type agriculture, water supply, and railway projects.

The reasons for these patterns are not clear. Whether an inefficient institution identifies bad projects or whether bad investments produce negative effects on institutional performance is hard to tell. In some cases the physical and the institutional development components are indistinguishable. A railway "project," for example, is merely a slice of the agency's total investment program over a certain period. The linkages between investments and institutional performance are so strong that one pushes or pulls the other: a badly operated railway will have difficulty implementing its investment program; the results will be higher operating costs and lower traffic; the worsening of its financial position will in turn affect its operating performance and the implementation of the investment program, and so on. This is typical of several railways reviewed in this study (in Colombia, Mali, Senegal, Turkey, and Yugoslavia).

In other cases the relationship is less apparent. It depends on the relative importance of the investment to the total operation of the agency: the less the importance the more diffuse the relationship. Many agricultural programs in Africa represent large proportions of the operations of the agencies handling them (the smallholder tea program in Kenya, the livestock projects in Madagascar and Zambia, and the oil palm projects in Cameroon and Côte d'Ivoire). In fact, most of the projects included in the sample represent a large proportion of the total investments of the agencies involved, and as such they affect the agencies in a pervasive way. There are fewer cases where the Bank-financed project is relatively unimportant. Sometimes a project has been too large for the technical and administrative capacity of the agency, and the strain was so great that neither the physical nor the institutional improvements could be implemented. Agencies that might not have been particularly weak relative to others in the country were overloaded by investment and institutional development programs.

In other cases the relationship between investment and institutional performance is less direct because the agency that makes the investment is not the one that operates the finished project. For example, the effectiveness of a highway agency is not directly related to whether a particular road has been built or whether the projected traffic levels were achieved; at least the relationship is less direct than in the case of a railway that buys a new locomotive or renews its track. In other kinds of projects, such as water supply, education, or financial institutions, the relationship between the success of the investment and institutional progress is stronger than in the case of highways.

A finding that needs further exploration is that in some types of agricultural projects the institutional development component was relatively unsuccessful and the institutions involved were weak, but the rate of return to the investment was quite high, around 20 percent. Within this sector a country pattern is valid: agricultural investments in most countries in Sub-Saharan Africa were not successful, a finding that has been confirmed by subsequent studies. In other regions, the most reasonable hypothesis is that the potential return on agricultural investments was even higher than what was possible to achieve in light of the institutional weakness.

The varying degree of difficulty in implementing different types of investment (equipment and machinery being easier to implement than civil works, and civil works easier than the provision of services) is consistent with the pattern found with regard to the performance of activities and subsectors. The Malawi Lilongwe Land Development Program of integrated rural development is a good example. The land development and the feeder roads—civil works—were completed on schedule, or even ahead of schedule, while the provision of services, which required special organizational arrangements for extension, marketing, and the supply of inputs, was considerably delayed. The most expeditious part was the acquisition of vehicles and certain pieces of machinery. The pattern is also strong among railway projects. Even in a successful one such as the Spanish railway, track renewal—a complex civil works operation—was much delayed although rolling stock was procured on schedule. The greatest difficulty was in setting up a new marketing operation to give the railway a more commercial outlook. Another classic example of this pattern is in irrigation projects. The main civil works are almost always ready before the tertiary canals are completed and long before there is a workable organization to take charge of water management.

Many other examples could be cited. In a Bolivia livestock project (as well as in several others) the infrastructure such as fencing and other facilities was in place before the provision of services and other inputs needed to improve cattle management. In education projects (in Colombia and Kenya) the "hardware," that is, the schools, was completed before the "software," the educational services such as the development of new curricula. In agricultural mechanization projects the tractors are always available before other inputs, such as fertilizers, or an improved extension service. In highway maintenance projects the machinery is always in place before the organization for operating the system or the trained staff. The only exceptions to this pattern were some education projects where the procurement of equipment and vehicles was more delayed than school construction because independent contractors completed the construction work as scheduled, while existing line agencies or new project units, which handled procurement, did not have sufficient experience to cope with the size of the program.

Overall, many of these findings were to be expected and by now have become part of the conventional wisdom, although the underlying reasons for them are far from clear. It was more surprising to find that sectoral and subsectoral patterns were stronger than country patterns, but this finding is new only in relation to institutional development. Twenty years ago Albert Hirschman arrived at similar conclusions with regard to variations in success among projects in different sectors and subsectors. He wondered why, for example, projects in telecommunications and power appear to be more successful in many respects than those in agriculture. Some of his analysis parallels the one here, particularly with regard to the concept of specificity developed in chapter 5, where his analysis and conclusions are used as additional evidence.[9]

Notes

1. See Warren C. Baum and Stokes M. Tolbert, *Investing in Development: Lessons of World Bank Experience* (New York: Oxford University Press, 1985), p. 333.

2. Geoffrey Lamb and Linda Muller, *Control, Accountability and Incentives in a Successful Development Institution: The Kenya Tea Development Authority*, World Bank Staff Working Paper 550 (Washington, D.C., 1982).

3. See, for example, Stephen Sandford, "Review of World Bank Livestock Activities in Dry Tropical Africa," World Bank Agriculture and Rural Development Department (Washington, D.C., January 1981).

4. See World Bank, *World Development Report 1983* (New York: Oxford University Press, 1983), p. 85.

5. See "The Road Maintenance Problem and Institutional Assistance," World Bank Transportation, Water, and Telecommunications Department (Washington, D.C., December 1981).

6. See "The Railways Problem," World Bank Transportation, Water, and Telecommunications Department (Washington, D.C., November 1982).

7. Other studies confirm the gist of this finding. For example, a review of organizational innovation and performance concluded that administrative innovations are adopted and implemented faster by high performance than low performance organizations. See Fariborz Dauranpour and W. M. Evan, "Organizational Innovation and Performance: The Problem of 'Organizational Lag,'" *Administrative Science Quarterly,* vol. 29 (September 1984), pp. 392–409.

8. This statement compares results that have been quantified by an ex post estimate of the rate of return on an investment with institutional results that cannot be quantified. Thus, the qualitative element in this comparison is important.

9. Albert O. Hirschman, *Development Projects Observed* (Washington, D.C.: Brookings Institution, 1967).

4 : The Standard Explanations

Why do we find certain patterns in the results of institutional development? A review of the literature and many talks with academics and practitioners yielded useful insights and partial explanations. But usually these sources were more concerned with questions of how to organize or how to manage under a given set of circumstances than with the question of why some institutions are more effective than others. A few answers to the "why" questions were implicit in the prescriptive approaches, but there was no coherent conceptual framework that could be used to find explicit answers.

The remainder of this study explores the "why" questions and the operational implications of the answers. In this chapter I analyze the reasons explicitly given by the project evaluators for the success or failure of institutional development, as well as some explanatory factors that are implicit in their work. These explanations correspond to those usually given in the developing countries and at the World Bank regarding institutional development. But many of them have turned out to be only proximate causes. Part II, which is the core of the study, analyzes in more detail two factors, specificity and competition, which help to provide a more coherent explanation of the experience to date in institutional development. But first I briefly review the state of the art in the field of institutional development. I will of course not summarize all the accumulated wisdom, but merely point out a few strengths and weaknesses as background for the analysis that follows.

The State of the Art

The "art" of institutional development covers several fields that might be encompassed by the generic name of organizational theory.[1] Under various labels—business administration, public or development administration, management science, public enterprise management—it deals with the basic issue of how to get groups of human beings organized for a purpose. The central point is that there is no accepted theory of organization, and it is unlikely that one will appear in the foreseeable future. Human behavior is probably the most complex of all subjects, and a satisfactory theory of organization would be tantamount to a unified theory of the social sciences. Probably there never will be one (just as well, perhaps) because social reality is always changing and theories in the social sciences cannot have the cumulative characteristics of those in the natural sciences. Theories have to be constantly adapted to new conditions and environments, and the theories themselves may influence, sometimes heavily, the social reality. Conversely, the natural sciences deal with a reality that is, for all practical purposes, immutable, allowing for cumulative knowledge. Thus, institutional development and the disciplines that relate to it are like economics before Adam Smith or physics before Newton—with the added difficulty that it is unlikely that a "social Newton" will ever appear. This, of course, does not mean that knowledge and progress are not possible. They are, and progress in the social sciences has been remarkable in the past two or three decades.

A large number of techniques is now available to help perform organizational and managerial tasks, and there are several approaches or schools of thought that implicitly give more or less weight to groups of factors determining organizational effectiveness. In addition, there are a few—very few—insights for deciding which combination of techniques and approaches best fit a particular situation.

The techniques can be divided into three groups: quantitative, systems, and social science. The quantitative techniques are derived mainly from mathematics and economics; they allow the quantitative evaluation of alternative organizational or management decisions or the logical analysis of organizational structures and procedures, but for the most part they do not take into account behavioral patterns. Techniques in this group include network and critical path analysis, programming, and financial analysis. Second, the systems techniques derive mainly from a combination of systems analysis and some of the social sciences; they allow the analysis of organizational structures and procedures in more precise work situations and include techniques such as manpower and organizational planning, job description, and job evaluation. Third, those derived mainly from the social sciences allow the study of structures, procedures, and management decisions with special reference to the behavioral responses of individuals and groups: job enrichment, group techniques, personnel development and selection, participation techniques, and communications.

The approaches or schools of thought have evolved from the interaction or tension between two opposite views. At one extreme is the rationalistic, mechanistic, formalistic, or deterministic view of an organization as a machine, heavily influenced by the model of the industrial world. At the other extreme is the view of an organization as a culture whose effectiveness is largely determined by the individuals and formal and informal groups that it comprises, by the way the members fashion their role, and by the relations among them. In between these two extremes is a spectrum of views: for example, the emphasis can be transferred from the purposes and motives of the organization to those of the individuals or groups that compose it; the organization can be seen as conditioned by a combination of the technology it uses and the needs, goals, and motivations of the individuals or groups that compose it; or the organization can be seen as heavily conditioned by the type of interaction with its environment (other institutions and the rest of the society). These approaches, as well as many others within this spectrum, are interdisciplinary, drawing from several of the social sciences. And the more an organization is seen as a culture and less as a machine, the more the analysis depends on the social sciences.

It must be clear, even from this oversimplified presentation, that there is a correspondence between techniques and approaches. Mechanistic or rationalistic approaches will tend to rely more heavily on techniques derived from mathematics and economics, while organicistic or cultural approaches will rely more on those based on the social sciences.[2]

Of the several disciplines in this field, those that seem to be more content with their accomplishments are management science and business administration. Their narrow focus has been questioned, however, because it does not adequately consider the broad political environment in which private activities take place, and in recent years there have been several attempts to fill the gap. When these disciplines have been applied to the institutional issues in developing countries, the experience has been generally poor; as a matter of fact, some writers on the subject say that institutional development is at a dead end.[3]

This is probably an extreme view. There has been a great deal of experience with techniques such as accounting, auditing, financial planning, job classification, training, planning, and organizational analysis, and if properly applied they could have positive effects. Experience is more limited with regard to the applicability of some of the approaches that consider an organization as a culture. Substantial knowledge has been accumulated from several well-documented cases and some practitioners—unfortunately only a few—have acquired considerable and useful experience.[4]

From the standpoint of the developing countries, however, the state of the art on which institutional development ought to be based has major shortcomings. First, the field has developed along two main lines: at one extreme the private sector, industrial-financial line of management science and business administration, and at the other the formalistic, legalistic line of public or development administration. (The introduction of principles of management science into development administration in recent years has brought the two fields somewhat closer together.) But public enterprises and many individual agencies in the public sector fall between these two stools. The simple and sometimes misguided application of the private sector model to the far more difficult world of public sector institutions has often been a failure.

Second, the disciplines have concentrated on the effectiveness of institutions at national, sectoral, or regional levels, but not enough has been done to organize clients or constituents (beneficiaries, target groups, and participants) at the local level and to improve the relationships between the institutions and their constituents. There is a gap between institutions and constituents that has to be bridged—as shown by the difficulties experienced in any type of delivery system in agriculture or health.[5]

Third, there has been a tendency to apply quantitative techniques derived from mathematics in situations where behavioral methods would have been more appropriate; for example, statistical techniques have been used excessively in personnel management. The "neatness" of these techniques has caused undue emphasis to be placed on the quantitative, on inputs rather than impact (the number of people trained rather than the effects of training; the number of farmers visited rather than the effects of the visits; the number of graduates rather than the effects of education, and so on).

Fourth, the disciplines such as development administration that focus more on the needs of developing countries have had a static flavor to them. They have concentrated on the establishment of structures that were expected to remain unchanged for long periods. Few insights are available into how to have an efficiently evolving public agency and into the process of institutional change.

A fifth shortcoming of particular importance in developing countries is the unsatisfactory treatment of the relationship between institutions and politics. Management science treats politics as just one more exogenous constraint. Although this approach is being questioned more and more as too simplistic, even in the developed countries, it is generally adequate for the private sector but certainly not for public sector activities.[6]

The Explanations

The so-called standard explanations, those derived from the evaluation studies, can be divided into five groups. In an order of increasing general relevance and of declining randomness these groups are:

Exogenous factors
Outstanding individuals or groups of individuals

Effective planning and implementation of
  institutional development programs
Effective application of management techniques
Adequate relative prices
Sufficient political commitment.

This list is a systematization of the factors explicitly or implicitly considered in the ex post evaluations. When the list is compared with the brief description of the state of the art just given, it is obvious that the evaluators did not follow any particular conceptual framework. They emphasized factors that were often outside the control of management and that can be considered aleatory. Other explanations have to do with internal factors, in particular the effectiveness with which management and organization techniques were applied. But the judgment about this application also depended on what the evaluators thought was appropriate. Some were mechanistic in their views, others organicistic. Although this might have been all right, there is no way of knowing whether the particular approach followed was adequate for the circumstances. And some of the frameworks were suspiciously simplistic in putting the burden of explanation on one or two internal or external factors.

In fact, the only comprehensive ex post evaluation of institutional development programs has been done by Samuel Paul. He analyzed in depth a small number of programs and concluded that a central condition for success is the ability of the top management of a program (and, by extension, of an agency) to practice what he calls "strategic management."[7]

Keep in mind that factors explaining the success or failure of institutional development programs may be different from those explaining absolute levels of institutional performance. This distinction is generally unclear and in most cases irrelevant; the high correlation between institutional effectiveness and progress in institutional development programs has already been discussed. Some factors, however, especially those discussed in this chapter, may be more relevant for one than the other. As later chapters delve more deeply into underlying causes, the factors discussed tend to apply more equally to the level of institutional effectiveness and to progress in institutional development.

Exogenous Factors

The exogenous factors in institutional effectiveness are those affecting a whole country, region, or sector over a given period. These can be acts of God such as floods, droughts, and hurricanes; political upheavals and uncertainties, including war; economic crises, including shortages; and major changes in economic policies such as currency devaluations and new import policies. Some of these factors can have a positive or negative influence: the jump in oil prices in the 1970s and the ensuing economic crises have been a curse for some institutions but a blessing for others.

Exogenous factors figure prominently in explanations of institutional effectiveness or progress. They are mentioned as directly affecting around 90 of the 175 cases reviewed. Their importance varies considerably, some institutions having been affected by several factors, while others have been mildly touched by one. As expected, no sectoral or country pattern emerges.

Acts of God were surprisingly few, with only six cases recorded in the sample, half of them in agriculture. A couple of agencies in West Africa were seriously affected by the Sahelian drought during the early and mid-1970s. Prolonged droughts also affected a power agency in Liberia and an agricultural credit project in India. But the most common and widespread problem was political upheavals and uncertainties. It was mentioned as an important factor in one-fourth of the cases reviewed, especially in East Africa and South Asia. The majority refer to political upheavals which reduced support for the institution (this issue is further elaborated below), necessitated staff changes, and delayed the provision of funds. In East Africa agencies in Burundi, Madagascar, Sudan, and to a lesser extent in Ethiopia, Zaire, and Zambia were affected by such changes. In West Africa programs were affected by the civil war in Nigeria and government changes in Ghana. In Thailand several agencies were affected, at first favorably, then unfavorably, by the war in Viet Nam. Agencies in Pakistan were seriously hampered by the civil war and the wars with India. Institutions in Syria and Jordan were affected by political developments in the Middle East. In Latin America, the uncertainties of land reform affected the functioning of agencies dealing with the agricultural sector in several countries. Conversely, in a few cases political problems had a positive effect; for example, the port of Dakar profited from the closing of the Suez Canal for several years.

Economic crises affected a smaller number of agencies—about 12 percent of those reviewed—especially revenue earning entities such as development finance companies, power companies, and railways whose financial solvency was threatened. This happened with a development finance company, ports, and railways in India during the economic recession in the early 1970s, with a development finance company in Korea during a slowdown in the economy, and with a regional development bank in Brazil's Northeast during a crisis there. Economic crises are also given as the main reason for shortages of funds for recurrent expenditures in several agricultural and rural and urban development programs. Changes in economic policies, including currency realignments (the most common) and import restrictions, appear as a principal factor for about one-tenth of the agencies studied, among them a power agency in Mexico, a pipeline company in Pakistan, a fertilizer complex in India, and an education agency in the Philippines. Import restrictions had a negative influence on several agencies in India, and changes in national and regional policies were a major handicap for the Yugoslav railway.

Several agencies were seriously affected by two or more exogenous factors and found it extremely difficult, if not impossible, to make progress. An agricultural credit in Senegal was affected by the Sahelian drought and a drop in groundnut prices; a private development corporation in the Philippines by floods and a recession in the country; a fertilizer company in India by exchange rate fluctuations and by supply distortions derived from the oil crisis, power shortages, and war with Pakistan. In many instances the same factors were very damaging for certain agencies in a country but had a mild effect on others, usually those in the industrial or financial areas.

In several cases, however, exogenous factors actually helped the institutions by improving their financial situation, generally through price increases. Sharply higher rice prices saved the finances of an irrigation project in Madagascar, and unexpectedly rapid economic growth helped accelerate institutional change in several agencies in Iran, Spain, Taiwan, and Trinidad and Tobago by improving their financial situation and making institutional reforms more palatable and feasible.

Leadership of Outstanding Individuals

In 33 out of 175 cases, the evaluations identified one individual, usually the project manager or the general manager of the agency in charge of implementation—in a few cases, a small team was mentioned—as the determining factor in whatever progress took place in institutional development and project implementation. In only a few cases, however, is it possible to distinguish clearly between very good managers, who appear frequently in the cases reviewed, and the outstanding individuals who are credited with changing the course of the programs or the agencies. The potential for tautology is high: managers of successful agencies are considered outstanding in many evaluations even though causality is not proven or even illustrated. Perhaps the thirty-three cases with outstanding individuals is an overestimation, and reliance on leadership alone is not very promising as a generalized method of achieving high institutional performance.

The only patterns are that nineteen of the thirty-three cases were in Africa (the factor is unimportant in other regions, except in agriculture in Latin America) and that twelve of the thirty-three cases were in agriculture. This concentration in Africa may be explained by the low level of institutional strength in the region. Most of the outstanding individuals were expatriates who were for a while the only, or among the only, skilled and experienced staff in the agencies where they worked. Their impact may therefore be magnified. If the same individuals were in bigger and more firmly established institutions in other parts of the world, their performance would be as good, but their presence would not appear as crucial. The lower the level of institutional effectiveness, the higher seems to be the potential impact of outstanding individuals.

In several cases there was proof that individuals did make a difference because a difficult situation improved after their arrival and deteriorated after they left. Sometimes the influence of an outstanding manager has been not so much to transform a difficult situation into a success, but rather to prevent further deterioration or help achieve an acceptable operational level. No matter how effective a manager, he cannot fight by himself factors such as a pervasive lack of funds in the country, an absolute dearth of skilled manpower, or a reduction in world prices. In more recent analyses of these factors, especially in the African context, practitioners have concluded that the weight of the exogenous factors outside the control of the manager has been so overwhelming that very few individuals could actually have made a difference. In a few cases the success was due to a combination of excellent managerial qualities with strong political support and access to the sources of political power. In practice, this has proved to be an unbeatable combination.

Several examples illustrate these points. A livestock project in Madagascar had problems from the start. In retrospect, it was badly designed and ill-adapted to the local needs and interests. Problems were not made easier by a team of foreign managers who were not attuned to the political realities of the country. The situation improved considerably, however, during the tenure of an interim general manager that lasted almost two years. After his departure the project deteriorated again and many of the technical and institutional achievements were lost.

In another livestock project (in Zambia), in spite of an unsuitable original design and several technical difficulties, there was a propitious beginning that has been attributed to a good project manager. Implementation began to deteriorate when that manager left and was replaced by a less satisfactory one. The project and the agency were bedeviled by all sorts of problems in addition to the original faulty design—frozen prices, staff losses, and disease—but the difference between the two managers seems clear.

The influence of managers was also apparent in a power project in Sudan. Institutional progress was nonexistent because of the poor advice and ineptitude of expatriate management consultants, but conditions deteriorated markedly when a competent general manager left the agency. A power company in Turkey had a cadre of competent staff and was functioning at a level of efficiency well above that in the rest of the country, but the institutional success was attributed to a large extent to an outstanding chairman with excellent managerial abilities.

In a number of cases the influence of excellent managers could not be disentangled from other favorable circumstances, although there was little doubt about their positive influence. For example, one reason the

Spanish railway showed tremendous improvement in the 1960s and 1970s was the excellence of its general managers, but other factors were as important. In such cases it was impossible to dispute the tautology that good institutions have good managers.

Several of these good managers, particularly in Africa, were in charge of project units rather than line agencies. Parallel project units generally function as independent entities, however, and are insulated from the difficulties plaguing the central administrations. Being successful under these circumstances is therefore less meritorious.

Good Planning

The importance of "good planning and careful preparation" figures prominently in the evaluations and is preached as the gospel in any new institutional development program. But what does this dictum mean? At first sight, it appears to rely heavily on the mechanistic kind of organization theory—a belief that if objectives are clearly defined, they will be achieved. This reasoning might be good in the case of an infrastructure project—although even there things do not always turn out as expected—but there is no guarantee that a well-prepared blueprint for institutional development will ensure success or even be an important factor in it. For good planning and careful preparation, it is indispensable to know how things ought to be done, and it is easier to define clearly how to build a road than how to improve an institution. Good planning requires the meticulous design of a whole process, not merely of one alternative, and the knowledge of how to modify one or more alternatives in the light of experience and changed circumstances and of how to build a consensus about the objectives and methods of the program.[8] Thus, good planning and careful preparation do not stand up under scrutiny as significant causes of success—at least not in the form presented in the evaluations.

The potential for tautology is again large: successful institutional development efforts were considered to be well planned and prepared, but in only a few cases was there a clear link between planning and success. The link was easier to establish in cases where planning and preparation were most appropriate—the introduction of quantitative techniques, such as accounting or information systems—and especially in well-established sectors, such as power (Malawi), telecommunications (Taiwan), and development banks (Korea). But even in these cases there is only an impression that the degree of preparation explains the success. Moreover, the definition of success is vague. It often means, for instance, that accounting or financial management was introduced, but seldom that the techniques were effectively used.

In several cases, however, good planning and preparation were important positive factors. The telecommunications agency in Burkina Faso owes its relatively greater strength largely to a comprehensive improvement program and detailed action plan. The success of the Muda irrigation project in Malaysia has been attributed, among other factors, to good initial preparation and to flexibility in adapting to new circumstances as the program advanced. The success of institutional development in the Spanish railway also is attributed to detailed preparation at the outset and to the modification and adaptation of the basic action plan as implementation progressed.

Of course, the implicit assumption is that the plans were appropriate. This brings up two other aspects of planning and preparation: persistence and flexibility. An important factor in the success of institutional development has been the continuity of effort over long periods, decades rather than years, and the capacity to adapt the institution to changing circumstances. Improving the effectiveness of an institution takes time, and progress is usually slow and uneven, depending on the political and economic environment and the availability of competent staff. In practically all the cases that succeeded, the program managers and the World Bank maintained the pressure over long periods, modified strategies to fit new realities, and built upon whatever progress had taken place. Flexibility also connotes the capacity for withdrawing, modifying, or reducing institutional development programs when political or economic changes make continuation of the program useless or even counterproductive.

I found many instances of persistence, but few of the flexibility just described. Institutional development efforts tended to continue in spite of clearly unfavorable conditions. For example, an administration interested in promoting universal primary education launched a program to strengthen the agencies dealing with primary schools. When political change brought in a government more interested in technical education, the program dealing with primary education ought to have been stopped or reduced. It was not, and resources were increasingly misused. Another example is an industrial development bank which was being strengthened but, after a political decision, was crippled by competition from sources of public finance at subsidized interest rates. In this case, too, the institutional development program should have been reduced or discontinued.

Why persistence has been more common than flexibility is a fascinating issue. There is no clear explanation, but bureaucratic inertia both in the developing countries and at the World Bank would probably rank high on a list of reasons. It is always easier to continue with the existing course than to change it.

Application of Management Techniques

In a number of evaluations good institutional progress and performance are credited to the use of appropriate management and administrative techniques and approaches. The same smell of tautology and double counting emerges here: what do the evaluators mean by appropriate management techniques and good managers; what is it that good managers do if they do not apply appropriate management techniques?

Part of these questions can be clarified at the outset. The distinction between managers and the application of management techniques is quite clear in the evaluations. "Techniques" refer to the role of management or administrative consultants and the preparation of special studies in these areas, as opposed to the role actually played by a good manager, already discussed. The distinction between techniques and good planning and preparation is less clear, because whatever solution is proposed in the good planning must, to be successful, be based on the application of appropriate management or administrative techniques. But an additional element in good planning and preparation is an orderly attempt to achieve institutional development objectives; that is, to design and process an institutional development project or component as if it were a physical investment.[9]

In several cases it seems to be merely assumed that the successful application of managerial techniques produced a successful institutional development program. In other cases, however, the relationship between the techniques and the results is clearly established, principally when well-defined techniques such as accounting and auditing, inventory control, and technical training were introduced. The linkage is less clear in the case of a whole new approach to the operation of an agency, since the very nature of such programs makes it difficult to pinpoint a direct link between their design and the actual results.

In Ethiopia, for example, the process of establishing and strengthening the highway agency has been going on, with World Bank help, for more than three decades. Progress has been slow, with ups and downs, but after several years the cumulative effects of the program began to be felt. The improvements are attributed mainly to consultants who helped set up the agency and its various functions. Many other cases of progress in the highway sector could be linked to the role of consultants, as in the remarkable advance in the planning, design, and supervision of construction in Brazil.

Sometimes the application of management techniques had a positive effect in an unexpected way. A water supply agency in Jamaica faced serious operational difficulties despite several attempts over a long period to increase productivity. Consultant studies were contracted to review various aspects of the operation, but the proposed solutions were not accepted at the time. After a change in management and the advent of a favorable political atmosphere, however, the proposals proved valuable in the design of a successful action plan. In other cases, the opportunity never arrives or negative factors are too overwhelming. For almost three decades many good consultants looked at practically all aspects of the Colombian railway operation and made proposals that, with hindsight, were right. Many of these proposals were useful in preventing further deterioration, but the time has yet to arrive when they will be fully adopted. Several negative factors—political intervention, inadequate salary policies, excessive and unregulated road competition, and lack of skilled staff—have been more important.

In other cases, progress was made in spite of negative factors. In a power agency in Argentina, consultants made important operational improvements even though government restrictions on tariff levels caused serious financial difficulties for the agency. As expected, when general conditions are favorable, good management advice has a greater positive impact; the Brazilian MBR Iron Ore Company is a case in point.

Relative Prices

One of the exogenous factors of success or failure often implied by the evaluators and sometimes made explicit is the degree of distortion in relative prices of crucial inputs or outputs. Distorted prices have acted as a powerful disincentive to institutional development programs because they deprive the institution of crucial resources and, more important, cast doubt on the continuation of its existence.

Examples abound: massive institutional development programs for railways which have tariffs so controlled that huge deficits are generated; programs to improve rural extension services for crops with controlled prices; projects to increase livestock production while meat prices are kept artificially low in the cities. It is difficult to estimate the proportion of institutional development programs affected by distorted prices, but this factor has been one of the most pervasive.

In retrospect, some of the situations are puzzling. That the wrong prices are a powerful disincentive is an obvious point that does not need much demonstration. As Peter Timmer has said, "Getting prices right is not the end of economic development, but getting prices wrong frequently is." Nevertheless, one finds time and again a peculiar form of delusion: although it is known at the outset that important prices are likely to continue to be distorted, a program of investment and institutional development is designed on the assumption that the disincentives do not exist, or can be overcome by some palliatives included in the project, or will suddenly be eliminated by a political system that has shown no interest in doing so.

The link between relative prices and institutional performance is complex and sometimes difficult to detect. According to economic theory, if prices are lower than the equilibrium prices, less output will be produced—but the implicit assumption is that operational efficiency will stay the same. However, if a public enterprise is forced to produce a level of output that generates a loss, with the deficit covered by the national budget, the whole system of incentives within the enterprise changes. The lack of incentives for internal efficiency induces negligence, and the result is lower productivity.

The linkage is clear for agencies which provide services to uneconomic activities. How can a government livestock service be effective in providing technical assistance and credit to ranchers if low prices deter them from increasing their output? Unless prices were considered in the original analysis, the program would have been mounted in expectation of much more interest in technical assistance and credit than actually existed. As a result, the agency and each of its staff members would receive signals that the services they were supposed to provide were not required. In combination with the monopolistic position of the agency, these signals would provide powerful disincentives to institutional performance.

Thus, the "wrong" relative prices will have negative effects beyond the standard shift in production and consumption patterns postulated by economic theory. They will result in a less effective use of the available resources. Moreover, the extent of ineffectiveness is likely to increase with *both* higher and lower prices. Higher prices generate disincentives similar to the negative effects of monopoly, and lower prices generate other disincentives along the lines described above which also reduce effectiveness.

Commitment

The main reason for institutional improvement given by the evaluators, and perhaps the firmest conclusion derived from the World Bank's experience, is a country's commitment to the objectives of an institutional development program. To a considerable extent this factor, as discussed by the evaluators, is specific to the operations of the World Bank and other development agencies. The Bank's objectives might differ from what the country is prepared to undertake. Sometimes the Bank is more interested in pursuing institutional objectives, while the country agencies might be more interested in simply receiving the funds to get on with their investments. For instance, they want funds to expand agricultural credit but not to reorganize the agricultural bank's financial management, or they are interested in financing new locomotives but not in reorganizing the railway's commercial department. More often, there is broad agreement between the country and the Bank about the institutional objectives to be pursued, but there might be important differences of opinion about the methods to achieve those objectives or the pace of progress expected.

Still, commitment to institutional improvement—with or without the Bank—is an essential ingredient of progress. The actors involved need a strong motivation. The strength of a country's commitment is determined by the length of its duration and the number of people who share it. Particularly important in the context of improving institutions is the time dimension. Since institutional development usually extends over the implementation period of a series of Bank-financed operations, commitment has to last for decades and variations in its intensity may affect progress considerably. A truly total commitment would involve the management and staff at all levels of the implementing agency as well as of other relevant agencies in the central government, such as the ministry of finance or the regulating agency in the case of a public enterprise. Such a coalition of commitment is seldom found, but the main risks occur in programs supported primarily by one individual or group of individuals in a position of power. If they leave or lose power, the whole program collapses. Experience shows the importance of constantly assessing the nature of this commitment over time and adapting to it accordingly. Even more important are strategies to build up and reinforce commitment during the implementation period of an institutional development program. (These concepts are further developed in chapter 8.)

In many cases a full commitment to institutional development was one of the ingredients of success although, as with the previous factors, it is not possible to establish a clear causality between institutional progress and commitment. In fact, the review of the World Bank's experience strongly suggests multicollinearity among these factors. For example, a program for which there is commitment will be allocated the best managers and consultants and will be better protected from negative exogenous factors. In even more cases institutional development programs did not win the wholehearted acceptance of the implementing staff, and therefore little or no progress was made.

Behind any commitment there is, of course, a host of political and social factors, which the evaluations seldom mention. The actual outcome of an institutional development program and the actual level of commitment to it is the result of a complex interplay of political and social elements, such as corruption, that are endemic to each case.

Notes

1. The complexity of the field can be grasped by perusing any textbook that attempts to cover it. See, for example, Richard W. Scott, *Organizations: Rational, Natural, and Open Systems* (Englewood Cliffs, N.J.: Prentice-Hall, 1981).

2. W. Graham Astley and Andrew H. van de Ven, "Central Perspectives and Debates in Organization Theory," *Administrative Science Quarterly* 28 (1983):

245–73; and Thomas Lupton, *Management and the Social Sciences* (Harmondsworth, Eng.: Penguin, 1971).

3. There have been many efforts (described in a vast literature) to improve public administration in developing countries and a number of attempts to improve the effectiveness of particular agencies. Management science is a U.S. invention, and practically all developments in this field have been heavily influenced by developments in the United States. I have tried to bring into this study different perspectives, but without much success. A promising alternative is current efforts to tackle the effectiveness of public agencies by explicitly taking account of the political environment.

See, for example, Moses N. Kiggundu, Jan J. Jorgensen, and Taieb Hafsi, "Administrative Theory and Practice in Developing Countries: A Synthesis," *Administrative Science Quarterly* 28 (1983): 66–84; Derick W. Brinkerhoff, "The Evolution of Current Perspectives on Institutional Development: An Organizational Focus," draft, USAID, Port-au-Prince, Haiti, March 1985; Marcus D. Ingle, "Implementing Development Programs: A State-of-the-Art Review," executive summary prepared for the Office of Rural Development and Development Administration, Development Support Bureau, USAID under contract AID/ta-147-612, Washington, D.C., March 1979; Milton J. Esman, "Institution Building as a Guide to Action," paper presented at the Conference on Institution Building and Technical Assistance, Washington, D.C., December 4–5, 1969; and William J. Siffin, "Two Decades of Public Administration in Developing Countries," in *Education and Training for Public Sector Management in Developing Countries*, Lawrence D. Stifel, James S. Coleman, and Joseph E. Black, eds. (New York: Rockefeller Foundation, 1977).

4. See, for example, Jon R. Moris, "What Do We Do about African Agricultural Development? The Role of Extension Performance Reanalyzed," paper prepared for the Bureau of Science and Technology, USAID, Washington, D.C., 1983; David K. Leonard and Dale Rogers Marshall, eds., *Institutions of Rural Development for the Poor: Decentralization and Organizational Linkages*, Research Series 49 (Berkeley: Institute of International Studies, University of California, 1982); and David C. Korten and Rudi Klauss, eds., *People Centered Development: Contributions Toward Theory and Planning Frameworks* (West Hartford, Conn.: Kumarian Press, 1984).

5. Geert Hofstede, "Motivation, Leadership and Organization: Do American Theories Apply Abroad?" *Organizational Dynamics* (Summer 1980):42–63.

6. Richard Heaver, *Bureaucratic Politics and Incentives in the Management of Rural Development*, World Bank Staff Working Paper 537 (Washington, D.C., 1982); Marc Lindenberg and Benjamin Crosby, *Managing Development: The Political Dimension* (West Hartford, Conn.: Kumarian Press, 1981); and Gerald M. Meier, "On 'Appropriate' Policy Technology for Development," in *Essays on Economic Development and Cultural Change in Honor of Bert Hoselitz* (Chicago, Ill.: University of Chicago Press, 1977).

7. Samuel Paul, *Strategic Management of Development Programmes: Guidelines for Action*, Management Development Series 19 (Geneva: International Labour Office, 1983). Strategic management attempts to achieve the congruence of four critical interventions: (1) the formulation of a strategy that is consistent with the objectives of the program and with the environment in which it is to be imple-

mented; (2) the creation or adaptation of an organizational structure that matches the strategy and facilitates its implementation; (3) the management of such functions as planning, monitoring performance, and motivating and developing human resources so that they are consistent with the strategy and structure; and (4) the continual orchestration of the first three interventions so that they reinforce each other even though environmental conditions change.

8. Warren C. Baum and Stokes M. Tolbert, *Investing in Development: Lessons of World Bank Experience* (New York: Oxford University Press, 1985), chap. 17.

9. See World Bank, *World Development Report 1983* (New York: Oxford University Press, 1983), chap. 9.

Part II

Alternative Explanations

5 Specificity

The explanations for institutional effectiveness and progress in institutional development programs discussed in the previous chapter undoubtedly have important operational implications, some of which will be explored later. A couple, such as the importance of relative prices or of outstanding individuals, are commonsensical, although their application in the real world is surprisingly limited. Others, such as commitment, are trickier.

Still, these factors do not provide a sufficiently satisfactory conceptual framework that fits the institutional development experience to date. Even comprehensive attempts, along the lines of Samuel Paul's, leave the impression that some key elements are missing. The frameworks are perhaps too aggregated and sweeping at one end of the spectrum, and too specific—or escapist—at the other when they indicate that each situation is different and that all solutions must be tailor-made.

The remainder of this study explores two other factors that emerged from the review as central explanations of institutional performance but that have not been given much prominence in the practice and theory of institutional development. The first I have called "specificity," and the second is "competition," but in a broader sense than the traditional economic concept. The concept of specificity is developed in this chapter and the next, and that of competition in chapter 7.

Focusing on these two factors forces a detailed analysis of the intrinsic characteristics of a wide range of activities. It highlights the institutional difficulties that plague activities at the low-specificity, noncompetitive end of the spectrum—those at the lowest levels of technology and those oriented toward people, such as the delivery of social services, agricultural extension, or health care. In developing countries these are the activities most closely related to the alleviation of poverty. Since low-technology agriculture turns out to be one of the most difficult activities to manage, the problems of rural areas in poor countries appear to be overwhelming, not only in a general way, as usually discussed, but in a very precise way. The introduction of these new concepts is therefore an attempt to turn institutional development efforts in new directions, just as economic development strategies have already moved away from the grandiose industrial projects and toward greater emphasis on agriculture and on improving the productivity of more traditional and basic activities.

Specificity and competition fit into a broad framework of incentives. Individuals within an organization, and organizations as units, operate in response to incentives, or influences, produced by various factors. Some are external to the organization, such as the political and cultural environment or the general economic situation; others are internal, such as the organizational and managerial structure. The degree of specificity belongs among the internal factors, whereas competition is both external and internal. Both factors will affect not only the performance of individuals and organizational units but also the overall institutional performance of a country.

The appropriate unit of analysis for institutional effectiveness is an activity within an organization—that is, a specific function such as production, planning, budgeting, accounting, marketing, maintenance, personnel management, or training. Each of these functions could be disaggregated into different types of production, training, or planning activities, but for present purposes disaggregation is not necessary. To study the behavior of an institution as a whole (as is necessary with regard to external competition) requires the aggregation of these activities, and with further aggregation sectoral or subsectoral characteristics can be defined.

To develop the concept of specificity, it is necessary to look at a number of activities in detail. Because the evaluation studies present information and analysis in an aggregated form, however, the following sections develop the concept mainly on the basis of analogies, with a limited number of examples from the Bank's experience. Of course, the hypothetical cases presented are not at all theoretical, but simplifications of realities that have been well documented.

The Concept of Specificity

Specificity is composed of several elements. One is the degree to which it is possible to specify the objectives of a particular activity, the methods for achieving them, and the ways of controlling achievement. Another element has to do with how the activity affects the participating actors. These two elements in turn define the degree to which actors can be rewarded for their performance on the basis of results. I postulate that the degree of specificity has precise effects on the actors and, as a result, on the performance of the institution.

These effects can be characterized by their intensity, the time it takes for them to become apparent, how widely they are spread over different people and activities, and the practical possibilities of tracing them. The hypothesis is that the higher the degree of specificity, the more intense, immediate, identifiable, and focused will be the effects of a good or a bad performance. Conversely, the lower the degree of specificity, the weaker, more delayed, less identifiable, and more diffuse will be those effects. The degree of specificity is an "automatic" determinant of institutional performance—that is, it operates quite apart from the internal incentives provided by management and the organizational structure or the external incentives produced by the political, economic, and cultural environment. It imposes a discipline which is derived from the intrinsic nature of the activity and which affects institutional performance in very specific ways.

Obviously, the degree of specificity is higher for some activities than for others. Activities in high technology, finance, and industry have high specificity, while those concentrated in low technology and related primarily to human behavior (social or "people-oriented" activities) have low specificity.

Consider three widely different activities: maintenance of jet engines, operation of a tractor, and educational counseling. Jet engine maintenance is a prime example of modern technology. It is a highly specialized and specific activity. Precise instructions are printed to define each step in great detail and spell out their sequence and frequency. The need for precision is so great that the factories producing jet engines get directly involved in the training and selection of the maintenance mechanics. Responsibilities are clearly defined and the organizational structure will be similar for all maintenance operations dealing with that particular kind of engine. The effects of a good or bad performance will be fairly immediate and dramatic: if the job was well done, the plane will fly; if it was badly done, the result will appear in newspapers around the world. Because of this, political influence or nepotism is unlikely to be very successful in obtaining jobs for unqualified candidates in jet engine maintenance. Influence might decide who is selected from among those qualified; perhaps the best person would not be selected, but the standards would not fall below a certain minimum. Nor would it be possible to adhere to certain traditions, such as strict seniority, because the best qualified would not always be the most senior.

In the case of tractors, detailed maintenance and training manuals also are produced, and factories often help organize training courses for operators and mechanics. Responsibilities among tractor operators and related personnel are also clearly defined, although not as strictly as for jet engine mechanics. Often the operator will be an amateur, such as a farmer. Thus there are many more organizational possibilities under which tractors are operated. Mechanical standards are also less rigid: tractors are not so delicate as jet engines, maintenance does not have to be so strict, and a breakdown is only a nuisance and seldom dangerous. Although the operations performed by the tractor will obviously have an influence on crop yields, it will be extremely difficult to establish the link between the quality of the tractor performance and yields. Many other factors will determine those yields, and the effects will not be apparent for several months. Tractor operators are not as skilled as jet engine mechanics. Some basic skills are required, but tractors can be operated—or, more precisely (and this is an essential point in the argument), it is commonly accepted that they can be operated—by people whose abilities vary greatly. The range between the best and the worst tractor operator is probably much wider than the range between the best and the worst jet engine mechanic. Appointments for tractor operators are therefore more subject to political or nepotistic influences and to cultural traditions, such as seniority.

At the other extreme, the tasks of educational counseling cannot be defined with the same precision that is possible for the maintenance of jet engines, or even of tractors. Certain targets can be defined: for example, a counselor could be assigned thirty-five students. But this is not equivalent to saying that a mechanic should work on thirty-five jet engines a month. The mechanic would know exactly what to do with each engine, but the counselor has no way of knowing *exactly* what to do with each student in each interview. The state of the art in psychology and related disciplines does not allow the detailed specification of the required tasks and sequences: the "optimum" counsel for a specific individual is just not written down in any manual. Counseling is basically an art, and counselors have to find the right approach by trial and error and modify it as they go along.

The effects of their advice could be far-reaching: a potentially excellent doctor could end up as a mediocre engineer. But it will seldom be possible to isolate counseling from the many other factors that have determined someone's educational and professional path. Counseling could have an influence tomorrow or ten years hence. As a consequence, it is practically impossible to trace the effects of the counselor's performance.

The range in performance between good and bad counselors is probably even wider than among tractor operators. Even though the requirement of professional training establishes some minimal standards, wide variations are possible. For example, after a change in government it would be perfectly possible to fire all socialist counselors and bring in conservative ones. The effect on quality is impossible to predict. But few would think of firing all socialist jet engine mechanics and replacing them with conservatives. Similarly, in counseling seniority is perfectly acceptable as a basis for promotion and may even be a sound qualification. But whether or not it is cannot be assessed, and nobody ever tries.

Many other examples could be mentioned. In nuclear power plants, the precision and specificity of many activities and the consequences of a bad performance are, if anything, even more dramatic than in the case of jet engine maintenance—or, for that matter, air traffic controllers. In the middle of the spectrum are a host of activities that use medium technology and have mild effects: textile manufacturing, food processing, and metalworking. Most financial activities, like those in high technology, share a high degree of specificity and technical control (through accounting, auditing, and financial management), and to a considerable extent their failure has immediate and dramatic effects. At the other end of the spectrum are most of the social or people-oriented activities related to education, nutrition, health care, and management, including coordination and the supervision of personnel. Also at this end are most low-technology activities, which in principle can be specified in detail and do have potentially important effects, but they allow more leeway in the skill with which they are performed, and their effects are difficult to trace and generally not immediate. Weeding, for example, is apparently a simple activity. But it can be done scientifically, with the most sophisticated techniques, equipment, and products (the optimal weed killer for a particular type of soil, crop, and expected weather pattern). It can be done with scientific but still very labor-intensive techniques (a highly developed routine focusing on the most important weeds, with a clear and well-analyzed sequence through the year). Or it can be done with no method, equipment, or products at all, with bare hands, as in time immemorial. And how can we measure precisely the effects of good or bad weeding? Can they be separated from those of other factors affecting agricultural production? How serious are the consequences of bad weeding?

These examples illustrate several hypotheses. First, for certain activities, particularly those related to high technology and finance, it is possible to specify with great precision the long-term objectives and the method for achieving them, for controlling that achievement, and, as a consequence, for rewarding the participants. Second, the effects of performance in the high-specificity activities are more intense and immediate, and more directly attributable to the people involved. Third, the intensity of an effect and how quickly it will influence the actors are essential elements in determining institutional performance because knowledge of results and clear identification and allocation of rewards and punishments are powerful motivational forces. Fourth, the degree of specificity of an activity has an important influence on how the participants—managers and workers—will define the nature and scope of their jobs and specific assignments. It will induce specific behavior of individuals which, when aggregated for the group that composes an organization, will determine specific patterns of organizational performance and behavior. Fifth, high specificity, by allowing fewer degrees of freedom, imposes more precise managerial and organizational arrangements. Obviously, wide variations are always possible, but less than in low-specificity activities.

Four questions serve as a basis for a more systematic treatment of the subject in the remainder of this chapter: (1) how much can the activity be defined and what is the length of time for which the definition applies? (2) what is the nature and intensity of the effects of a good or bad performance, and how soon do they materialize? (3) how are the participants affected, and how is responsibility shared among them? and (4) how do the participants react to the incentives derived from those effects? The third question can be turned around somewhat: to what extent can participants or organizations transfer the effects of their actions to other participants or organizations? What proportion of the effects must remain within the decisionmaking unit and what proportion can be transferred to others?

Thus, the concept of specificity consists of four components:

○ The potential for specification, which can be divided into the potential for defining objectives, methods, and control systems and the length of time for which these definitions are valid.
○ The nature of effects—that is, their intensity, timing (whether immediate or delayed), spread among actors and activities, and traceability.
○ The ways in which the two previous components affect the motivation and behavior of the participants.
○ The types of action undertaken by the participants in response to these effects; the different ways that actors interpret their jobs.

This definition encompasses the characteristics of the activities (the objectives, methods, and effects), together with the consequences of those characteristics for the people involved. Strictly speaking, the degree of specificity is defined only by the characteristics of each activity, which in turn define the nature and intensity of the incentives derived from the degree of specificity. Nevertheless, to explore the operational consequences of these concepts, it is also necessary to study the reaction of the participants to those characteristics.

Potential for Specification

To what extent can an activity be defined? In principle, any activity can be divided almost infinitely into specific tasks—for example, the different tasks performed in the maintenance of a jet engine—but such detail is not necessary for this analysis. It is enough to focus on the general characteristics of an activity, without bothering with the variations among tasks.

Objectives

One could argue that objectives can be defined with a similar degree of precision for all activities in the high-specificity/low-specificity spectrum. For example, objectives in a certain period could be to maintain X jet engines, operate tractor services over Y hectares, and counsel Z students. But this apparent similarity breaks down when we look into these activities in greater detail and with a broader perspective. Once it is decided to maintain X jet engines, it is unlikely that this objective will change significantly and that it will be decided not to maintain them or to do it at a different standard. With tractor services, many factors—such as weather conditions and price changes—could modify the original objective. In educational counseling, the specific objective for each student cannot be determined until counseling has actually begun, a fact that may influence the number of students seen in a given period, since some will require more and others less time. A similar case is that of a personnel officer in a large corporation. Part of his activities will be routine, such as keeping records, undertaking performance evaluations, or recruiting. But a sizable and unpredictable portion of his time will be spent in handling specific personnel matters: conflicts, personal crises, and resignations.

Time

Attention now shifts to the time dimension, because the issue is not only the extent to which objectives can be specified, but also for how long. The possibility of defining objectives for long periods was one of the main advantages of factory production: the same type of cloth could be manufactured for three or six months. The planning periods in some high-specificity activities such as airplane production and shipbuilding are becoming longer and can cover several years. However, the relevant periods are usually shorter in the low-specificity activities, which depend more on the vagaries of human behavior or the political process and, in the case of low-technology agriculture, on the weather. In practice, this means that in high-specificity activities a higher proportion of actors can undertake similar tasks for a longer period of time than in low-specificity ones.

Methods

The importance of the time dimension becomes clearer in regard to specifying the methods for achieving objectives. The advantages of high-specificity processes are underscored by considering two examples,

a textile factory and almost any type of agriculture, say, wheat production. It is easier to specify the right method for manufacturing textiles
than for growing wheat. The technology for specific types of textile production is practically universal, with only a few variations from country
to country. Once the machinery is in place, its operation is fairly standard; inputs are clearly defined and the technical processes are probably
explained in a good manual or by a technician. If the industrialist can be
reasonably assured of markets and inputs, he will be all set for at least
several months of production.

In contrast, a farmer trying to produce wheat cannot buy an exact technical package, as the industrialist can. Some general methods for
producing wheat are widely applicable, but the exact process has to be
specified for each plot to take account of soil, topography, climate, and
other conditions. In developing countries, this is generally a process of
trial and error, in which a production technique is discovered after many
painful experiences. As a result, farmers are understandably very reluctant to change it. But even without the complication of exogenous factors,
agriculture will generally be more complex and less specific than manufacturing. In a one-year cycle, the textile manufacturer does more or less
the same thing every day, except the few times the machines are stopped
for maintenance. The agricultural process, however, requires that different tasks be performed at different times of the year—plowing, seeding,
weeding, harvesting, milling—and the exact content and sequence of
them may vary considerably. If something extraordinary happens, such
as unusual weather or a plague, the method for achieving the objectives
becomes considerably more complicated. The cycle has to be changed
and a specific method devised to cope with the situation. Sufficient exogenous factors occur to require that methods and activities be redefined
almost daily. The more modern the technology, the more specific and
"industrial" are the agricultural processes and the greater their indepen-
dence from exogenous factors. Conversely, low-technology agriculture is
more affected by exogenous factors and requires more frequent changes
in methods.

What about the methods of the educational counselor? His situation is
even more ambiguous than the farmer's. There is no accepted science of
educational counseling. The counselor has to draw on his own knowledge to decide which approach to follow with each person. The same
approach might be followed with most of the students in a group, or it
might have to be different for each one. If counseling continues for a long
period, the method will probably have to change in unpredictable ways
depending, for example, on the student's reaction to previous counseling, his academic path, family factors, and so on.

Among low-specificity activities, methods are less universal, lack generally accepted standards, and are applicable without changes for a

shorter time. But the range of feasible alternatives increases and, in practice, the possibility of knowing all of them decreases. The method for maintaining jet engines is, for all practical purposes, unique. Minor degrees of freedom can be tolerated, but significant shortcuts and sloppy work cause fatal accidents. With textile production there is also basically one method for a particular machine, but greater leeway than with jet engines: maintenance can be postponed and certain standards reduced without ostensible effects, at least in the short run. With low-technology wheat production the range of alternatives expands. Several feasible ways of cultivating a specific plot of land all yield more or less the same amount of wheat. The farmer appears to have considerable freedom in performing the different tasks from day to day or week to week (again without ostensible effects) and many more possibilities for reacting to events in the course of the agricultural year.

The panoply of alternative methods expands even more in educational counseling. The many feasible ways of performing this activity range from dictatorial counseling based on a thorough knowledge of the student's potential to modern coaching designed to help the student find his own preferences and limitations. At the level of individual counseling sessions, the variety of methods is even wider.

Control

The final element involved in the concept of specificity, the ability to control achievement, is a result of the ability to specify objectives and methods and thus to verify achievement. As with other aspects, controlling achievement is easier with high-specificity, more difficult with low-specificity activities. One reason is the intangibility of the output in low-specificity activities; usually it cannot be verified, and the products are less homogeneous. A particular operator in a factory may perform one clearly identifiable activity with a specific output. An educational counselor performs a wide variety of activities, which do not result in tangible outputs that can later be verified with precision.

Three Examples

Although the purpose here is not to develop a complete taxonomy of activities according to their degree of specificity, three other examples should be reviewed: activities of financial institutions in general, activities of a central government organization, such as a regulatory body or a line ministry, and marketing.

Financial activities can be classified among those with high specificity: objectives and methods can be specified with reasonable certainty, absolute precision is required in the handling of operations, and a strict set of controls ensures a high degree of discipline among those involved. Objectives can be specified for considerable periods and the range of methods for achieving them is limited.

The case of government line agencies is more complex. Their objectives, at least in broad outline, will be determined outside the agency by the political system, and the stability of that system will determine how long those objectives remain and with what precision they are defined. Some of the methods might also be politically determined, in which case the agency becomes a mere administrator of policies and methods, without many degrees of freedom. For example, in an agency regulating education, the general policy might be to reorient secondary education toward an academic curriculum, and the method for achieving that objective might be to control the secondary school curriculum and to review final exams. Most probably, the decision to focus on the academic stream would have a heavy political component, but the method for implementing the regulation would be decided at the technical level within the agency. Judging the achievement and effectiveness of a regulatory agency is difficult because the agency will be pursuing multiple objectives that might be contradictory. Under these conditions, the achievement of one objective becomes almost impossible to trace.

Marketing is relevant in this analysis because it brings the demand side of the equation into play, a not unimportant aspect in many public sector activities. Marketing is considered to be of intermediate to high specificity. Objectives can be specified very clearly, but the methods for achieving the objectives can vary considerably and are at the heart of the difference between good and bad marketing. In spite of the proliferation of quasi-mechanical marketing methods, the activity becomes really people-oriented because it attempts to change behavior. Thus the exact method for achieving success in a marketing effort will have to be tailored to the particular circumstances and people involved.

Marketing is essential to many activities in the public sector. Aside from the obvious ones in public enterprises, it is central to people-oriented activities such as agricultural extension and health care, with the added complication that in most cases the services are not trying to identify and supply a demand already existing, but are attempting to create a demand through changes in behavioral patterns.[1]

Agreement

This description of a high- to low-specificity spectrum is oversimplified because it assumes that all the people involved agree on objectives (goals) and methods (means). A disagreement, or the possibility of disagreement, about either will in practice reduce the degree of specificity. Thus at the high-specificity end of the spectrum an extreme case would be one in which there is complete agreement about objectives and methods. At the other end, an activity in which there is disagreement about objectives and methods would be an extreme case of low specificity.[2] The spectrum in between is really more complex than implied in the preceding analysis.

One consequence of extending the concept of specificity to include the extent of agreement about objectives and methods is that the analysis can take account of country commitment, one of the reasons given for progress in institutional development programs. In addition, it is possible to clarify what is meant by methods and their relation to the range of technologies for the different activities. "Disagreement about methods" could refer to uncertainty about those methods. This fits nicely with the specificity spectrum, in which lower levels of specificity are associated with increasing levels of uncertainty. Several examples, such as the case of marketing, follow this pattern well.

As expected, the World Bank's experience provides many examples of disagreements about objectives, methods, or both, either among officials within the country or between country and Bank officials. The specificity issue is well reflected in the patterns found; in higher specificity activities there was often disagreement about objectives but not often about methods. With several railways, for instance, discussions centered on the type of service they should provide and on their role as a public enterprise, but seldom was it necessary to debate methodologies for track renewal or locomotive maintenance. Similar findings appear with respect to telecommunications and electric power. The patterns are more complex with lower specificity activities: in the case of several educational institutions and agricultural credit agencies there were disagreements about both the objectives and the methods pursued; in many other projects, especially agriculture and livestock, there was considerable agreement about objectives (such as increased production) but serious differences about the technical and institutional approaches for achieving them.

Nature of Effects

High-specificity activities have been defined as those in which the effects of a good or a bad performance are intense, immediate, identifiable, and focused. Conversely, the effects of performance in low-specificity activities are weak, delayed, less identifiable, and diffused. The effect of an activity can thus be analyzed in relation to four characteristics: its intensity (whether strong or weak), timing (whether felt immediately or over a long period), spread (the number of persons or activities affected), and traceability (whether it can be identified and isolated from other influences). Different combinations of these characteristics define a broad spectrum of degrees of specificity.

Examples of the Four Characteristics

In jet engine maintenance, the effect of a bad performance will be intense and dramatic; at worst, failure of one or more engines may result in a plane crash. The effect will be immediate in the sense that, given the way in which a jet engine operates, a maintenance failure will be detected in a short time. The technology allows a reasonably accurate identification of the causes of an accident, and responsibilities can then be established. A failure will directly and indirectly affect a large number of people and activities: directly, those in the plane; indirectly, the airline, the manufacturer, the government regulating agency, and so on. In short, the effect is quick, intense, widespread, and easily identifiable. Fundamental to this analysis is the fact that in most cases the failures, not the successes, provide the element of discipline. If jet engines are well maintained and planes fly normally, no particular dramatic effect takes place, but the nature of the potential failure defines the intensity of the effect and the resulting discipline.

Among other high-specificity activities, those related to nuclear power would be an even more dramatic example. But many other cases present similar characteristics, such as the transport of liquefied gas, some activities in the chemical industry, pharmaceuticals, and certain types of mining operations. Surgery comes immediately to mind, but with a difference. Although the effects of bad surgery are as intense and immediate as they can be, they affect primarily one person, and generally so many factors affect the outcome that it is difficult to trace the specific cause.

In activities in which failure has an immediate and dramatic effect, there is a high level of redundancy in the technologies and mechanisms used: back-up landing gears, double or triple sets of controls, and so on. As accidents have demonstrated, this raises special managerial problems, because staff have to be trained to observe punctiliously procedures that might in fact be neglected without any immediately visible consequence. The importance of the immediate and directly traceable effects can be seen when contrasted with two very broad policymaking activities that fall at this end of the spectrum: establishing macroeconomic policies and controlling environmental pollution. In both cases the effects are extremely intense and widespread, but not necessarily immediate, and it will generally be difficult to trace them and to assign responsibility for them. The shape of their specificity is more insidious.

Continuing along the spectrum of specificity, the effects of a bad performance in a textile factory will be less intense. The extreme case of a breakdown of the machinery merely means closing the factory for a time, with a financial loss confined to those directly involved. As with all machinery, the effects of a bad performance will probably be apparent rather quickly, and responsibilities can be assigned to those involved. Thus the shape of the effects is similar to that described for jet engines, but with less intensity.

In the case of weeding, the effects are even less intense because bad weeding does not halt production or cause an accident. The potential damage will depend on how badly the weeding was done. It is not a "binary" activity like that of industrial machinery which either functions or does not. The effect of bad weeding will not be immediate; it will unfold slowly—insidiously—over the agricultural season and even beyond. The damage will not be widespread but will affect mainly the farmer.[3] And it will be extremely difficult to trace the cause and differentiate it from the myriad of factors that finally determine the actual yield. Agricultural technology, even under the best of circumstances, does not permit a precise conclusion that in a particular case yields were X percent lower because weeding was done one way or another or were Y percent lower because weeding was delayed ten days.

For counseling, even a hypothetical illustration is difficult. The direct spread is clear: it affects the person being counseled. The intensity of the effect is subject to wide variations: it could be decisive in setting the career path of an individual, but it could have a less intensive or even negative effect, which materializes over a long time and is difficult to isolate from that of many other factors affecting the career path of the persons being counseled. A similar analysis can be made for many other low-specificity activities such as education, personnel management, or family planning. A detailed study will show that the effects of these activities might be intense, although not in the immediate, dramatic way of some of the high-specificity activities, but they will always be hard to separate from those of other factors and will take much longer to materialize.

Financial institutions also conform in this respect to the characteristics of high-specificity activities. The results of failure are intense and quite immediate—financial statements have to balance, and operating losses are generally known soon—although perhaps not as dramatic as in the case of an equipment failure. Since everything should be recorded, it is easy to trace the effects of specific actions in great detail. They would directly affect a limited number of individuals involved in an operation, but indirectly a large number.[4]

The analysis is more difficult with regard to a government body, for example, a regulatory agency in education. It is unlikely that the operation of the agency will have effects of high intensity except in cases of major changes in educational policy, but such changes would probably be attributed to decisions made not by the agency but at a higher political level. The effects, particularly of the more routine regulatory activities, will not be immediate but will spread over a long time. And they will be extremely diffuse, covering the entire educational system; the weaker, slower, and more widespread the effects, the more difficult they will be to trace.

Marketing is again in an intermediate position. The impact of actions could be quite intense but not as dramatic as in some of the technological activities. The effects are very traceable and materialize rapidly.

The actual intensity of the effect of many activities is determined by the culture and the situation: some societies are more stoic than others. For example, in some countries a power failure is a common occurrence, a mistake by a hospital routinely accepted; in others, a power failure is a major event and a hospital mistake the cause for a civil suit. These cultural differences tend to even out the degrees of intensity of effects among activities so that it becomes difficult to use high-specificity activities as a means to improve performance. Tolerance of failure is part of the vicious circle that has to be broken.

The Generation of Incentives

Once the potential effects are identified, it is necessary to assess which ones actually act as incentives for the people involved to improve their performance and which ones are "lost" or filtered because there is no mechanism that links the incentive to the participants even if the effects can be traced. In general, effects that are difficult to trace or that materialize after a long time will be lost as incentives. In many cases, the institutional mechanisms themselves cause the loss of some incentives. Inadequate rewards and punishments within an organization, for example, reduce or eliminate feedback and leave participants in the same position regardless of whether the impact of their actions is positive or negative.

The point here is that different activities generate various types of incentives to institutional performance. Even though an activity generates an incentive, it will not necessarily act as such for the people involved because it might be too diffuse, weak, or lost in the transmission. The analysis suggests again that the higher the degree of specificity, the lower will be the proportion of incentives that are lost.

One last issue is the relationships among the four characteristics of effects. For each effect, which is the dominant characteristic? Are they additive? What are the tradeoffs among them? The answers to these questions are enormously important from an operational point of view, but the issue has not yet been explored. Each activity generates (or "emits," to take an analogy from the physical sciences) a number of effects, the characteristics of which depend on the activity itself. These effects may produce incentives to institutional performance, but many of them are lost. The question is whether the intensity, timing, spread, or traceability is the main determinant of the incentive or whether they operate jointly. For example, in locomotive maintenance, is the threat of an accident or a breakdown the main inducement of better performance, or is it also the fact that the accident might happen fairly soon and can be traced to maintenance? How different are these characteristics in terms of generating incentives?

Two extreme hypotheses can be explored. One is that the characteristics are fully additive, that is, that the threat of accident acts as an incentive in addition to the short timing, the relative traceability, and the narrow spread. Casual observation suggests that this is a plausible hypothesis. The other extreme is less likely, although it can easily be seen how in different cases one of the characteristics will be the dominant one: in nuclear power plants it will be the intensity, in many administrative functions (or in a concert) it will be the timing. For some clearly identifiable individual actions, it might be the narrow spread of the effect.

How the Actors Are Affected

We must now turn some of these arguments around and focus on the workers and managers in each unit who receive these incentives. How is a worker affected by an activity for which objectives cannot be clearly specified? What happens to his motivation if the effects of his actions are not noticeable in the short run but materialize over a long time and, in any case, can hardly be traced since he shares responsibility with several workers? In other words, how are workers' motivations affected by the characteristics of the activities they perform?

Answers to these questions will be possible only after a deeper analysis of how the many factors influencing performance affect the individuals actually working in an institution. It is generally accepted that the activities performed by individuals will affect their motivation on and off the job by shaping their personalities and general outlook—some would say their degree of modernization. It is not altogether clear, however, what effects specific activities will have.[5] The aggregation of these influences is crucial for understanding the workings of an institution. The main point is that the activity generates "automatic" inducements because of its very nature, and these influences are stronger with high-specificity activities and weaker with low-specificity ones.

Potential for Specificity

Even the most precise activities allow some leeway for interpreting the pace, timing, and other aspects of the job to be performed.[6] The leeway increases if the objectives, methods, and control mechanisms are less precise and the impact weak, delayed, and diffuse. The jet engine mechanic may be able to change the pace of his work or make some minor variations in sequencing, but by and large the tasks will have to be performed as prescribed. But a personnel officer could redefine the specific objectives of his assignment and the methods followed almost daily. This means that his performance cannot be controlled as precisely as that of the mechanic. Management will therefore have to rely on indirect indicators to assess his performance—for example, what the staff say about the personnel officer. His performance depends largely on his self-motivation and on indirect, general incentives, such as salary levels, opportunities for promotion, and status. The mechanic may have all those incentives, too, plus the inherent discipline of the activity. It is likely, then, that, *on average*, performance will be better and more uniform among jet engine mechanics than personnel officers. There might still be excellent performances among personnel officers, but they will probably be by outstanding individuals. The variability in performance would be larger.

This difference in the amount of leeway for defining jobs is a fundamental point. It is the opening through which cultural and political factors influence the operations of an institution. It is also the opening through which individual differences become more apparent. In a high-specificity activity, the scope for cultural and political influences is smaller. The jet engine will have to be maintained in almost exactly the same way whether the society is socialist or capitalist, Muslim or Christian, modern or primitive. Cultural traits might affect the pace at which the operation is performed, but in the end it will be the same operation. And, as pointed out earlier, politicians exert minimal influence on this type of specialized personnel.

Low-specificity activities such as counseling, however, will be heavily influenced by the culture of the society, by the way in which individuals relate to each other, by the standard methods of persuasion, and by whether it is legitimate to give advice at all. Such influence is inevitable because it is not possible to deal with social issues outside the cultural environment in which they take place. In intermediate activities cultural influences are more difficult to trace. In a textile factory, for example, technological requirements are flexible enough to allow variations in performance. Cultural elements such as seniority or particular work habits may therefore be incorporated into the operation without any apparent loss in performance, although the hidden cost could be extremely high in the long run.

Characteristics of Effects

If the effects of an activity are weak, slow to materialize, widely spread over individuals and activities, and difficult to trace or distinguish from other factors, they will offer much less positive incentives for operational effectiveness than will activities whose effects are strong, immediate, directed to few individuals and activities, and easily traceable to those responsible. This proposition is based on widely accepted behavioral patterns. There are exceptions in the case of strongly motivated and efficient individuals and those possessed by a "revolutionary spirit" (that is, the excitement and commitment engendered in large numbers of people by rapid changes at the national or agency level), but these exceptions do not invalidate the general proposition. In general, an air traffic controller or someone in charge of the security of a nuclear power plant will have an automatic inducement to perform adequately because of the inherent characteristics of the job. And the inducement will be stronger than that for a bureaucrat doing a minor clerical job. The more immediate the effect, as with air traffic controllers, the stronger the inducement. It is human nature to discount the future: effects that will materialize next year are less valuable as incentives than those materializing tomorrow.

Similarly, if effects cannot be traced or are mixed with those of other actions, the discipline of accountability disappears. A very good secondary school teacher may have a positive and lasting influence over a student's command of the language, and twenty-five years later that student may get a promotion mainly because of his ability to write clearly. But how is that success going to be linked to that teacher? And how is the teacher going to be rewarded?

Another characteristic of an effect is its spread, and some would say the importance of who or what is affected (as when the jet engine mechanic is in charge of the president's plane). If the impact is widely distributed it will not offer much of an incentive, but if the impact is narrowly focused the incentive could be powerful. Mistakes by travel agents, doctors, stock brokers, or bankers usually result in rather dramatic reactions from their clients. At the other extreme are the mild and widespread effects produced by a minor bureaucrat regulating or controlling an unimportant activity, members of a committee without much influence, and certain advisers without power or authority. For these people, the incentive for performance is so tenuous that it is irrelevant.

At a more aggregate level, people's behavior is the result of the interplay of these different types of effects. The most glaring example is the relative lack of success of maintenance and preventive programs in low-specificity activities, especially when the effects of bad maintenance and lack of prevention take a long time to materialize and the actual results—accidents, breakdowns, or illnesses—are difficult to link to the lack of maintenance or prevention. In the short run nothing happens. This lack of an obvious impact is at the heart of the difficulty in promoting maintenance and preventive activities in developing countries: there are no inauguration ceremonies for the good maintenance of roads or for preventive health care. It takes a major cultural adjustment, which has been identified as one characteristic of modernization, to absorb the notions of prevention, maintenance, and damage control.

No matter what a country's level of development, activities with these characteristics have historically suffered from serious difficulties in getting going. The most obvious example is environmental concerns. Although the effects of environmental policies could be very intense and vital, they may materialize only after a long time and be too widespread to be of direct concern to any group in particular. Progress has been made in these areas mainly in response to accidents and obvious and widespread damage.

In all previous discussions a linear relation between incentives and performance has generally been assumed; that is, stronger and better incentives are thought to result in higher levels of institutional performance. But there is sufficient evidence to conclude that this is not the case. Additional incentives will result in higher levels of performance only up to a point, after which more incentives will become dysfunctional and result in actual declines in performance. The "incentive function" will probably follow the shape of a normal bell curve. But how do we assess the differences in the shape of the incentive function for different combinations of effects. Again, this question remains unexplored. Common sense would suggest that very intensive effects would result in narrower incentive functions, and mild effects in wider ones.

One last area worth exploring is the response to the incentives engendered by different types of activities. A reasonable hypothesis is that the higher the professional and educational level of those involved in the activity, the less important this kind of incentive will be in explaining performance. Unskilled workers doing menial work would be very much influenced by the incentives derived from the nature of the activity, whereas the performance of high-level researchers or senior managers might be almost totally independent of the nature of the activity. This hypothesis is strongly supported in the literature on organizational psychology by the "needs based" approach, which postulated the existence of a hierarchy of needs: the lowest being the physiological needs, then safety and love; the highest being esteem and self-actualization. Professionals presumably have their "lower" needs taken care of and are therefore much more likely to be concerned with the "higher" needs for esteem and self-actualization.[7] In fact, it has been argued that a main objective of the lengthy training period for professionals and managers is precisely to reinforce commitment to the high performance standards that are unlikely to be adequately rewarded in the daily flow of incentives.[8]

Reactions of the Actors

In analyzing how people normally react to incentives, I rely heavily on Leibenstein and Simon.[9] Traditional microeconomic theory has neglected the internal workings of a productive unit. It assumes that the smallest unit of analysis is an organization, which will make optimal use of the resources available to it. Both Leibenstein and Simon have made a major contribution to the theory of organization by questioning some of the behavioral assumptions on which the theory is based and by applying some of the tools and principles of microeconomics to the study of productive units.

All members of an organization, from the chairman of the board to the last worker, should be seen as decisionmaking units. Each decision can be considered as a "project," with its stream of benefits and costs. Obviously, people do not consciously act this way—at least not all the time—but this is a useful way of focusing on the issue.[10] People will react to different types of stimuli in terms of their objectives.

The analysis in this section is based on the following assumptions. First, human behavior conforms more to Simon's notion of "administrative man" than to the notion of "economic man" on which economics is based.[11] Members of organizations make decisions affecting themselves and the organization on the basis of incomplete information. They attempt to find not an optimal solution in the economic sense, but one that is acceptable in the light of their own aspirations and the known possibilities. Behind this behavior there is also an assumption of rational behavior and rational choice.

Second, individuals give high priority to their own interests and try to achieve them with minimal effort. Under normal conditions individuals have a hierarchy of priorities, beginning with those that affect them directly (a concept that can be extended to include their family or friends), the organizations to which they belong, and broader units such as the city, region, or nation. This scheme does not give much weight to the "revolutionary spirit." I believe in it, but not as a permanent and pervasive motivation. Experience shows that it peaks over relatively short periods—when the revolutionary change takes place and shortly thereafter—but declines rather rapidly; it is randomly distributed among the members of a community and very uneven in the number of individuals affected and the intensity and duration of the effect. More difficult to include in this scheme is vocation, the special interest that induces individuals to continue certain activities even when the incentives are below the levels normally required to elicit a certain performance. If the educational and training systems in a country are strong, the pattern of vocations will reflect those programs. But if professional and training programs are weak, as they are in many developing countries, vocations will be randomly distributed, with negative consequences for institutional performance.

Third, individuals try to make their environment more controllable and predictable. This behavior coincides with that of institutions, but the specific objectives and the methods of achieving them might not be the same for an organization and the individuals that compose it. A corollary is that, on average, individuals do not desire an absolute or excessive degree of freedom, but rather a "reasonable" number of rules and regulations as a form of protection. (Just what constitutes a reasonable number is culturally determined.) These rules and regulations allow individuals to channel their actions within relatively narrow limits and help control their environment.

Central to individuals' attempt to control their environment is the way each person interprets his job. The Leibenstein-Simon literature considers several motivational factors, such as the structure and the "culture" of the organization, but does not deal explicitly with specificity as influencing job interpretation. Leibenstein, however, lists several characteristics of a job: the activities to be performed, the pace and quality of the performance, and the timing. This categorization permits a closer look at how specificity as such allows different degrees of freedom in job interpretation.

Job interpretation will be the result of how the automatic inducements of the activity combine with motivational forces that are determined by personal interests and with the style of management. This interaction is crucial in determining performance. For example, very strict budgeting and control mechanisms will probably have a negligible motivational effect on air traffic controllers; these mechanisms would be redundant because of the discipline imposed by the activity itself. Strict quantitative controls on a basically unquantifiable activity, such as counseling, may even have a negative motivational influence. But they are essential for good performance in intermediate activities such as marketing.

As a matter of fact, specific signals (given through managerial and organizational rules and regulations), as Leibenstein has indicated, have motivational effects. Overly specific signals, such as strict controls on attendance and output, may reduce trust and motivation; more general signals, such as exhortations by managers, may improve motivation, but increase the risk of a lower level of performance. The "automatic" inducements derived from specificity do have a motivational effect, but are probably more neutral than direct managerial signals. (A study of these differences would be a useful exercise.) A potential handicap of the low-specificity activities is that, in principle, they require stronger managerial signals to achieve higher levels of performance. Stronger signals or tighter controls will ensure a minimum performance, but they increase the likelihood of negative motivational effects and greatly reduce the possibility of above-average effectiveness.

A fourth behavioral assumption is derived from Leibenstein's "selective rationality," which postulates that, in general, individuals will try to minimize the pressure to which they are subjected and reduce the amount of calculation in their decisionmaking. Experience suggests that the degree of rationality increases as pressure increases: a crisis or an unusually strong demand helps wonderfully to concentrate the mind. Thus, it is likely that in high-specificity activities the intrinsic pressure from the activity will create a high degree of rationality at the outset, before any managerial pressure is applied. Again, this means that low-specificity activities require stronger managerial pressure to achieve a higher level of performance.

Leibenstein also developed the concept of "inert areas," defined as follows: "The inert area idea reflects a fairly common set of experiences: those in which it is possible to improve a situation in some respects but not worth the effort to do so. By an inert area, I have in mind a set of effort points whose associated levels of utility are not equal, but in which the action required to go from a lower to a higher utility level involves a utility cost that is not compensated by a gain in utility."[12] This concept is particularly useful for analyzing differences in potential performance among activities. The inert area for an individual will be closely related to the discipline or pressure exercised by the activities being performed (or by a competitive atmosphere, as discussed in chapter 7): lack of specificity makes for larger inert areas. Of course, inert areas will be determined not only by the nature of the activity but also by the personality of the people involved.

Some general hypotheses related to these inert areas have been developed. Risk averters will tend to have broader inert areas, while innovators and entrepreneurs (who could be someone in a bureaucracy) will tend to have narrower ones. Supervisors will try to narrow the inert areas, and peers to broaden them. Following the line of reasoning developed in this chapter, the hypothesis is that the inert areas of individuals dealing with high-specificity activities will be narrower than those of individuals working in low-specificity activities. There is probably a spectrum going from very narrow inert areas in high-specificity activities in the private sector to very broad ones in certain low-specificity activities in the public sector. This analysis again points in the same direction: individuals with large inert areas require stronger incentives to achieve a higher level of performance. But they have large inert areas for precisely the same reasons that make it difficult for them to have sufficiently specific and strong incentives.

In the end, each individual will arrive at an equilibrium position about the level of effort that he is willing to make and about the particular way he defines his job in light of his own motivation and the incentives to which he is subjected. This analysis can be expanded to broad groups within an organization to derive further differences between high-specificity and low-specificity activities.

Toward a Specificity Index

In principle, a "specificity index" could be built which would serve to rank activities according to the degree of discipline that they impose on the people involved. Such an index is attempted in table 1 (pp. 70–71) for several activities defined at different levels of aggregation. The first category includes broad activities, such as accounting and personnel, that are standard in most medium-size or large organizations; the second category includes more narrowly defined activities, such as highway maintenance, and those restricted to particular industries or subsectors, such as air traffic control and agricultural extension. Each activity is ranked according to the degree of specificity and nature of effects; each receives a total of eight rankings, which have been given equal weight to form the index of specificity for each activity.

The results at this stage are purely indicative, based largely on the general information available about the nature of those activities. The preparation of such an index is in itself a major research project. Each of the eight characteristics needs to be defined much more precisely and a basis for comparison established among activities. For example, the spread of the effects is a complex concept that has to be linked with intensity: a particular activity could affect a large number of people, but at different levels of intensity. There is also a serious potential for multicollinearity; for instance, the possibility of controlling objectives is closely correlated with the nature of effects in general, and especially their traceability. Other problems concern the level of aggregation: the more aggregated the definition of activities, especially in attempts to categorize subsectors, the more difficult these problems become. Research to determine the best levels of aggregation is another complex and worthy project.

Although any committee would modify the numbers in the table, perhaps drastically, even at this preliminary level a few patterns begin to emerge. First, as expected, the spectrum of activities from high to low specificity appears quite clearly, with high-technology ones at the high-specificity end of the spectrum, and education, personnel, and other people-oriented activities at the other end. Air traffic controllers appear at the high end, and rural primary education at the low. The fact that the preparation of such an index needs further work is reflected in some of the results, which do not seem to reflect reality accurately. One would have expected somewhat larger variations, for instance, between air traffic controllers and locomotive operators.

Second, in practically all cases the degree of specificity seems to be equal to or higher than the effects of the activity as a factor determining the index. It is hard to attach much significance to this result because the rankings are unweighted averages and probably do not adequately capture the potentially more dramatic effects such as those derived from a nuclear plant failure. But, in general, it makes sense that the degree of specificity, which is more directly under the control of the activities themselves, would be more important.

Third, the difference between the subtotals for degree of specificity and nature of effects is larger than the average for activities such as rural primary education, plantation agriculture, and road maintenance. On the one hand, these activities produce effects that are difficult to encapsulate and to use as incentives for higher performance, but on the other hand they have a good possibility of defining objectives and methods (although not as good as most activities).

Fourth, one or more of the eight characteristics are particularly weak or strong for some activities—that is weak and strong from the point of view of providing incentives for achieving performance. The possibility of controlling the achievement of objectives is especially weak for many of the "softer" activities. Traceability seems to be another weak spot, as is the spread of the effect (for example, in planning, road maintenance, and primary education). At the other extreme, the possibility of defining objectives is among the strongest points, with few exceptions.

What is the practical use of attempting to build a specificity index? It helps to understand in a more precise way the incentives derived from the intrinsic nature of any one activity, so that a management strategy can be defined to make full use of the strong points and to devise managerial and administrative measures to compensate for the weak aspects or to mitigate their potentially negative effects. The ranking of activities, once it is sufficiently perfected, could be important for the internal management of institutions, helping to differentiate the treatment of activities at different points in the specificity spectrum so that special attention could be given to the low-specificity activities to ensure an acceptable level of performance. Similarly, at the macro level, rankings could be used to distinguish among broad activities and subsectors needing to be strengthened.

Table 1. Toward a Specificity Index

Activity	Degree of specificity					Nature of effects					Total
	Objective	Method	Control	Length of time	Subtotal	Intensity	Timing	Spread	Traceability	Subtotal	
General											
Accounting	4	4	4	4	16	4	3	4	5	16	32
Planning	3	3	2	3	11	2	3	2	3	10	21
Financial management	4	4	4	3	15	4	3	3	4	14	29
Personnel management	3	2	2	2	9	3	2	4	2	11	20
Training	4	3	3	3	13	2	3	4	2	11	24
Legal	4	5	5	4	18	4	5	4	5	18	36
General administration	4	4	4	4	16	3	4	3	4	14	30
Specific											
Low-technology and rainfed agriculture	4	3	3	2	12	3	2	4	2	11	23
Plantation agriculture	4	4	4	4	16	3	2	3	3	11	27
Rural primary education	4	2	3	3	12	2	1	2	2	7	19
Technical education	4	3	3	4	14	3	3	3	3	12	26
Agricultural extension	3	3	2	2	10	4	3	3	2	12	22
Health services	4	3	3	3	13	3	3	2	3	11	24
Jet engine maintenance	5	5	5	5	20	5	5	4	5	19	39
Road transport	4	4	4	4	16	4	4	3	4	15	31
Road maintenance	4	4	3	3	14	3	2	2	3	10	24
Counseling	3	2	2	2	9	2	2	4	3	11	20
Tractor operation	4	4	3	3	14	3	3	3	3	12	26

Irrigated agriculture	4	4	4	3	15	4	4	3	4	15	30
Locomotive operation	5	4	5	4	18	4	4	4	4	16	34
Railway manual track maintenance	4	3	4	4	15	4	4	4	4	16	31
Railway signaling	5	5	4	5	19	5	5	4	4	18	37
Air traffic control	5	5	5	5	20	5	5	5	5	20	40
Nuclear plant maintenance	5	5	5	5	20	5	5	5	4	19	39
Textile machine operation	5	4	4	4	17	4	4	3	3	13	30
Billing utilities	4	3	4	4	15	3	3	4	4	14	29
Car repair	4	4	4	4	16	4	4	3	4	15	31

1 = low specificity; 5 = high specificity.

Note: The components of the degree of specificity are defined as follows:

Objectives. The extent to which objectives can be defined. A high ranking means that objectives can be specified both in general terms and in great detail. A low ranking means that objectives can be specified only in very general terms.

Methods. The degree to which methods for achieving the objectives can be defined before beginning an activity. A high ranking means that those methods can be defined in great detail. A low ranking means that methods are unclear or uncertain or need major adaptations during operations.

Control of achievements. The degree to which it is possible to control the achievement of the original objectives. A high ranking means that close control is possible and relatively easy. A low ranking means that control is difficult.

Length of time. The length of time for which the definition of objectives, methods, and controls will hold true without requiring modification. A high ranking indicates the possibility of defining them for long periods; a low ranking reflects the need to modify objectives, methods, and controls frequently.

The nature of effects is characterized by the following:

Intensity. The strength of the effect on the people or equipment involved.

Timing. Whether the effects of the activity materialize immediately after actions take place, or whether they materialize weeks, months, or years afterwards.

Spread. Whether the activity affects one, a few, or a great many people or pieces of equipment. The spread could be uniform or could differ in intensity and timing among the people and equipment affected.

Traceability. Whether the effects of the activity can be traced, either by isolating them from the effects of concurrent activities or by isolating the actions of one person from those of others.

Notes

1. See Richard Manoff, *Social Marketing: New Imperative for Public Health* (New York: Praeger, 1985).

2. Thompson and Tuden developed some time ago a model of decision-making which focuses, broadly speaking, on objectives and methods. This model is a good indicator of the exponential increase in the difficulty of decisionmaking from a situation in which there is agreement to one in which there is disagreement. It shows how a clear situation results in a simple method of decisionmaking, while an unclear one presents almost insurmountable difficulties. See James D. Thompson and Arthur Tuden, "Strategies, Structures and Processes of Organizational Decision," in *Comparative Studies in Administration*, James D. Thompson, Peter B. Hammond, Robert W. Hawkes, Buford H. Junker, and Arthur Tuden, eds. (Pittsburgh, Penn.: University of Pittsburgh Press, 1959), pp. 195–216, and the discussion in chapter 9 below.

3. The measure of spread effect used here refers exclusively to one unit of production or a single action: one farmer doing bad plowing, one textile industry, one airplane. Obviously, if all farmers in a country are doing bad weeding, it would be a different phenomenon.

4. This does not preclude the fact that in many countries financial activities, particularly accounting, are done quite poorly. It has been argued that accounting is one of several activities that may be important for "bureaucratic hygiene" and the long-term general health of the organization but that have no immediate impact on the achievement of the institution's goals. These activities might, in fact, run counter to some of the current goals of the people who control the institution. See David K. Leonard, "The Political Realities of African Management," *World Development* (1987).

5. To illustrate this point, consider the case of identical twins who have shared the same school, house, city, environment, and so on, but separate at age eighteen to train for different careers. One becomes a mechanic in the maintenance of jet engines and the other, a primary school teacher. (Many scientists claim that identical twins would never do such a thing, but since this is merely a "thought experiment" it need not be scientifically accurate.) The question is, what differences in personality and outlook, or *weltanschauung*, are the twins going to have after five, ten, and fifteen years? There seems to be agreement that there will be some difference, but not on what the difference will be. Will the mechanic be more methodical and generally more efficient; will the teacher be more imaginative and have a broader outlook on life?

6. Many of these points have been developed in more detail by Leibenstein in his exploration of X-efficiency. See Harvey Leibenstein, *Beyond Economic Man: A New Foundation for Micro-Economics* (Cambridge, Mass.: Harvard University Press, 1976), and his *General X-Efficiency Theory and Economic Development* (New York: Oxford University Press, 1978).

7. See A. H. Maslow, "A Theory of Human Motivation," *Psychological Review*, vol. 50 (1943), pp. 370–96.

8. See Jaques Elliott, *The Measurement of Responsibility: A Study of Work, Payment, and Individual Capacity* (London: Tavistock, 1956).

9. Leibenstein, *Beyond Economic Man*, and Herbert A. Simon, *Administrative Behavior*, 2d ed. (New York: Macmillan, 1957).

10. This is an old problem in the social sciences, particularly in economics. When a specific behavior is postulated, it does not mean that each and every individual in the society will act that way all the time, but only that the behavior represent an average for a group of individuals.

11. The contrast between these two concepts has been analyzed in detail in several places. Simon's concept of bounded rationality is similar to Leibenstein's idea of selective rationality. See Herbert A. Simon, *The New Science of Management Decision* (New York: Harper, 1960).

12. Leibenstein, *Beyond Economic Man*, pp. 111–12.

6 Technology and the Degree of Specificity

In the previous chapter the notion of specificity was developed in the abstract, as an independent concept. The main purpose of this chapter is to link it with related concepts and approaches that support it, and to explore the relations between the nature of the technologies and the degree of specificity. A discussion of special cases and the World Bank experience illustrates these linkages.

The underlying concept of specificity began in earnest with the Industrial Revolution. Although before the eighteenth century there were machines and mechanisms that required careful attention and operation in a well-defined sequence, they were simpler than modern machinery, the effects of breakdowns were not as dramatic, their use was not so widespread, and they certainly did not constitute the salient characteristic of the society. The advent of the Industrial Revolution produced some fundamental changes in those activities that were touched by it. The number and complexity of machines increased enormously. Workers were forced to adapt to the requirements of machines; as Marx said, the machines set the pace. Not only did they set the pace, but they also imposed a method of working and defined work standards.

The main advantage of machines, from the point of view of an organization, is that they can be directly controlled by the producer. Of course there is a need to buy raw materials, maintain machines, and train workers, but the methods of production are known and controllable, which is a great advantage over agriculture. At the time of the Industrial Revolution (as in most of the developing world today) agriculture was much more dependent on exogenous factors, and it was impossible to define exactly the best production method for each piece of land and for each day. When modern technology became available, it was possible to project output with a fair chance that it would materialize, to specify the inputs and the sequences for achieving the desired output, and to review whether the production targets were being met, and if not, why not.

This degree of specificity created more precise standards of performance than had previously existed, based on the widespread ability to control the production process. These standards ushered in a new industrial concept of effectiveness or performance that has taken hold not only in the industrial sphere, but also in other activities, whether applicable or not. It has taken hold because of the precision of the new standards and because of the extent to which they have spread.

Ironically, however, the impact of machines on the attitudes and motivations of the workers has not been studied in much detail. Most studies of the effects of machines concentrate on the immediate operations in the workplace and the mechanical performance of human beings.[1] And the science of ergonomics, or social engineering, deals with how to adapt machines and working environments to obtain the maximum productivity out of individuals.

Industry, Modernity, and Organization Theory

The concept of modernity seems to be derived in part from the degree of specificity of the industrial process. Manning Nash has defined modernity as "the social, cultural and psychological framework which facilitates the application of tested knowledge to all phases and branches of production."[2] He claims that human history has experienced three major revolutions—the development of culture and tools, the beginning of agriculture, and the rise of industry—and indicates that industry has spread less widely than the first two. He sees the main purpose of economic development as enabling countries to join this third revolution: "the concern with economic growth and modernization is hence an interest in discovering the conditions under which different societies and cultures can enter this stream, take the social and economic aspects of it as well as the technological, and domesticate them so they operate or are accommodated to the social systems and cultural patterns doing the incorporating."[3]

These ideas trigger three points. First, contrary to what Nash claims, the Industrial Revolution is spreading extraordinarily fast, certainly much faster than the other two, because it is more powerful, more incisive, and more likely to break through cultural, political, and social barriers. After all, the Industrial Revolution is only 250 years old. Second, the basic characteristics of what is considered "modern" are universal; they apply in all countries regardless of the cultural and political patterns and are a consequence of the industrialization process just described. (To be modern is to emphasize planning, to be forward looking and open to innovation and social change, and to attach importance to time, efficacy, calculability, and technical skills.) Third, the attitudes associated with modernity are similar to those associated with an effective institution and all its activities.

These arguments have received further support from Inkeles and Smith, who have tried to identify the factors that determine the formation of a "modern man."[4] They concluded that the two most important factors are the school and the factory. Unfortunately, Inkeles and Smith did not go in detail into why industry and the educational system explain modernity. The influence of the education system is readily understood, but the role of the factory must be explained by the arguments developed here: modern is seen as virtually synonymous with industrial. Individuals' educational progress with regard to their attitudes and general outlook—that is, with regard to their potential modernity—continues during their lifetime, particularly in their work. Occupational experience alone might be sufficiently significant to explain modernization. In addition, however, the modernizing attitudes introduced by the Industrial Revolution have been incorporated into the education system regardless of whether the society as a whole has modernized. This is why the school and the factory together are probably the most powerful factors in achieving modernization. In fact, Clark Kerr had concluded in the 1960s that patterns of industrialization are similar everywhere in spite of country differences, that industrialization has proved to be more powerful than cultural patterns, and that with industrialization management becomes more professional, workers become more conservative, and the relations between them are similar everywhere.[5]

On the basis of this analysis activities can be divided into three groups: the high-specificity or industrial and financial ones that are based on modern technology and methods and fit the standard pattern of modernity; activities that have the potential to become modern and industrial, but which at present use primitive techniques to which modern industrial standards cannot be applied without modification; and low-specificity, mostly people-oriented or social activities that cannot ever be measured by the same standards. Within this triad, there is a historical difference between activities in the first two groups, and a basic and permanent difference between the first and the third groups. This does not mean that low-specificity activities cannot be modernized. They can be and have been, but alternative methods and an altogether different concept of modernity have to be followed.

Within organization theory itself, the perennial discussion between formalistic and behavioral approaches is a reflection of the tension between the machine and human beings. Organization has been considered indispensable for putting economic rationality into practice. In Weber's terms, technology pushes toward a rational-legal form of organization—in his scheme, the truly modern form—while people-oriented or social activities tend to drift toward more traditional forms of organization.[6] The whole development of organization theory can be interpreted as an attempt to build a theoretical structure that will parallel and also serve the technological developments of the industrial age.

The concept of specificity is linked to theories of organization that put special emphasis on technology and the technical core as determinants of the structure of organizations (but, interestingly, not their relative effectiveness). A main proponent of this view was Joan Woodward, who studied the organizational implications of different types of industrial production.[7] She reviewed three major types: unit (a tailor, artisans), batch or mass (a car assembly line), and process (an oil refinery). Her work was expanded by Perrow and Thompson.[8] Perrow refined the concepts used by Woodward and expanded their scope to include nonindustrial activities. He focused his analysis on the number of exceptional cases in the activity and its degree of uniformity. Thompson focused on the degrees of variability or uniformity of inputs and outputs (thus linking technology to the environment), classifying activities according to the combination of uniform and variable inputs and outputs. He also developed the concept of the "technical core," which an organization tries to protect from the environment as much as possible. This concept is used later in this study to denote the technological characteristics related to the main activity in an organization.

These approaches are first cousins to the concept of specificity, which tries to take some of these notions one step further by focusing on the differences among activities and on the conditions that accompany weak institutional structures. Another approach that follows a similar line is that of Leibenstein, who states that one of the reasons for a less than effective use of existing resources (X efficiency) is the impossibility of being absolutely exact in the process of transforming a specific group of inputs into a specific group of outputs.[9]

Characteristics of Technology

It is necessary to explore somewhat more the concept of technology to indicate the basis on which intertechnological comparisons of specificity can be made. Three dimensions are important. First is the degree of certainty or predictability of a technology, which has been defined as "the variability of the items or elements upon which work is performed or the extent to which it is possible to predict their behavior in advance . . . Specific measures of uncertainty include uniformity or variability of inputs, the number of exceptions encountered in the work process, and the number of major project changes experienced."[10] Second is the complexity of technology, which has several definitions, but the most appropriate for our purposes contains three elements: number of components, degree of differentiation among components, and degree of interdependence among them. The greater the degree of each characteristic, the greater the technological (and organizational) complexity.[11] Third is the degree of interdependence, which refers to the nature and degree of interaction among the different processes and units that compose a technology. This interdependence of processes and units could be pooled (each contributes independently to the technology), sequential in time, and reciprocal (the elements of a process relate to each other as both inputs and outputs).[12]

Disaggregating the nature of the technology is important in developing the concept of specificity. For example, agricultural processes are characterized by greater uncertainty than industrial processes and display a type of sequential interdependence, but they might be less complex, especially at lower levels of technology. Technologies in the social sciences will have a high degree of uncertainty or unpredictability, but they could have varying degrees of complexity and most likely a reciprocal type of interdependence.

Because technologies with very high levels of specificity tend to be more international and uniform and more independent from the local culture and social environment, they might create a technological enclave separated from the rest of the economic system. The need for special skills, for example, means that workers will be hired to a considerable extent on the basis of merit, and the selection process will be less influenced by local cultural and political factors. The counterpoint is that low-specificity activities are more locally oriented.[13]

Many low-specificity activities provide services, a fact that considerably complicates their organizational and managerial problems. Because their output cannot be stored in the same way as goods, the activities are more exposed to exogenous factors and more dependent for their performance on organization and management. For example, interdepartmental coordination is a serious problem. Transport services suffer from the same difficulty, although to a lesser extent because equipment can be stored more easily than staff. Services are also more difficult because progress depends more on behavioral changes. For example, a technological improvement can be straightforward and fast: substituting one machine for another can be done in a relatively short time, and the effects on output will be available very soon (start-up difficulties, which can take a long time, are disregarded here). But implementing a change in personnel policies and methods in the same factory could require months or years, depending on how the employees react to it; and how they react will depend on a host of factors about which few generalizations can be made.[14]

Programmed Decisions

Another line of argument refers to programmed and nonprogrammed decisions.[15] Programmed decisions deal with routine activities or with situations for which standard approaches are available. Nonprogrammed decisions deal with nonroutine, nonstandard problems. It stands to reason that, on average, a high-specificity activity will have a lower proportion of nonprogrammed decisions than a low-specificity activity. This does not mean that decisionmaking in low-specificity activities may never be standardized. This is being done, but probably at a high cost in terms of real effectiveness. If, for example, the personnel policy of an agency imposes strict rules that decisions be made according to a programmed form, not arrived at by individuals, it might help to keep the place going, but most probably it will not induce the best use of the human resources available. The important practical point here is that in many low-specificity activities, nonprogrammed decisions are made at the lowest levels in the organization, by extension agents, teachers, or health workers. The proportion of nonprogrammed decisions will increase if the agency is in addition going through a period of rapid change.

The use of computers supports this hypothesis. Which activities can be computerized and what are the requirements and effects of computers? Routine activities, such as some types of clerical work, and areas of high specificity are the easiest to computerize; less easy are activities related to the maintenance of equipment and to civil works. The most difficult are those dependent on human behavior. The less dependent a decision is on human behavior, the easier it is to computerize. Whole areas related to programmed decisionmaking can eventually be made highly dependent on computers. There is, however, a tendency to transform decisions that ought to be nonprogrammed into programmed ones to minimize the "distorting" effects of human behavior. Simon reflects this hope very clearly when he writes: "the changes now taking place [in the new techniques of automation] mean that the manager will find himself dealing more than in the past with a well-structured system whose problems have to be diagnosed and corrected objectively and analytically, and less with unpredictable and sometimes recalcitrant people who have to be persuaded, prodded, rewarded, and cajoled."[16] This analysis also suggests that low-specificity activities will not (or should not) be able to profit as much as others from the progress in computers and automation.

On a different plane, studies of the effects of computers tend to confirm the hypothesis regarding the effects of high-specificity. One early study found that, after clerical activities were computerized, certain jobs were routinized but required greater skill because the computer demanded greater accuracy and reliability.[17] Computers are the epitome of the need for specificity and clarity of objectives (at least with existing technologies): instructions and program design have to be unambiguous, otherwise the results are clearly and immediately wrong.

Learning by Doing

Perhaps the most important additional argument to support the link between technology and specificity is the concept of learning by doing.

Quite surprisingly, a formal treatment of the obvious fact that people learn not only at school, but also at their place of work and at home, is very recent. Kaldor was one of the first to consider explicitly a "technical progress function," which includes constantly improving knowledge and know-how generated by the activity itself.[18] A more complete treatment of learning by doing has been made by Arrow. He analyzes learning as a by-product of ordinary production. This learning, when combined with formal education, greatly accelerates the creation of skills and know-how: "technical change in general can be ascribed to experience . . . it is the very activity of production which gives rise to problems for which favorable responses are selected over time."[19] From the point of view of development, the implications of Arrow's analysis are: "1) increases in skill and knowledge are the main keys to growth; 2) exposure to new situations speeds learning; and hence 3) rapid replacement of obsolescent equipment is a sound investment in people and, through people, in economic growth."[20] These implications should be further extended by analyzing the effects of learning by doing on individuals working in high-specificity and low-specificity activities and then the effects of organizational and managerial learning derived from the same two groups of activities—that is, learning by individuals and by institutions.

The Spread Effects of Technology

An extension of this analysis has to do with how the effect of the institutional discipline imposed by high specificity may spread to other activities. In a telecommunications agency, for example, high specificity may exist only in its technical departments. The discipline imposed by the technology will be reflected in the functioning of its technical core. But what about the other departments? Is the billing department also influenced by that discipline, and by what mechanisms? Are more remote departments such as personnel affected, or even related activities outside the telecommunications agency, such as suppliers? Are the accounting and personnel departments of a low-specificity agency less efficient than the corresponding departments of a high-specificity unit? Which types of technologies or activities have the highest and the lowest spread effects?

Since this subject has not been explored, it is only possible to postulate some hypotheses and a few promising lines of inquiry. The most direct way the discipline spreads is through daily contacts between groups in the high-specificity (technical) and low-specificity departments. If the technical groups have achieved a high level of performance, it is unlikely that they will tolerate too much of a differential in the lower-specificity departments, particularly if some of them produce important inputs to the technical process. In the old example of jet engine maintenance, the technical personnel will exert considerable pressure on the group that provides spare parts; most likely it will be under the same wing as the technical operations. This group in turn may pressure the financial sections to release funds in time to ensure the steady supply of parts. Several groups that are directly linked to the technical activity will therefore be induced to perform well, but what about those dealing with the people involved? Will payroll or personnel departments function better? This is hard to tell. Pressure for high standards might also be expected here, but perhaps less pressure than that affecting the activities related to the technical core. There are too many examples of utilities that perform relatively well at the technical level but have appalling billing departments.

Then what about the activities such as the sales department that are even less directly related to the technical core? Airlines have a special aura because they are "modern," but the nontechnical activities may operate with their own dynamic. Many people who have been frustrated by inefficient customer services have prayed that the technical side of the airline operation is considerably better. The performance of customer service departments may still be much better than the average institutional performance in the country, in part for the reasons indicated above, and in part because of the effects of competition if it is an international service. (The difference in quality between an airline's national service, where it has a monopoly, and its international one, where it is subject to competition, is quite noticeable.)

This phenomenon is common in the experience of the World Bank. The technical departments in a railway can have many problems but still achieve a level of operational performance far superior to the average for the country, but the marketing and administrative departments can be quite poor. Conversely, a line ministry can be ineffective but have an excellent computerized statistical department.

These issues can be raised not only with regard to units within an institution, but also among different entities. If spare parts are supplied to an airline by a different company, it will be this company which profits from the high-specificity discipline. One can conceive of a technological input-output matrix of the economic system to show the linkages between activities with different levels of specificity (see chapter 8). One hypothesis is that the higher the proportion of high-specificity activities in the economic system, the higher will be the chances of increasing the country's institutional effectiveness.

Special Cases

A few special cases shed more light on the links between technology and specificity and the concepts that have been developed here. These are low-technology agriculture, the delivery of education and health services, and railways.

Low-Technology Agriculture

The previous arguments suggest that low-technology agriculture might be one of the most difficult, if not the most difficult, activity to manage. The activity itself emanates little discipline, and in the case of subsistence agriculture it is not exposed to any sort of competitive pressure. Moreover, low-technology agriculture is influenced by environmental conditions and subject to the vagaries of the weather, pests, and plagues; the lower the technology, the less these conditions are under the control of the farmer. Objectives can be defined in broad terms (to plant wheat), but the short-term daily or weekly objectives are much more difficult to specify clearly because they will be determined to an important (but unpredictable) degree by exogenous factors. Each day could be different. Production methods are specific to a particular plot of land. Even if wheat is planted throughout the region, individual decisions on how to go about it should, in principle, be made according to the peculiar characteristics of each piece of land, its soil, salinity, drainage, sun, and so on. This is seldom done with low-technology processes. At most, the farmer's methods will evolve through trial and error, sometimes over many years. In the language of management science, the proportion of nonprogrammed decisions is very high.

Institutions related to low-technology agriculture (extension, credit, input distribution) are managerially complex because they must deal with large numbers of individuals and relatively large areas. To use an industrial analogy, agriculture is like a huge factory scattered over several thousand square miles, trying to produce a homogeneous output with technologies that have to be timed and slightly modified—perhaps daily or weekly—to suit the fancy of the workers and of the environment. And of course the workers are not subject to any institutional discipline but operate independently and have very low educational levels.

Although farmers might be extremely well motivated because their efforts make the difference between starvation and survival, low-technology agriculture as such is not a good source of institutional discipline because it does not produce effects of immediate and dramatic intensity. Many of the effects of a good or a bad performance unfold very slowly; some of them, such as erosion control, could take years to materialize. And as indicated before, it is impossible to disentangle the effects of a particular action from that of other factors affecting production.

The specific effects on the behavior of farmers are difficult to identify and have remained a bit of an enigma to those studying them. Several authors have analyzed differences in mentality and the specific rhythms and motivations that agriculture imposes on farmers.[21] But little has been learned about the effect of low-technology agriculture on the managerial behavior of farmers (as opposed to their economic behavior and the notion of the "rational farmer") and on the agencies dealing with agriculture. The difficulty of arriving at a workable production routine makes subsistence farmers understandably reluctant to embark on experiments so risky that they threaten the well-being of their families, although they have often demonstrated their willingness to undertake minor experimentation.[22]

Closely related to agriculture and sharing several of its characteristics is the provision of services to rural populations. In rural activities such as agricultural extension, health and nutrition, family planning, even some types of education, a large number of agents operate independently over extensive geographical areas, so that it is complicated to control their performance. The messages or technologies that these agents deliver are not always well defined, and they have to be adapted to the individuals or groups who are intended to benefit from them. The effect of these services is often difficult to trace and to link back to the agent that delivered them.

Education and Health

At first glance, one might think that education could be "modernized" much along the lines of an industrial or financial activity. The objectives—teaching particular skills to a group—can be specified, and the teaching methods can be established and tests designed to determine whether the skills have been acquired. This is true, but only if it is assumed that the individual students are so similar that they react equally to the teaching methods and tests. Neither students nor teachers are similar, however, and different teaching methods and tests will generate wide variations in learning. More important are the large differences between actual and potential learning: from a particular teacher using a particular teaching method, some students will learn close to their potential while others will remain at a much lower level. The reasons are obvious: the optimal teaching technique has to be tailor-made for each student and teacher and adapted daily to the particular circumstances of each. All aggregations, in persons and in time, will generate distortions, and large aggregations will generate large ones. It is no surprise that the best educational systems have small classes to profit from group dynamics and tutorial activities and to deal with the unique characteristics of each individual.

This does not mean that everything in education needs to be tailor-made to each individual. Considerable uniformity has been achieved with standardized curricula and tests. This kind of objective-oriented measure can act as a powerful disciplinary force while at the same time encouraging more differentiation in educational methods among students.

But the objectives vary among different types of education. If the purpose of technical training is to impart simple technical skills to a relatively homogeneous group (similar in educational background, social environment, work experience, and so on), it could be treated almost as a high-specificity activity, although differences among individuals would still be crucial in determining the effectiveness of specific teaching methods. But when moving from technical training to, say, primary education, the possibilities of aggregation are reduced. Recent trends in education theory focus more on the effects on learning of the characteristics of each individual, the teaching methods, and the social environment. More emphasis is being given to looking beyond the mere drill of a formal, uniform teaching program to attempt the fuller development of the individual. Jean Piaget wrote in 1973 that universal education had taken on a "far greater responsibility than simply to assure each one reading, writing and arithmetic capabilities; it is to guarantee fairly *to each child* the entire development of his mental faculties and the acquisition of knowledge and of ethical values . . . children can be taught an almost infinite variety of knowledge as long as the level of sophistication is adjusted to their age and development" [emphasis added].[23] There is in education a tendency to abandon general methods for an attempt to adapt teaching to the characteristics of each individual.

A similar analysis can be made regarding health care. A purely mechanical view of curative medicine is that doctors rely heavily on standard diagnostic tests to identify the cause of an illness and then try to find a cure for it. These characteristics would support the view that health care is a high-specificity activity with well-defined procedures and effects that are of high intensity, immediate, and readily traceable. If a more holistic view is taken, however, the health of an individual is seen as the result of the interaction between his physiological and psychological functions and his environment. Then the possibility of high specificity diminishes drastically, and the cure has to be tailor-made to each individual. In addition, certain unique characteristics of health services affect the way they are managed. The medical aspect of health care takes precedence over all considerations. The discipline is so strong, the techniques are so inflexible, and their effects so intense that they have greatly delayed or prevented the introduction of managerial methods that are generally accepted elsewhere (although basic techniques such as accounting are a possible exception). Doctors, not managers, are in charge of hospitals.

Railways

The last special activity to be reviewed is railways. In general, railways have a low level of institutional performance, and institutional development programs have made little progress among them. These negative results have been confirmed by several evaluations of railway operations undertaken by the World Bank and other agencies. At first sight railways appear to be an exception to the scheme proposed here, but a closer look indicates that the framework is useful for analyzing that activity.

In relation to the level of institutional performance in each country, railways have been more a financial than a technical failure. Evaluations and other studies conclude that the technical level is relatively high, but performance is uneven. This is to be expected. The level of specificity and technology among the many different activities in a railway varies considerably, from the relatively high-specificity operation of modern equipment (locomotives) to simpler activities such as labor-intensive track maintenance and some types of operations within the terminals. These variations in specificity are reflected in variations in performance among the activities.

At the financial level, poor performance can be explained by the distortion of competitive pressure as an inducement for better performance. Historically, railways were heavily regulated during the period in which they had a monopoly. When the more flexible and managerially decentralized road transport began to offer competition—rather recently in many developing countries—railways were caught with their hands tied by regulation and by the inefficiencies inherent in a monopolistic activity. The resulting operating deficits have reduced or eliminated the incentive derived from competition and led to a decline in operational performance.

In addition, railways are extremely complex to manage, particularly in the context of the capabilities of most developing countries. Thousands of different operations of varying importance, requiring from one man to several hundred, have to occur simultaneously to achieve the ultimate objective of delivering passengers and freight from one place to another. Because these operations are scattered over extensive territories and involve large numbers of individuals, they are difficult to control. In this respect, railways are closer to agriculture than to industry. The more mechanized the railway, the more it is possible to create work centers, analogous to factories. Railways with intermediate technology will typically have more lonely station masters or far-flung maintenance gangs, which generally reduce their level of specificity. In addition, as national, countrywide undertakings, railways are exposed to the problems raised by Hirschman of having to contend with staff from different regions—a serious problem in culturally heterogeneous countries.[24]

The World Bank's Experience

The overall findings from the review of the Bank's experience (chapter 3) support the linkage between technology and specificity and the hypothesis that high specificity provides a powerful incentive to institutional performance. It seems reasonable to assume that the sectoral and subsectoral patterns found in that review follow the high-specificity to low-specificity spectrum: for example, telecommunications at the high end of the scale and education and services at the low end; the technical and operational activities at the high end and the people-oriented ones at the low. The implementation of investment components will follow the same pattern, with the acquisition of equipment the fastest and the establishment of service delivery mechanisms the slowest to be accomplished. Figure 6 in the appendix illustrates the close correlation between degree of specificity and institutional performance. The very close correlation between institutional performance and progress in institutional development programs could also be taken as supporting evidence.

Although none of the Bank-financed institutions in developing countries deal with the extreme examples of high specificity, such as nuclear power plants or aircraft maintenance, there is enough of a sample to identify such a pattern. More than the actual statistical basis, it is this pattern accumulated over the years in the Bank's general operational reviews and ex post evaluations that gives credence to the hypothesis of the role of specificity.[25] Perhaps the clearest evidence is from institutional development and institutions in Sub-Saharan Africa. Progress has been slow and uneven, but the clear cases of success are mostly in the areas of relatively higher specificity or those in which specificity has been effectively simulated. Some examples are a few airlines, particularly with respect to their technical operations (such as Ethiopian Airlines), several of the telecommunications companies (such as those in Burkina Faso and Ethiopia), power companies (such as Tanzania's TANESCO), and several mining operations (as in Botswana and Zaire). Studies have concluded that the strength of these institutions has been their technical core and, very important, their ability to absorb technical assistance, the concentration of professionals in them relative to the total in the country, and the corresponding accumulation of political power that protected them, within limits, from the vagaries of political change.

Other successful cases in Africa are at the high-specificity end of agricultural production and somewhat akin to industrial activities. They include plantations for homogeneous cash crops such as cotton and tea and several projects in oil palm and cotton production in West Africa. In contrast, many difficulties have plagued agricultural and livestock projects in Sub-Saharan Africa, especially integrated rural development projects. Livestock projects have been a particularly glaring example of a low-specificity activity that often gave rise to serious disagreements between the country and the Bank about not only the objectives to be pursued but also the technologies and approaches to be followed. The coincidence in the success stories of a high level of specificity and a high level of commitment reflects the fact that low specificity gives more scope for "lack of commitment," which in the Bank's parlance refers to disagreements about objectives and approaches.

The Bank's experience also highlights the relative success of the technical core in most activities, including financial ones. In several cases the technical core was so important and so well protected that the level of institutional performance and progress was high for the institution as a whole, even in heavily negative environments (pipelines in Bolivia, power companies in Central America, and industries in Pakistan). In other, more numerous cases, the overall level of performance was not satisfactory or improved very little, but the operational performance of the technical core remained high in relation to the average level in the country. Such cases include railways, industrial concerns, and power companies.

Another source of evidence, also derived from the Bank's experience, is Hirschman's analysis in *Development Projects Observed*. To a large extent, his whole discussion supports these arguments: his contrast between industry and infrastructure and agriculture, his concepts of latitude and discipline, and his analysis of the discipline imposed by high technology and by time-bound and even location-bound activities. The examples he cites are equally supportive: the case of the Damodar Valley Authority in India, which had to return to its technical core to survive, the telecommunications system in Ethiopia, or the electric power agency in Uganda.

Notes

1. See, for example, P. M. Fitts and M. I. Posner, *Human Performance* (London: Prentice-Hall, 1973).

2. Manning Nash, "Cultural Meanings—The Widening Gap between the Intellectuals and the Process," in *Essays in Economic Development and Cultural Change in Honor of Bert Hoselitz*, Manning Nash, ed. (Chicago, Ill.: University of Chicago Press, 1977), p. 21.

3. Ibid., p. 19.

4. Alex Inkeles and David H. Smith, *Becoming Modern: Individual Change in Six Developing Countries* (Cambridge, Mass.: Harvard University Press, 1974).

5. Clark Kerr, *Industrialism and Industrial Man: The Problems of Labor and Management in Economic Growth* (New York: Oxford University Press, 1964).

6. Max Weber, *The Theory of Social and Economic Organization*, A. H. Henderson and Talcott Parsons, eds. (Glencoe, Ill.: Free Press, 1947).

7. Joan Woodward, *Management and Technology* (London: Her Majesty's Stationery Office, 1958) and *Industrial Organization: Theory and Practice* (New York: Oxford University Press, 1965).

8. Charles Perrow, "A Framework for the Comparative Analysis of Organizations," *American Sociological Review*, vol. 32 (April 1967), pp. 194–208; James D. Thompson, *Organizations in Action: Social Science Bases of Administrative Theory*

(New York: McGraw-Hill, 1967); and James D. Thompson and Frederick L. Bates, "Technology, Organization, and Administration," *Administrative Science Quarterly*, vol. 2 (December 1957), pp. 325–42.

9. Harvey Leibenstein, *Beyond Economic Man: A New Foundation for Micro-Economics* (Cambridge, Mass.: Harvard University Press, 1976).

10. Richard W. Scott, *Organizations: Rational, Natural and Open Systems* (Englewood Cliffs, N.J.: Prentice-Hall, 1981), p. 211.

11. Todd R. LaPorte, "Organized Social Complexity" and "Complexity and Uncertainty: Challenge to Action," in *Organized Social Complexity: Challenge to Politics and Policy*, Todd R. LaPorte, ed. (Princeton, N.J.: Princeton University Press, 1975), pp. 3–21 and 332–56.

12. Thompson, *Organizations in Action*.

13. This is a subject on which considerable work has been done. Albert O. Hirschman discusses it extensively in *Development Projects Observed* (Washington, D.C.: Brookings Institution, 1967).

14. See Fariborz Damanpour and William M. Evan, "Organizational Innovation and Performance: The Problem of Organizational Lag," *Administrative Science Quarterly*, vol. 29 (1984), pp. 392–409.

15. Simon, *The New Science of Management Decision*.

16. Ibid., p. 132.

17. Thomas L. Whisler, *Information Technology and Organizational Change* (Belmont, Calif.: Wadsworth, 1970).

18. Nicholas Kaldor, "Capital Accumulation and Economic Growth," in F. A. Lutz and D. C. Hague, eds., *The Theory of Capital*, Proceedings of the International Economic Association Conference (London: Macmillan, 1961).

19. Kenneth J. Arrow, "The Economic Implications of Learning by Doing," *Review of Economic Studies*, vol. 29 (1962), pp. 155–73.

20. M. J. Bowman, "Education and Economic Growth: An Overview," in Timothy King, ed., *Education and Income*, World Bank Staff Working Paper 402 (Washington, D.C., 1980).

21. See, for example, Nicholas Georgescu-Roegen, "Economic Theory and Agrarian Economies," *Oxford Economic Papers*, vol. 12, no. 1 (February 1960).

22. Robert Chambers, *Rural Development: Putting the Last First* (London: Longman, 1983); and Paul Richards, *Indigenous Agricultural Revolution: Ecology and Food Crops in West Africa* (Boulder, Colo.: Westview, 1985).

23. *New York Times*, September 23, 1980, p. C4, article by Fred M. Hechinger.

24. Hirschman, *Development Projects Observed*.

25. A good index of the formation of this pattern is the annual reviews of project performance audits prepared by the Bank's Operations Evaluation Department.

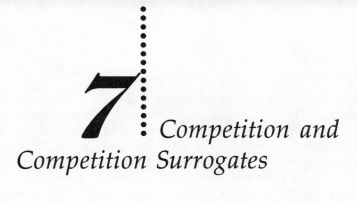

7 Competition and Competition Surrogates

Competition as a factor influencing institutional performance has been studied for a long time, mainly by economists who have used typologies based on market structures (oligopolies, monopolies, and competition). In this chapter the analysis of competition is extended to different types of nonmarket competition, which are considered in the context of developing countries. Interactions between specificity and competition are discussed, as well as the relations between those two factors and other elements determining institutional effectiveness, in particular the political environment and specific cultural traits.

Definitions

The American Heritage Dictionary (1973) defines competition as "a striving or vying with another or others for profit, prize, position, or the necessities of life." The economic concept of competition is much more precise.[1] It entails a large number of participants who are well informed and act independently from each other, without any power to influence the price of inputs or outputs, who have easy entry to or exit from the market, and who have homogeneous products.

The concept of competition can be expanded to encompass not only the economic definition, but also three other types of pressure that can have effects on institutional performance similar to those of economic competition. I have called them competition (or market) surrogates because, although economic competition is the most important form, the other three forms are able to exert pressure when market competition is not possible or not desirable. The expanded concept thus encompasses, first, the economic concept—that is, external competition faced by an entity from similar entities attempting to provide the same or similar goods or services; second, external pressures derived from clients, beneficiaries, and suppliers; third, external pressures derived from the political establishment or from the controlling or regulatory agencies; and fourth, internal competition among different people or units within an institution.

This group or family of pressures can affect an institution in similar ways, generating incentives for higher levels of performance. At any given time, each entity will be subject to different combinations of these four types of pressure. The important operational issue is that the three competition surrogates can be directly influenced or modified so as to strengthen the incentives they provide. This is particularly important in many developing countries, in which the role of economic competition is still limited.

The conventional economic type of competition has been so thoroughly studied that it does not need to be reviewed here, but the three surrogates require more complete explanations.

The first surrogate refers to external pressure from clients, beneficiaries, and suppliers, who take action to demand higher standards of operational performance from a particular institution. This pressure could be exerted on entities in the private sector, but it is particularly relevant for public sector agencies which are not or cannot be exposed to competition in the marketplace. Much has been written about the relations between public entities and their clients, especially in the context of the provision of services, but little about the potential impact of suppliers, especially if they perform at a high level or belong in the high-specificity category. Such suppliers could demand, at least from parts of an entity, a level of performance that is above the average level of the entity as a whole. This pressure is generally weak, but not negligible in certain activities.

In a developing country, for example, a few industrial plants and the power and perhaps the telecommunications agencies could pressure some of their clients to perform at higher levels. In addition, they could exert more direct pressure on their own suppliers. Other examples of industrial or agricultural activities with large numbers of suppliers include tea processing facilities (the KTDA has already been discussed), agricultural marketing boards, sugar factories, and flour mills.

Yet another source of competitive pressure on clients is the financial system, especially banks. In many countries banks and other financial institutions could be induced to oversee and control the performance of many of their borrowers in greater detail than normal. If it is not practical to do it for all of them, even a selective attempt could produce significant results. Banks are among the elite institutions in any country, and they generally have the capacity to monitor their clients' performance more carefully and the power to make their influence felt.

The second competition surrogate, political pressure, emanates from the political establishment (elected officials or their equivalent at all levels) or from some regulatory or control agencies. A subtle difference is suggested here between direct, obvious control and a form of pressure whereby the political establishment relates to an agency as a client or shareholder rather than as a controller. If well directed, this type of pressure could have a positive rather than a negative effect on institutional performance. Similarly, relations between a regulatory or parent agency and a particular entity could have more of a competitive than a controlling flavor to it, with the central government acting as a client or shareholder rather than as an owner or regulator. This difference in the relationship has specific operational consequences which are discussed below in chapter 9.

The third surrogate, internal competition, has to do with whether an entity, through its organizational structure and management style, uses a degree of competition among its personnel and units to achieve a higher level of performance.

This classification of competition and competition surrogates has been made on the basis of the sources of those pressures. An additional perspective can be obtained by exploring the nature of the pressure itself, which falls into three basic categories—economic, political, and administrative—as shown in the matrix in table 2. The purpose of this matrix is to indicate the kind of pressure that is predominant for each source, since the category has a bearing on the type of impact that can be expected. The pressure could also be a mixture of categories. For example, pressure from clients on a government agency would most likely be both economic and political, whereas pressure from a regulatory agency on a public enterprise might be purely administrative, but most likely will also be political.

At any given time a country's institutional structure will have a network of these pressures, of different levels and intensities, which will condition the effect of competition and competition surrogates on overall institutional performance. The interaction among units facing different degrees and types of competitive pressure will be one of the mechanisms through which those pressures might be enhanced and transferred from one unit to another. Just as it was possible to conceive of a technological

Table 2. Competition and Competition Surrogates

Source	Predominant category of pressure		
	Economic	*Political*	*Administrative*
Economic competition			
Competitors	X		
Competition surrogates			
Suppliers	X	X	
Clients	X	X	
Politicians		X	
Regulators		X	X
Internal			X

X indicates the category of pressure that is likely to predominate for each source.

input-output matrix with regard to specificity, a competitive input-output matrix could be designed to depict the nature and intensity of the pressures on different groups of units, and the interactions among the groups. Whether or not such a matrix is formally available, it must be understood that such a network of interactions exists and that it must be the basis for any strategy at a national or sectoral level to enhance the effects of competition and competition surrogates on operational performance.

At a less sophisticated level, a profile of the economic structure of a country according to the level of competition in its different markets would be extremely useful. A similar assessment could be made with respect to competition surrogates. At a time when increasing emphasis is being put on the role of competition to increase general economic efficiency, it is also important to assess its potential for improving institutional performance. It seems that the lower the level of development, the more limited are competitive markets and the smaller is the potential for competition (and competition surrogates), at least in the short and medium run. In some of the countries in Sub-Saharan Africa, for example, most economic activities may be outside a market economy or not exposed to any form of competitive pressure.

The whole spectrum of pressures encompassed by the concepts of competition and competition surrogates either have a positive effect on institutional performance or can be directed to have such an effect. The two external competition surrogates (pressure from clients and suppliers and from the government) have been the subject of extensive work among organization theorists, who mainly described them and explained how they work, but said very little about how they can be manipulated as incentives to increase institutional performance. Two lines of inquiry are relevant in this respect. The first is a concern with "task environment," a term used by organization theorists to refer to all aspects of an institution's environment that are "potentially relevant to goal setting and goal attainment"; Dill focused on four groups in the task environment of most organizations: customers, suppliers, competitors, and regulatory groups.[2] The second line of inquiry, the "resource dependence approach," emphasizes the importance of the environment—the institutions and groups with which an entity interacts and the social and economic system in which it operates—and how it relates to and impinges on a particular institution. This approach has helped develop strategies that enable institutions to deal with their environment.[3]

Mechanisms

Competitive markets force higher specificity and help to generate effects of higher intensity that are attributable to the market and that materialize quickly. Different degrees of competition will generate effects of different intensity. In nearly perfect markets, a marginal producer who faces increased costs will have to act almost immediately to reduce them, otherwise he will lose his place in the market. In most cases, effects are less immediate and a single unit has some degree of monopoly which allows it to react more slowly and less drastically.

In general, competition provides an incentive, or pressure, in a way similar to that of specificity. It reduces the areas of discretionary behavior for the individuals and groups in an organization, and it imposes a discipline that results in a higher level of performance. But the exact mechanisms through which that happens still need to be explored (and a productive exploration it would be). Economic competition and the competition surrogates may affect an institution either directly, through the stimulus produced, or indirectly, through the actions of management. A sudden increase in competitive pressure—say, an abrupt lowering of its protective trade barrier—will seriously challenge both the enterprise as a whole and each of its members. Actions will be taken to tighten operations within the existing managerial and organizational structure. But the pressure could and should change the way in which the industry is organized and managed, which will in turn have an effect on personnel that has to be added to the original effect. Thus the impact could be divided in two parts: a primary one within the old managerial and organizational structure and a secondary one derived from a possible change in that structure. A primary effect could be greater quality control within the existing structure, and a secondary one several managerial and organizational measures to change the output mix. In general, the extent to which external competition acts as an incentive will depend on the nature of the institution affected, that is, its organizational and managerial structure.

If the exact mechanisms through which economic competition influences institutional performance remain partly unknown, the lack of knowledge is even more acute with regard to the two external competition surrogates (clients and suppliers, politicians and regulators). These pressures are more complex. First, because they emanate from an individual or a particular group they are much more personalized. This means that they might penetrate more easily and deeply into an institution because they are based on direct human interaction. Second, they are more heterogeneous and refer to more specific and more varied activities at all levels of the institution. One extreme example is an entity producing a homogeneous output that loses its tariff protection—a homogeneous, impersonal, all-encompassing kind of economic pressure. At the other extreme are cases in which one supplier forces one person or unit in an organization to perform better, or one irate user of a government agency pressures one lower-level official to improve his

Table 3. Characteristics of External Competition and Competition Surrogates

Examples of pressure	Measure of effect on an institution		
	Degree of personalization	*Degree of comprehensiveness*	*Levels affected*
Economic competition			
Tariff reduction, one product	Impersonal	Very large	All
Price reduction, one of several products	Impersonal	Possibly large	Probably all
New competitors	Impersonal	Large	All
Competition surrogates			
Beneficiaries, clients, and suppliers			
Individual client	Personal	Generally small	Few, probably low
Large beneficiary organization	Mainly personal	Possibly large	Probably all
Small supplier	Personal	Small	Low to medium
Weak client organization	Mainly personal	Medium	Low to medium
Politicians and regulators			
Powerful politicians (individual or group)	Personal	Large	Probably all
Regulatory agency	Mainly personal	Partial to large	Probably all
Auditing and control	Mainly impersonal	Large	Probably all

performance. In between, there is a whole spectrum of pressures of different kinds and levels.

Table 3 lists several examples of competitive pressures and indicates three measures of their probable effects on institutions: the degree of personalization, that is, whether the pressure materializes through impersonal channels or through identifiable individuals or groups; the degree of comprehensiveness, that is, whether the specific pressure will affect the entire institution or only parts of it; and the levels (low, medium, or high) within the organization that are affected by the pressure. It is apparent that the pressures exerted through competition surrogates are much more erratic than those of economic competition.

Whether the pressures act as incentives to increase the operational performance (or reduce the organizational slack), and whether they can also force a redefinition of objectives or goals are other questions to be answered. It is clear from experience that economic competition does both; what is less clear is the role of the competition surrogates, especially in low-specificity activities in which goals and methods are not clearly defined or there is disagreement about them.

Well-directed pressure from clients, beneficiaries, suppliers, or regulators would generally operate along the lines indicated above to increase operational efficiency. But if those groups are not homogeneous and if the pressure is uneven, the institution could become fragmented or fall into the hands of elites. Producer cooperatives have a poor record in this respect; often most of their benefits have accrued to a small group of powerful farmers or to a political group.[4] Similarly, a large institution providing a variety of goods or services might be subjected to pressure from several groups; the group with the most power might distort the production pattern of the institution and turn it away from the original objectives. In many cases, for example, agricultural credit programs that are intended to benefit the poorest farmers are instead diverted to the benefit of middle-income farmers who are better able to pressure the institution. For the same reason, sites and services programs directed to slum dwellers often end up benefiting the middle class.

Whether competition surrogates act as incentives to improve performance and to modify goals in the same way as economic competition will depend on the kind of pressures to which an institution is subjected and the nature and complexity of the institution itself. It will also depend on the intensity of those pressures. A reasonable hypothesis is that the more homogeneous the institution and the pressures, and the greater the intensity of those pressures, the more competition surrogates will resemble economic competition in their effects on efficiency and goal definition. As intensity diminishes and heterogeneity increases, the effects of the surrogates become less predictable and probably act more to improve efficiency than to modify goals.

In this analysis of the mechanisms through which competition surrogates operate, one can detect again a handicap for the low-specificity activities, because greater leeway in defining objectives and methods results in greater heterogeneity in the activity and consequently less predictable effects of competition surrogates. Clients or politicians could put pressure on a farm mechanization service to direct more services to rich farmers than to the poor, who were originally intended to benefit. But pressure from the same sources could also achieve some improvements in the efficiency of the service. In the case of an educational service, pressure groups could influence negatively not only the objectives but also the educational methods to be pursued.

Within a productive unit the tightening effects of internal competition can be achieved through organizational and managerial measures designed to generate a competitive atmosphere among individuals and units. Many people would say that the nature and degree of internal competition is primarily a matter of management style. It can indeed be related to the style of senior management, but it also depends on whether the organizational structure induces competition among different units producing similar products and whether incentive mechanisms promote competition among staff; it can be related to the content and orientation of the training programs and to other aspects of the institution.

Some entities are intrinsically more amenable to a higher level of internal competition than others. The potential increases with size, much as the potential for external competition increases with the size of the market. In an entity composed of highly specialized streams producing completely different lines of goods or services, some competition is always possible, but it will probably be limited to intrastream competition, mostly at the supervisory and managerial level. Activities providing largely individual services, such as a large consulting firm, have more scope for internal competition. An entity that is geographically decentralized can make the regional units compete with each other with regard to standards of performance. In some extreme cases, the goods or services being produced can be made to compete among themselves in the market. In general, there are two types of internal competition. One is generated by administrative and managerial measures designed to make internal units compete among themselves on the basis of predetermined performance standards. The other derives from the possibility that two or more outputs produced by an institution can compete among themselves in a market or market-like situation. The second type is of course more difficult to find in reality.

Limitations of Competition

The effectiveness of competition and competition surrogates in inducing institutional performance may be limited by cultural conditions. Competition increases the potential for conflict. It does not necessarily generate an attitude of confrontation, but in many circumstances it does. And conflict raises difficult situations for management. Competition may work well in many western societies, where its virtues are extolled and the potentially negative effects have been incorporated into the fabric of society in a way that (it is claimed) reduces their importance. But in societies where collaboration and avoidance of conflict are paramount, the effects of carelessly introducing competition could be counterproductive. In these societies, the relevant factor would be collaboration rather than competition. The practical implications are extremely complex, because traditional societies functioning in a collaborative environment are subject to competitive pressures from external forces, and some adaptation is necessary. Deciding where to keep the old arrangements and where to adapt to the new circumstances is a difficult process that few societies have managed to accomplish successfully. Japan has absorbed the advantages of competition selectively, without destroying the basic collaborative structure which serves the country so well. This dilemma is well known, but has not been systematically explored—an important omission, given the number of market-like solutions being propounded in developing countries.

If the cultural context is important for economic competition, it is even more so for competition surrogates, especially those with a high degree of personalization (see table 3). Personalized pressures will be, by definition, more culture specific than impersonal ones. The traits of the particular society will determine the way such pressures are exercised (for example, covertly or openly, formally or informally), and the relative importance in the society of the groups or individuals applying the pressure will determine how much influence they have.

In addition to having to adapt competition surrogates to the relevant cultural traits in each society, it is essential to learn how to prevent such pressures from being perverted or corrupted. There are too many cases of extortion in the supervisory or monitoring system or of corrupt political intervention to assume that such functions can be easily modified to become an enlightened tool of management. A serious analysis of the specifics of each case is needed before attempting to harness competitive pressures as incentives to better performance.

Competition could have other drawbacks as a factor inducing institutional performance. One of them, discussed at length by Leibenstein,[5] is that, although more competition (or competition surrogates) reduces the area of discretionary behavior of the actors within an organization, it also increases what he calls entropy, the tendency to loosen up operations and avoid the tightening effects of competition. The intensity of entropy will depend not only on the individuals involved but on the cultural environment. If the potential for entropy is high because the traditional atmosphere is not competitive, an increase in external competition might produce a net positive effect on effectiveness, but an additional attempt to increase internal competition through organizational and managerial measures could be counterproductive.

Another potential drawback is analyzed by Hirschman.[6] He says that, when confronted with the ineffectiveness of an entity, the clients (or beneficiaries) could follow two courses of action: "exit" and "voice." Exit means to abandon the entity and stop using the goods or services produced; voice means to protest and act to improve the entity and upgrade the quality of the goods or services. Exit is impersonal and characteristic of economic markets: if someone is not satisfied with a particular brand or service, he merely exits and consumes a different one. This is easily done and painless from a personal point of view. Voice, however, involves direct action—a distinction that is essential for an understanding of its cultural implications. Because individuals seldom choose this option and act alone, voice requires some form of organization, and as such it becomes political. Thus, exit generally is more applicable to market situations and voice to government goods and services and to monopolies.

The usefulness of these concepts for the analysis of the effects of competition and competition surrogates is immediately apparent. For example, a decline in the effectiveness of an education system that is a government monopoly could be tackled in several ways. One of them is to open up the system to services provided by the private sector; another is to organize users associations to elicit better performance; yet another is to embark on broad organizational reforms. Which will be the most successful? No generalizations are possible, but some of the potential pitfalls of each solution can be discussed in the light of Hirschman's analysis. If the cultural environment is such that voice is not normal behavior, users associations (such as the parent-teacher associations common in public schools in many countries) will not be effective; on the contrary, if such solutions are forced on the system, they will be ineffective or fall into the hands of groups with specific political objectives and be shunned by those who could make a real contribution to the improvement of the system. If competition is created by encouraging private schools, potentially useful groups might choose to exit and create a pocket of high-quality education in the private sector. The outcome could be a reduction rather than an increase in the effectiveness of the public system. If this is the case, standard organizational and managerial measures applied to the public system will be only marginally effective. A better alternative might be to keep the public monopoly and make a special effort to take advantage of the voice potential within the specific cultural context—for example, by adapting some of the competition surrogates discussed here and by restructuring the system.

Which strategy to use depends on the type of activity and the cultural environment. For goods and services that are minor items in the consumer's shopping basket, exit would be a more expeditious alternative than voice. The role of voice increases with the importance of the item for the user or beneficiary and with the diminishing availability of alternatives: the higher the importance and the fewer the alternatives, the higher the potential role of voice. Government monopolies of durable goods or housing offer good examples. In some societies in which popular participation, consumer groups, and similar grass-roots organizations are well organized and effective, voice could play a potentially large role in ensuring the adequate performance of a number of institutions. In other societies, where protest and group actions are not traditional, exit may have to bear most of the effort for a long time, while attempts are made to develop the voice mechanisms that will fit the particular cultural structure.

People-oriented, low-specificity activities will probably find it difficult to make wide use of the simpler exit alternative to induce institutional effectiveness. Many people-oriented activities are totally or partially in the hands of governments or operate under heavy monopolistic conditions. Some form of voice has to be used—usually a more costly, cumbersome, and problematic alternative.

In some instances, the possibility of exit can be promoted so much that the entity has no chance to react. Railways in developing countries are a classic case. As previously discussed, many operated for a long time as virtual monopolies. The rapid advent of road transport in recent decades, accelerated by vast programs of road construction, caught the railways completely unprepared for operating in a competitive atmosphere. Most of them reacted badly, and traffic losses and heavy deficits left them at the mercy of the ministries of finance. In addition to the purely political restrictions (for instance, the obligation to maintain uneconomic services) the ministries placed further limits on the railways' operations; for example, ceilings on salaries made it impossible to attract and retain the high-quality staff necessary for an effective operation in a competitive atmosphere. This, in turn, induced further deterioration of the railways' position and bigger deficits, generating a vicious circle that few railways have been able to break successfully. The payment of the deficits by the treasury has not offered any inducement to improve performance, since it wiped out whatever disciplinary effect could have been expected from the increased competition. In such situations voice becomes a potentially crucial element that, unfortunately, is seldom used. In its absence in the case of railways perhaps a slower exposure to road competition would have been appropriate.

The concepts of exit and voice can be extended to internal competition. Each individual or group has the alternative of exit or voice. In response to increased competitive pressure, personnel can react either through exit or voice behavior, which will result in the entropy, or effort to loosen up, that Leibenstein describes. Because actions are more personal, voice becomes the logical mechanism and exit a last resort. Except in cases of high unemployment, an agency will not have a monopolistic power over its workers. If excessive pressure is created, those that exit are staff with other opportunities, the best and precisely those who could have made an important contribution to improved performance by exercising the voice option. It might be decided, for example, to improve the performance of a government entity by reorganizing it and changing the management style to augment the degree of internal competition. But if these are the only measures taken and other negative factors remain, such as ceilings on salaries, cumbersome procedures and regulations, or excessive political interventions, a likely result of increased internal competition will be an exodus of the best people from the organization. The experience with institutional development corroborates this hypothesis: in numerous cases a partial set of measures has resulted in the loss of the most valuable staff. As a consequence of the recent economic crisis many institutions in Sub-Saharan Africa are glaring examples of this phenomenon.

The effectiveness of competition and competition surrogates in inducing higher levels of performance is also limited in the case of public sector institutions unless their survival is threatened. Until a few years ago, few public entities faced this threat. More recently, however, many countries have begun to liquidate certain government activities or transfer them to the private sector; the elimination of public activities has become politically acceptable.

Competition (and competition surrogates) works by threatening an organization's survival; if it does not adapt it might be forced into bankruptcy or the equivalent.[7] If a public enterprise faces the possibility of going out of existence, competition would affect it in the same way it does a private firm: the organization would try to adapt in order to survive. The big difference is that a public enterprise does not directly control some of its basic policy parameters. The survival of the enterprise thus requires in most cases a change in government policies. Often these policies are overloaded with so many objectives that they do not meet any one of them satisfactorily or resources are inadequate to meet the goals. If the government is interested in the enterprise's survival, it should alter its policies so as to help the enterprise continue.

The question of enormous practical importance is how economic competition will affect the performance of public sector activities that are not threatened with extinction. In addition to railways, other public endeavors that are unlikely to be disbanded in most countries are education and health services, telecommunications, water supply, and urban services. There has been no systematic analysis of this experience, but the information accumulated suggests that economic competition has had a positive effect on performance in many cases, negative in others (again, the railways). If survival is not at stake, however, there has been little inducement to modify or reduce objectives. Given the push toward a broader use of markets throughout the world, regardless of whether the productive units are publicly or privately owned, research in this area should have the highest priority.

A related question which also has no answer has to do with the effect of competition surrogates on performance when survival is not threatened. There have been cases of positive effects on performance from pressure by clients and regulatory agencies—the latter particularly with regard to public enterprises. It stands to reason, however, that the effects will be considerably diminished in the absence of danger.

On the basis of the arguments already presented, it also stands to reason that low-specificity activities with complex objectives and uncertain technologies will require stronger incentives to improve performance and simplify goals. Incentives derived from competition and competition surrogates might be insufficient. Moreover, in the case of disagreement and uncertainty about objectives and methods, there is the risk that decisionmakers might move politically rather than professionally to resolve at least some of the disagreements. In other words, they might apply political strategies of bargaining and authoritarian allocation to a situation that really requires professional debate, experimentation, and evaluation. Conversely, when objectives and methods are clearly defined and there is agreement about them, decisionmakers will more easily formulate the necessary answers to competitive pressures.

In summary, competition and competition surrogates are double-edged weapons, apparently far more complex than specificity as a factor inducing institutional performance. They are potentially very powerful when combined with high specificity, but in circumstances such as those just discussed, which seem to be common in developing countries, the excessive or misdirected use of competition and competition surrogates could have negative effects. Moreover, there is theoretically an optimal degree of competition for a set of activities at any given time, beyond which the positive effects on institutional performance would decline. The factors determining that optimal level are the nature of the activity, the management style, the general competitive environment, and, perhaps the essential point, the cultural traits of the society.

The World Bank's Experience

The Bank's experience supports the previous analysis. Most institutions that were exposed to some form of competition had a higher level of institutional performance than those that were not, railways being the exception. Most of the Bank's operations deal not with institutions that are exposed to competition, however, but with government agencies that have a monopoly or near monopoly, either by design or by the nature of their activities. Of the 159 principal agencies reviewed, only a few were exposed to a considerable degree of competition. The competitive activities were mainly in industry, finance, some subsectors in agriculture, and railways. The concern here is with whether the agency, not the activity served by it, operates under competition. Although road transport or agriculture could be very competitive activities themselves, the highway department or the national extension service might not.

The Bank evaluation studies deal almost exclusively with external competition. The clearest cases are among railways. If a railway that faces increased competition is given sufficient freedom to readapt the scale and structure of its services to the new realities, as happened in Spain, it usually benefits from the new environment, although with some delay. But in several countries (Colombia, Senegal, and Turkey) the operational framework given to the railways was so contradictory that there were negative effects from competition.

State-owned enterprises are particularly important. They range from large national monopolies or near monopolies in utilities (power and water supply), through large industrial and transport concerns and marketing companies, all the way to small retail operations. These enterprises are in the hands of the government either for political or ideological reasons or by default because bankruptcy had threatened to close what had been a private enterprise. In recent years the Bank has promoted a new approach for dealing with public enterprises. Among the factors determining the performance of the enterprises only some—often quite a small proportion—are in the hands of the managers, and a larger proportion is under the control of the central government agencies that regulate or oversee those enterprises. The Bank has therefore begun to focus more on the nature and effectiveness of the relations between the central agencies and the public enterprises as a way of inducing a better performance. Whenever feasible an effort is made to expose the enterprises to a competitive environment.[8]

A related pattern that emerges from the Bank's experience is a positive correlation between a financial surplus and a high level of institutional performance, including rapid progress in institutional development programs. Causality has not been proven, but these cases indicate that payment of deficits tends to act as a disincentive to better performance. The reasons for covering the deficit may be numerous and valid—such as that services should continue to be provided for strategic or social reasons—but the actual effect is to reduce the potential of competition as an incentive for better performance, especially in cases where the accounting and costing procedures are incapable of distinguishing between subsidized and nonsubsidized activities. In addition, the nature of central government and nonrevenue agencies prevents them from taking advantage of economic competition as a potentially powerful mechanism for inducing their own internal effectiveness.

The Bank evaluations were even less informative with regard to competition surrogates, although experience has been growing considerably in recent years. The cases reviewed offered few examples of pressures from clients or beneficiaries. For some of the agencies providing infrastructure or services, the competitive nature of their users or clients does not seem to have much influenced their effectiveness, which suggests that the potential of these competition surrogates has not been tapped. For example, in only a couple of instances has the road transport industry organized itself to press with a common voice for better maintenance of roads. In more cases small farmers and villagers have pressed for the maintenance of feeder roads and even participated directly in the maintenance activity. A similar phenomenon can sometimes be found in irrigation systems or some of the services involved in the sites and services components of urban development programs.

A different form of client pressure has come from big industrial or mining concerns in relation to railways, ports, and utilities. Many of the railways in the sample have been induced by a large client to provide a specialized service that is highly efficient in relation to the rest of the railway operations; similar cases appear in ports and power companies. Especially with railways, however, the difference between the efficiency of these services and that of the bulk of their operations has persisted over long periods. The gap illustrates not only the importance of this kind of pressure, but also the difficulty of transferring these incentives even within the same organization, unless special efforts are made to do so. In other cases the influence of large clients with monopsonic power seems to have been detrimental—for example, agricultural marketing boards have imposed freight rates that forced small truck operations into bankruptcy. In other fields where the potential for competition surrogates is large, such as education and many agricultural institutions, there is little evidence that they have been used at all. The evaluations do not register any significant case of pressures exercised by suppliers, and none has been found in subsequent experience.

The topic of client pressure has, however, received a great deal of attention, but from different perspectives. Community participation often includes elements of this kind of pressure and has been an important component in many World Bank–financed programs. Of the many varieties of community participation, the one that is relevant here is the organization of formal or informal groups not only to mobilize workers for community efforts, but also to deal with central government or local authorities from a position of greater strength.[9] At a more general level, pressure from clients and users of such government services as export promotion, licenses, and registrations has been channeled in Brazil to help improve the provision of those services.[10]

Instances of pressures to induce higher performance emanating from the political and regulatory establishment were much less apparent among the evaluations, probably because they did not focus on this issue. Aside from the purely political interventions, central government and regulatory agencies appear in the evaluations to focus mainly on issues of control. Perhaps the most direct type of competition surrogate that has evolved in recent years is the performance contracts between the public enterprises and the central regulatory agencies.[11]

Internal competition through administrative and managerial actions was virtually absent from the sample. In no case has this approach been consciously pursued by an entity, although in a few cases something similar has been tried: for example, among the various units of a railway (Spain), among branches of development banks, and among the regions covered by an agricultural extension service.

Little attention has been paid to the issue of competition with regard to small farmers, although in many developing countries, particularly the poorer ones, they are a substantial proportion of the population. Because subsistence farmers are largely outside the market economy and a competitive environment, they are deprived of one of the potentially most important inducements to improve their productivity. The higher the proportion of their production that is marketed, the higher will be their exposure to competitive forces, even if only indirectly. Often, however, these farmers' only external contacts are with public institutions that are among the most ineffective. They therefore receive little pressure or feedback to improve their performance. It could be argued that the struggle for survival gives subsistence farmers an even stronger incentive than would competition, but experience shows that major improvements in their productivity take place mainly when they move from subsistence to cash crops.

Interactions

The interactions between specificity and competition and the political and cultural factors that influence institutional performance are so complex that they alone could be the topic of several major studies. As indicated, specificity tends to reduce the influence of cultural factors. This hypothesis can be extended to competition, which produces the same effect. Specificity and competition also change the nature and scope of the political influences on institutional performance.

The empirical evidence is not sufficient to predict how the nature of the political influences will change from the low-specificity to the high-specificity activities. However, a few hypotheses can be stated. Political decisions are more pervasive and intense the smaller the amount of knowledge available and the larger the extent of change. Thus political intervention is likely to be more intense in low-specificity activities. In the high-specificity ones, the technical side of the operation is less open to direct political intervention. Conversely, the technical content of most of the low-specificity activities, such as education or rural extension, is not so clearly defined as to be free from politics. In electric power, it is possible to conceive of political intervention in the tariff level and structure, in staff appointments, especially at the senior level, and in the decision of whether to build a new plant. But political intervention on the technical aspects of the operation—for example, maintenance standards—is highly unlikely. Moreover, a very strong technical cadre will resist political influences, even in areas outside the purely technical part of the operation, or will channel them to their advantage.[12] Often high-specificity (and in most cases highly competitive) activities acquire political power themselves and become capable of negotiating with other centers of power. Conversely, in low-specificity activities, where the technical aspects are less clear-cut, political intervention can be extended to practically the entire activity. In education, for example, politics may influence not only the whole spectrum of demand—who gets what education—but also the composition of the curriculum and even the teaching techniques.

A parallel hypothesis is that political influences will be stronger in situations where large numbers of individuals are involved, as in many people-oriented activities, and especially if the link between the activity and the individuals is direct and visually evident, as in the case of students and teachers. Furthermore, many people-oriented activities (education, training, extension services) can easily be used to achieve political objectives. In principle, these objectives can be pursued in myriad ways, including the distribution of industrial goods, but perhaps the best possibility of exerting long-run political influence is through some of the people-oriented activities. In most countries many of these activities are in the hands of the public sector and most operate at a deficit; they therefore require continuous contributions from the budget. In the review of the Bank's experience, a positive correlation was found between the degree of political intervention (that is, overt intervention cited in the evaluation documents) and the existence of a deficit or the fact of being a line agency of the central government.

Political influences are related to political commitment. In developing countries governments tend to be very supportive of the "modern" activities in the economy, in part because of the concentration of economic resources in them. Sometimes these modern activities are politically and economically so important that the political establishment intervenes excessively, as happens in the case of many public enterprises. Conversely, many people-oriented activities, although subject to all sorts of political interventions and controls, may be peripheral to the main interests of the political establishment and receive little support. In the more extreme cases, if the government is not really interested in social development these people-oriented activities might actually be opposed by politicians, although they might still be subject to heavy political intervention.

Similar hypotheses can be advanced with regard to the influence of cultural factors, and for the same reasons. The nature of the influence will depend on the specific traits in each society. Some cultural traits encourage better institutional performance, and others discourage it. There is, however, surprisingly little in the literature to help distinguish the favorable traits from the unfavorable. A promising line of inquiry is to establish which cultural traits have a significant influence on institutional effectiveness, identify the mechanisms through which that influence operates, and—a central element—determine how, in a given society, those traits interact with the incentives induced by the intrinsic nature of various activities and by the competitive environment. A society will change drastically as it modernizes. But just how the change occurs—which cultural traits will remain, which will disappear, and which will be modified—is a largely uncharted area.

Within an organization the so-called informal groups provide a good illustration of these issues. Informal groups are formed on the basis of friendship, common interests, or professional, religious, tribal, or regional affinities; they exist outside the formal structure, but have a potentially crucial influence on the performance of the institution. Which informal groups are formed will be determined largely by cultural factors. A review of informal groups in a transitional society—one in which most activities are still traditional but some are modern—would reveal the effects of new technologies on the composition and nature of these groups. If the hypotheses postulated here are correct, these groups will change drastically, adapting to the requirements of working with a new technology and discarding or modifying some of their cultural traditions and values. Some of these traditional values might be strong enough to withstand the influence of the new technologies at least for a while, especially if the technologies are being introduced slowly or inefficiently.

Notes

1. See J. M. Clark, *Competition as a Dynamic Process* (Washington, D.C.: Brookings Institution, 1961).

2. William R. Dill, "Environment as an Influence on Managerial Autonomy," *Administrative Science Quarterly*, vol. 2 (March 1958), p. 410.

3. See Jeffrey Pfeffer and Gerald R. Salancik, *The External Control of Organizations* (New York: Harper and Row, 1978).

4. Stephen B. Peterson, "Government, Cooperatives, and the Private Sector in Peasant Agriculture," in *Institutions of Rural Development for the Poor: Decentralization and Organizational Linkages*, David K. Leonard and Dale Rogers Marshall, eds., Research Series 49 (Berkeley: Institute of International Studies, University of California, 1982), p. 113; and Goran Hyden, *Efficiency vs. Distribution in East African Cooperatives: A Study in Organizational Conflicts* (Nairobi: East African Literature Bureau, 1973).

5. Harvey Leibenstein, *Beyond Economic Man: A New Foundation for Micro-Economics* (Cambridge, Mass.: Harvard University Press, 1976).

6. Albert O. Hirschman, *Exit, Voice, and Loyalty* (Cambridge, Mass.: Harvard University Press, 1970).

7. There are differences of opinion about how the threat of extinction operates to induce higher performance in the system. Some argue that competition eliminates institutions with inappropriate forms (natural selection) rather than forcing them to reform internally. Others argue that much reform can occur (rational selection) without going to the extreme of eliminating institutions. Both explanations are partially true, the former principally for small entities and the latter for bigger ones. See Howard E. Aldrich, *Organizations and Environments* (Englewood Cliffs, N.J.: Prentice-Hall, 1979); and Michael T. Hannan and John Freeman, "The Population Ecology of Organizations," *American Journal of Sociology*, vol. 82 (March 1977), pp. 929–64.

8. Mary M. Shirley, *Managing State-Owned Enterprises*, World Bank Staff Working Paper 577 (Washington, D.C., July 1983).

9. See Samuel Paul, *Community Participation in Development Projects: The World Bank Experience*, World Bank Discussion Paper 6 (Washington, D.C., 1987).

10. *Programa Nacional de Desburocratização: Desburocratização Idéias Fundamentais* (Brasilia: Presidéncia da República, 1982), especially articles by Helio Beltrão, Guilherme Duque Estrada, João Geraldo Piquet Carneiro, Heitor Chagas de Oliveira, Aguinaldo Guimarães, and Alvaro Pessôa. See also Helio Beltrão, "Debureaucratization and Freedom," Brazil National Debureaucratization Program, April 1982; processed.

11. John R. Nellis, *Public Enterprises in Sub-Saharan Africa*, World Bank Discussion Paper 1 (Washington, D.C., 1986).

12. Political intervention can be on the supply side or the demand side of the operation. Intervention on the demand side is more common and could serve legitimate social and political objectives by determining which groups get electricity or certain health or educational services. Of greatest significance for this analysis is political intervention in the supply of goods and services because it can have a more direct negative influence on the effectiveness of the operation.

Part III

Operational Conclusions

8 National Strategies to Increase Institutional Capacity

Usually, strategies for improving institutional performance focus on individual agencies or groups of them. This study, however, suggests that performance can be improved through countrywide policies and measures that affect most or all agencies. In fact, experience indicates that major improvements in performance often materialize in a country only after national policies and measures are established or modified. This chapter deals with national strategies; the remaining three, with strategies at the agency level.

When competition and specificity are taken as central explanations of institutional performance, the first and probably most important corollary is that low-specificity and noncompetitive activities cannot, by definition, achieve the same level or kind of performance as high-specificity and competitive ones. The effectiveness of low-specificity and noncompetitive activities has to be measured by different standards. The standards will vary most between a high-specificity activity that operates in a competitive atmosphere and a low-specificity one that operates as a monopoly.

In view of this difference, resources tend to flow toward high-specificity and competitive activities. Financial resources generally flow to them because they offer greater potential for growth and control. Human resources gravitate toward them because the financial rewards and status are higher and, for certain individuals, because technological and financial activities are intellectually more satisfying. The combination of factors, in particular the monetary rewards and the status, attract the "best and the brightest" to careers in high-specificity and competitive activities; a vicious circle begins when these people further enhance the development of the related disciplines and the effectiveness of the institutions and, consequently, increase the gap between the high-specificity, competitive and low-specificity, noncompetitive activities. (This point has been made mainly about managerial talent.[1])

This permanent gap also makes many of the low-specificity, people-oriented activities unattractive to the private sector. Most services are therefore provided by the public sector—except for some, such as education and health care, which can be profitable when directed to the highest income levels or, as often happens, when they are given privileges by the government. The handicaps inherent in the public sector tend to increase the differences between the two kinds of activities. In addition, to reduce the size of the public sector governments have begun to transfer many of their high-specificity, potentially competitive activities to the private sector, thus further increasing the intrinsic differences between the two sectors.

A second corollary of using the concepts of specificity and competition is that institutional improvement in low-specificity and noncompetitive activities will take longer than in high-specificity and competitive ones. If velocity of change is taken as a measure of performance, low-specificity and noncompetitive activities will be ranked as doing poorly. Evaluations of their performance will therefore have to use different measures.

A third corollary has to do with the possibility of substitution between specificity and competition as factors inducing better institutional performance, although at this stage the concepts are not sufficiently precise to allow the actual measurement of substitution rates among them. A similar degree of institutional improvement can be achieved by using different combinations of these two factors. It might be possible to increase the technological level through investments, or to expose the entity to more competition, or to introduce organizational and managerial changes. Some indication of the nature of substitution rates has been given in previous chapters, but much more work is necessary to establish the mechanisms through which substitution among factors takes place.

A related issue is the degree to which the role played by each factor can be modified over time. Perhaps technology, defined in a broad sense, is the most difficult factor to change in the context of the high- to low-specificity spectrum. By definition, it is impossible to adopt a high technology for a people-oriented activity, but within a high-specificity activity it is possible to switch fairly quickly from an intermediate to a high technology, given the resources to do so. The evolution of the degree of competition is more difficult to predict. On the basis of purely economic factors one can make a reasonable projection of market conditions or anticipate the introduction of some of the competition surrogates, but the political framework for competition could change drastically and unpredictably. For example, a highly protected market could be suddenly opened to international competition or the legal framework for a particular activity substantially modified.

A fourth corollary is that improved institutional performance is part and parcel of the process of modernization. Unless a country becomes "modern" it cannot raise its performance to the level now prevailing in the developed world. This means a transformation of the society being developed. Increased institutional effectiveness is only one element of modernization, however. The difficulty is that countries are trying to speed up their institutional development before being fully industrialized and before having a widespread competitive atmosphere—that is, without two of the most powerful inducements for increasing institutional effectiveness.

This makes the technical/people-oriented dualism implicit in the high- to low-specificity spectrum even more difficult to tackle. It is a more basic and permanent form of dualism than that of developed and developing countries. The technical/people-oriented dualism exists in all societies, independently of their level of development. Poor developing countries, however, have a small proportion of high-specificity activities and, to break out of their poverty, they require a large number of people-oriented activities such as rural extension services and primary education. The challenge is for them to modernize as fast as possible, but without unduly changing the character of their people-oriented activities.

Elements of a Countrywide Operational Strategy

The analysis in previous chapters suggests three general, countrywide approaches for improving institutional performance that should be part of a national strategy: a greater awareness of the issues, an emphasis on the low-specificity subsectors and activities, and a strategy to minimize the need for institutional capacity.

Increased Awareness

The need for greater awareness of the issues related to institutional development on the part of the political authorities and managers in a country may appear to be obvious, but in practice it is often neglected. Although many are aware of the importance of institutional performance in achieving development, there is a certain despair about what can be done to improve it, and the issue is often pushed aside in discussions about development strategies. That despair derives from the difficulty of improving a country's public administration or of getting certain agencies to perform adequately; it is seldom related to the inconsistency of the policies that define the environment in which the agencies have to function or to the inherent difficulty of achieving progress in particular activities. The authorities might complain about the problem of improving a rural extension service, but they will overlook the fact that salaries of extensionists are much too low or that the extension agency is overregulated and has little operational freedom. There is also a generalized lack of awareness that activities and institutions differ in their potential and in the difficulty of the problems they present; instead there is a tendency to treat them all in the same way.

Sometimes politicians and managers are reluctant to deal explicitly with any problem, such as institutional weaknesses, that could be seen as a sign of the backwardness or inadequacy of their society. The refusal of some governments to discuss openly, for example, their implementation problems is not justified if viewed from the proper historical perspective. A traditional society has performance standards which are different from those induced by industrialization and modern technology. Great progress could be made if key decisionmakers would change their attitude toward these issues and face insufficient institutional capacity as just one more of the resources lacking in a developing economy.

What can be done to increase the general level of awareness? Considerable progress has already been made. The international development community is increasingly focusing on institutional capacity as one of the missing elements in any successful development strategy. This was inevitable in light of the accumulating evidence that development programs fail because of institutional and managerial weaknesses and that institutional development programs continue to have mixed results. Since the economic crises of the early 1980s, the emphasis on the adequacy of macroeconomic policies has highlighted the fact that policies may be well designed, but they are seldom well implemented and monitored, largely because central government agencies lack the ability to do so. It has become clearer to many politicians and economists that a congruent set of policies is a necessary but not a sufficient condition for effective economic management.

The multilateral and bilateral development agencies have launched several initiatives. An important milestone was the World Bank's *World Development Report 1983*.[2] Some developing countries are paying more attention to this issue and are tackling various aspects of their institutional capacity. Still, the general attitude is one of skepticism; policymakers and economists have reluctantly agreed that institutional capacity is indeed an important factor, but remain to be convinced that something can be done about it. The best argument in these cases is success—not just a few successful cases, but a pattern of success even if only in limited areas. More could be made of the many successes in the past three decades of institutional development efforts. After all, most countries would not want to return to the administrative capacity they had a generation ago. But despite some success, as discussed below, there are not yet enough examples to form a consistent pattern.

Three steps can be taken to publicize the issue of institutional capacity among politicians, administrators, economists, and academics dealing with developing societies. One is to have more so-called high-level policy seminars, along the lines of those sponsored by the World Bank's Economic Development Institute. These seminars focus on a variety of policy and strategy issues and are attended by individuals from all the groups just listed, but especially politicians. Similar seminars could be organized by national institutions and concentrate on national problems, including conceptual issues and experiences, along the lines of the *World Development Report 1983*, successful strategies, and the costs of not having adequate institutional capacity. Similar seminars or workshops for lower-level government administrators have focused specifically on the diagnosis of institutional constraints, with considerable success.

The second step is to increase the efforts of all relevant entities, especially the academic community and the international development agencies, to measure and document the costs of institutional weakness and the cases of success, so that they can be disseminated more widely. Surprisingly little progress has been made in designing methodologies to measure the effects of poor performance of individual institutions, although a wealth of data is available, even in developing countries. There has been even less progress with regard to methodologies to assess the costs of poor performance in sectors and subsectors of national economies. A clearer notion of the resources involved will help sharpen the minds of politicians and managers.

The third step is to make better use of the press and other channels of communication, in those countries where that is feasible, to raise the awareness of these issues among all segments of society and to underscore the urgent need to find solutions. The international and bilateral development agencies could play an important role as catalysts, either by disseminating their own experiences or by encouraging the professional establishment in the country to disseminate theirs.

A broader awareness of the importance of increasing institutional capacity would in itself be significant because much could be done simply by following existing approaches and known solutions more systematically and persistently. There is no need to wait for major breakthroughs to achieve progress. The right political and professional support at the right time could achieve much.

Emphasis on Low-Specificity and Noncompetitive Activities

If increased awareness is the first order of business, the second is to give priority in institutional development strategies to the low-specificity (low-technology and people-oriented) activities. This priority is vital for countries at lower levels of development, particularly if their high-technology activities operate as enclaves. The real intellectual challenge will be to design solutions for these activities without simply copying those that have worked in the high-specificity ones. Several biases will have to be overcome, such as the tendency to assume that progress will be made merely by introducing partial organizational improvements and a few management techniques or by concentrating on the quantifiable aspects of an operation and on planning and design instead of on implementation.

This last point may need some elaboration. "Hard" investments—in infrastructure and machinery—can be designed in great detail because actual implementation is likely to be quite close to what was planned. With institutional development in the low-specificity activities, the opposite is often the case. This means that planning and design have a different meaning; they cannot be a blueprint. In institutional development programs for low-specificity activities, design, planning, and implementation coincide in time, because institutions and circumstances are constantly changing. The state of the art and the complexity of the subject do not allow an initial solution or blueprint to be fully implemented as originally defined. What is necessary is to set up ways in which the individuals involved can participate in the implementation and redefinition of objectives and methods as implementation progresses and knowledge and experience accumulate. The suggestions made in this and the following chapters point in that direction, and considerable work has already been done by academics and practitioners in this field.[3]

A question that arises now is whether this proposed emphasis on the institutional aspects of low-specificity and noncompetitive activities makes sense as a development strategy, since it neglects the modern sectors. To this, there are several answers. First, the low-specificity and noncompetitive activities in a developing economy will represent the largest proportion of the total activities, and the less developed the country, the larger that proportion; the strategy thus attempts to tackle the largest and weakest segments. Second, the modern and competitive activities will, if my hypothesis is right, take care of themselves pretty well (relatively speaking, of course), and their effectiveness can be improved much more than those of the low-specificity and noncompetitive activities with relatively minor efforts. Third, as indicated before, since many of these activities deal with the rural areas and the poorest segments of the population, emphasizing them is tantamount to reiterating the priority attached by the development community to the eradication of poverty; it coincides with the emphasis given to agriculture in the most recent development strategies; and it strengthens the argument that development programs oriented to agriculture and poverty eradication are among the most productive.

Perhaps the most difficult obstacle to this strategy is the long-standing belief in all societies, including the developed ones, that hard technology deserves the highest priority. To conclude that low-specificity activities are the most important and in many ways the most difficult requires an intellectual jump which will be hard to achieve in practically all developing societies. At present, attitudes and incentives are oriented in the other direction. A myriad of examples could be cited in which engineers and other technical professions receive the highest salaries and the greatest prestige or where exceptions are made for this type of activity. But very few examples can be cited of special efforts to improve the remuneration and quality of teachers, health workers, or staff in institutions operating people-oriented activities in rural areas. Developing societies are dazzled with technology, but their real breakthrough will come at the other end of the spectrum. After all, human resources are more important to development than natural resources or technology.[4]

Minimizing Institutional Needs

Institutional capabilities are not only one of the most important resources for development, but also one of the most scarce, if not the scarcest. It should be explicitly considered as a separate resource in the design of development strategies. Countries often embark on large-scale attempts to increase the availability of this resource through education, training, or importation of skills; in this sense, it is a constantly changing resource. But how to minimize the need for institutional capability is seldom explored. It is not an easy task, and a full analysis, or even the preparation of a taxonomy of the institutional intensity of different types of activity, is beyond the scope of this study. Some illustrations, however, will suggest a particularly important line of policy in this respect.

Take, for example, road and rail transport. As previously indicated, railways are highly management-intensive, whereas road transport, if it is in private hands, is likely to be operated by many small, independent operators which, overall, are less management-intensive. Even if road maintenance is included, road transport probably requires less managerial capabilities than railways. Thus it might be more effective for a country with very limited managerial resources to avoid railways, because a badly run railway is a less economic proposition than a well-run road transport service, even if the railway appears to have a comparative advantage for certain traffic. But assessments of comparative advantages assume an adequate operation, which is seldom the case. It is not difficult to find examples, especially in Africa, of badly run railways which are justified primarily for certain bulky, long-distance traffic. If a serious economic and managerial analysis were made, however, it would conclude that most or all railway operations could be performed more effectively by road transport.

Another example is the centralization/decentralization dilemma. A centralized approach is usually taken when a wider span of control is required to coordinate local units, achieve economies of scale, or avoid fraud or corruption. Any number of examples could be given, from centralized purchasing units set up to reap the benefits of bulk buying to political organizations established to consolidate control. But centralized solutions might be more management-intensive in the long run, especially if they recognize local variations and require mechanisms capable of quick interaction between the center and many distant satellites. The negative effects of excessive centralization are too well known to repeat them here. It is important, however, to impress one effect upon the political establishment: if centralized solutions do not function well, they defeat their original purpose and might exacerbate the damage that they were designed to prevent. Minor corruption at local levels, for instance, might be replaced by massive corruption in central places, or an ineffective centralized operation could end up weakening the political control for which it was originally designed.

Decentralization is probably less management intensive in the long run, but it raises the problem of coordination. Sometimes the needs of coordination are more complex than those of control. Taken to an extreme, decentralization implies the creation of fully independent entities and the establishment of operating rules so that coordination takes place automatically. This is seldom the case, and decentralized decisionmaking requires the creation of some central mechanisms of control and coordination, which will have higher authority and will tend to function better than "automatic" coordination mechanisms among independent entities. Thus there is a ranking of institutional complexity in this respect. Fully centralized arrangements are probably the most management-intensive, especially when the organization is large and geographically dispersed. Interagency coordination is probably next, especially if the level of authority behind it is low. In the short run, however, the transition from a centralized to a decentralized structure might be very management-intensive because of the need for specialized skills.

As always, there are tradeoffs between the potential benefits of complex institutional solutions and the costs of using scarce institutional resources. If the resources are not available, the potential benefits will not materialize. The problem is that institutions and managerial capacity are not as visible a resource as capital or labor. A classic example is that of highway construction and maintenance. In purely economic terms, if it is assumed that managerial resources are available, the choice of technology for highway construction might be labor-intensive with low construction standards in keeping with projected traffic levels and budgetary constraints. But this solution could have two problems. First, labor-intensive technologies might require a great deal of management. Second, low construction standards assume adequate maintenance, an eminently management-intensive activity. If the managerial capacity is not available and maintenance is not performed, the original economic calculations are meaningless. The rate of return estimate could have been based on a technical lifetime of fifteen years for the road with adequate maintenance. If maintenance does not take place and the road is destroyed after four years, probably other technical solutions would have been more appropriate.

The issue of institutional intensity is more glaring in the case of economic policies. Different ways of achieving policy objectives have different levels of institutional intensity. For example, if the objective is to reduce the deficit in the balance of payments of a country, one way of achieving it is through market forces, which would require the devaluation of the local currency. The institutional requirement of this alternative is relatively modest: probably a small group of economists and other professionals located in the central bank. At the other extreme, the full control of imports, exports, and foreign currency transactions would require a large bureaucratic establishment, probably with a staff of thousands in a medium-size country, to process, authorize, and control each transaction, with the risks of inefficiency and corruption. A similar analysis could be made for other policy objectives, such as market prices as opposed to price controls or free entry to an activity as opposed to licensing. A central point to remember is that the market mechanism is a substitute for institutional capacity, and private sector alternatives are often less management-intensive than public sector ones since many small private operators can replace a large and unwieldy government organization in many sectors, including agriculture (provision of extension services and marketing), education, health, and transport. Interest in this subject has increased considerably in recent years. Some would argue that the institutional complexity of the market, when considered systematically, is not much less than that of a government operation. But the market does not require complex planning, and it reduces the role of a number of large government institutions, precisely those that are difficult to improve in developing countries.

Two other examples are discussed below and in chapter 11. One has to do with the choice of technology and the other with project and program design and complexity. The notion that institutional capacity is a scarce resource, that it should be considered independently, and that its use should be optimized should provide a new perspective for the design of development strategies. A taxonomy of organizational solutions, from the simpler to the more complex, to typical problems would be an important contribution.

National governments in general and individual institutions in particular must recognize the need to simplify their goals in order to adapt them to the institutional capacity of their country. When that capacity is particularly weak, as in many countries in Sub-Saharan Africa and elsewhere, the real choices are quite dramatic—but the choices become apparent only after a detailed analysis of the institutional capacity, and such an analysis is seldom made. A good indicator of the size of the problem is the enormous requirements for technical assistance in developing countries. Because of weaknesses in the rest of the institutional system and numerous deficiencies in the technical assistance itself, the impact of this assistance has been negligible and in a few cases negative.

Overloading an institution with goals that it cannot achieve increases the management difficulties in a more than proportional way, especially in the case of low-specificity activities in a noncompetitive environment. The converse, then, is that an arithmetic simplification of goals will produce a geometric increase in the chances of getting the programs and the activities implemented. Many indicators, such as the failure of programs and the ineffectiveness of technical assistance, point toward the imbalance between objectives and institutional capacity. The naked fact is that many developing countries can undertake with a reasonable chance of success only a few programs at a time; going beyond that limit will exponentially reduce the likelihood of success in any of them.

A similar need for a drastic simplification of objectives is apparent with regard to individual institutions, especially those in the public sector that are close to the low-specificity, noncompetitive end of the spectrum. What this means for the internal performance of the undertakings is analyzed in chapter 9. Here, the crucial issue is that for the agencies in the central government, by definition, and for public enterprises, the simplification of goals is in the hands of the regulatory agencies and the political establishment. Strengthening the capacity of those agencies that define the goals—the core agencies in the government—becomes the highest priority. If these "nerve centers" do not work, the chances of achieving this simplification are very low.

Macro Implications of Specificity and Competition

Specificity

At the macro level specificity has important implications for appropriate technology, a concept which needs to be considerably revised. Appropriate technology has been defined mainly with regard to the use of capital and labor on the assumption that both factors of production are used effectively. But this assumption does not hold. The concept of appropriate technology therefore needs to be modified in two ways. First, a third factor of production, institutional capacity, has to be added to capital and labor. Second, high-specificity technologies have a strong modernizing effect that should also be considered in the selection of a technology. Although the advantages are difficult to quantify, the use of a high-specificity technology whenever feasible might be an important tool for achieving modernization and for ensuring better institutional performance.

Institutional capacity ought to be added as a separate factor of production because there is often an inverse relation between capital intensity and institutional requirements: the higher the capital intensity, the lower the managerial requirements. It is therefore likely that capital will be used with greater effectiveness than labor and that labor-intensive techniques will face serious managerial problems. In such a case, actual increases in output *and* employment might be lower in the medium run with labor-intensive techniques than with relatively more capital-intensive techniques.

These considerations suggest that often the best technology will be more capital-intensive than one chosen in accordance with a standard economic capital-labor analysis. How much more will depend on the particular situation and set of technologies. Appropriate technologies should be designed not only to adapt them to the available capital, labor, and institutional capacity, but also to maximize their modernizing effects. If these four factors—capital, labor, institutional capacity, and modernization—were taken into account together, it is likely that the technologies chosen would be quite different from those being selected at present.

In simpler terms, countries want to modernize and they will do so through the use of modern technologies and approaches. Any strategy that consciously delays modernization has to be viewed with extreme caution, particularly if it is based on an intensive use of an intangible but nonetheless important resource such as institutional capacity. In the literature in this field there has been for a long time an awareness of the organizational and managerial implications of intermediate technologies,[5] but little if any attempt to incorporate the modernizing effects of technology into the argument. The real challenge for developing countries is how to organize and manage the low-technology and people-oriented activities so that they have a modernizing influence on the individuals working in them, but introduce the kind of modernization and technology that is compatible with the activity. In this respect, the definition of appropriate technologies is complementary rather than contradictory to the increased emphasis on low-specificity, noncompetitive activities proposed in the preceding section. Moreover, these arguments remain valid no matter what definition of modernization is used. The term is heavily weighted by historical and cultural baggage, but no one at this point thinks of modernization in terms of big steel plants. Whichever concept of modernization is adopted, however, all are linked to the use of some form of technology and more systematic methods of production, in which case the previous arguments continue to apply.

Another aspect of specificity at the macro or global level is the possibility of making use of the whole productive structure of a country, since it contains a spectrum of activities from high to low specificity, to improve institutional performance. At lower levels of development, the structure will tend to be closer to the low-specificity end of the spectrum; at higher levels, the structure will become wider and shift toward the high-specificity end. It should be possible to induce higher levels of performance by the lower-specificity activities through pressure from or contacts with the higher-specificity ones.

How could this be done? One possibility is the technological input-output matrix proposed in chapter 6. The principle behind such a matrix is that increased contacts between high- and low-specificity activities have a positive effect on institutional performance. Those contacts have to be identified within the economic system, and managerial and organizational ways have to be found to increase the number and intensity of the contacts and to enhance their positive impact on the operational effectiveness of the lower-specificity activities. At this stage this is just an idea to be explored at three levels. First, the nature of the matrix has to be developed conceptually to identify the links between activities at different levels of specificity and the nature of the interactions. Work in this respect could begin by defining a matrix for small groups or clusters of activities rather than for the whole institutional system. Second, some taxonomy of the nature of these links is necessary to describe what kinds of interaction between high- and low-specificity activities do in fact act to discipline the low-specificity ones, which modalities are followed, and what is the intensity of the effects. Not all links are similar and surely some have a higher potential for improving performance than others. To establish such a taxonomy requires detailed study of linkages among activities. Third, with a preliminary understanding of the nature of these interactions, measures could be designed to enhance their positive impact or to generate other positive interactions: new links could be established, others made more formal, or special training programs designed. The question is how to make normal contacts among activities a more effective disciplinary factor for institutional performance.

A similar but partial approach would be to identify within the productive system of a country the clusters of high-specificity activities and the links among activities that are especially suitable for inducing better performance in the low-specificity activities with which they relate. The activities that immediately come to mind are the same ones mentioned in other contexts: airlines, power and telecommunications companies, and financial institutions. Many industrial activities have similar potential, as do the armed forces and even some activities in agriculture.

Competition

A few qualifications are in order with regard to the use of competition as an incentive for operational effectiveness. The first has to do with the issues raised by Hirschman: there is no point in opening up an activity to competition, especially in the public sector, if it will induce a loss of the best customers or beneficiaries and therefore actually decrease effectiveness. Second, although a broader competitive atmosphere may be established, the rules of the game for each entity are not always similar; some hold an unfair advantage, as in the classic case of road-rail competition. Any time a public entity is exposed to competition, there is a strong likelihood that different units will play under different rules. It is much more difficult to establish homogeneous rules for a mixed public and private market than for a market in which only private units are competing. The recent literature on public enterprises and the need to establish "contracts" between the central government and each enterprise goes into this issue in detail.[6]

The third qualification relates to cultural factors. The effectiveness of competition as an incentive will be enhanced or limited by specific cultural traits: most modern societies readily accept competition and offer little social resistance, but traditional societies might be more reluctant to react to this kind of incentive. It is generally assumed that the relationship between competition and operational effectiveness is linear, but it is not at all clear that more competition will always result in higher operational effectiveness. How far the relationship will hold before some sort of cultural barrier is hit or Leibenstein's entropy ensues is at this stage anybody's guess, but conditions will vary from country to country or market to market. An interesting hypothesis to explore is that the "efficiency" of competition as an incentive will increase with higher levels of modernization. This is put very simply in figure 1. A country (or a sector) at a low level of modernization, M_1, will experience an increase in operational effectiveness as the degree of competition increases, until a point at which the competitive atmosphere clashes with cultural factors to such an extent that some actual reductions in performance begin to appear. At a higher level of modernity or development, M_2, competition can help take operational efficiency to a relatively higher level, and the potential reductions caused by cultural factors will be less. At an even higher level, M_3, competition will not have a noticeable negative effect, although its positive effect might decline or become negligible after a certain point. The figure can also be used to illustrate the effectiveness of competition for an activity or group of activities at different levels of specificity.

What can be done at the macro level to make full use of competitive pressure to achieve higher institutional performance? From the discussion in the previous chapter and from the experience of many countries in recent years, it should be clear that the extension of competition to its

**Figure 1.   The Effectiveness of Competition as an Incentive
at Various Levels of Modernization (M)**

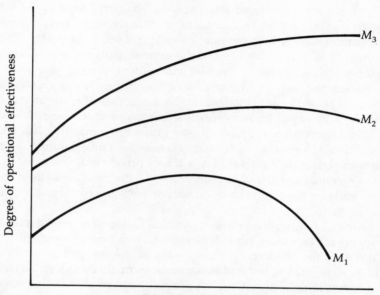

Degree of competition

use in improving performance is only partially related to the ownership
of the means of production. Markets and other forms of competitive
environments are equally feasible in capitalist or socialist societies.

Still, the extent to which different types of competitive pressure are
used is very much a matter of government policies. The extent to which
any economy is open to international trade and to competitive pressures
from abroad is a well-known and much discussed issue. I can only stress
again that an open economy is likely to have positive effects on the performance not only of the activities exposed to international competition
but also of many others directly or indirectly related to them. The competitive input-output matrix becomes a handy instrument for tracing
these activities. Another policy is related to the role of monopolies in the
economy: a pro-monopoly bias tends to close the economy and reduce
the role of competition. Many governments are ideologically inclined
toward keeping certain activities in the hands of monopolies, especially
in small economies, and attempt to reduce their negative effects through
regulation and special controls. A change in this bias would greatly
increase the competitive atmosphere in these countries.

Another related macro policy of the central government defines the
framework for the operation of public enterprises. Again the spectrum of

policies could go from a highly controlled, interventionist, monopoly-oriented approach to one in which public enterprises are allowed to operate with a maximum of freedom and a minimum of intervention from central government agencies. The former will certainly not be conducive to a competitive atmosphere; the latter will greatly help it. A fundamental element of the policy should be that public enterprises cease operation if market conditions require it. As indicated in the previous chapter, if the survival of an enterprise is not being threatened, the incentives derived from an increased competitive atmosphere will be lost or dysfunctional. In practice, if government policy assumes the continuous existence of the enterprises, it should not bother very much to improve their performance. Here the prediction is easy: not much will happen.

Another aspect that should be taken into account in considering competition as an incentive is the extent of market-like conditions in a country. Most discussions of the subject seem to assume implicitly that market-like conditions are pervasive. In fact, the true extent of these conditions varies considerably. Very simple estimates, such as the proportion of gross national product (GNP) attributed to subsistence agriculture, the size of the public sector, and the extent of monopoly in other activities, would quickly indicate that in many developing countries the scope of economic competition is quite limited. In these cases, a potentially useful complementary strategy is to identify the segments of the economy that operate in a truly competitive environment (which might be called the "centers of competitive excellence") and see whether they could help extend the positive influence of competition to other activities to which those segments are related.

Governments could also attempt to have general policies with regard to the external competition surrogates (competitive pressures within an organization cannot be the subject of global government policies). The objective is to help transform the whole network of relations of institutions, clients, suppliers, regulators, and so on into a form of pressure that will have a positive impact on institutional effectiveness. How much any policy can achieve will depend on the particular circumstances of each country. As examples of what might be done, a government could actively encourage the formation of groups of clients and beneficiaries of all or some of the public agencies; it could help agencies set up special units to get more feedback from clients and beneficiaries; it could give clients and suppliers extensive training to improve their capacity to deal with public agencies; or it could make extensive use of participant-observer methods to assess the potential role of clients and suppliers in this respect.[7]

How to change the role of regulatory agencies and the political establishment is a more difficult task and the outcome is more dependent on conditions in each country. Only an active policy on the part of the government could turn regulatory agencies from a role of authoritarian control to one of encouraging better performance. A similar turn is possible with respect to controller and auditing agencies.

At the macro level, some would consider the budgeting process in the public sector the ultimate potential competition surrogate. Whether the budget can be used as an effective instrument for achieving higher performance will depend on the objectives of the political establishment and the role and objectives of the technocracy that actually manages the budget. In theory, there is no reason why the budget should not play such a role, but most countries would have to make major modifications in their current practices if they were to put the budget to this use. However, the design of such a system is outside the scope of this work.

More generally, a government could attempt to define a "competition policy," which would specify the role of competition and competition surrogates in the public and private sectors. Such a policy has a good chance of enhancing the impact of these incentives on institutional performance by making use of the synergy implicit in these different forms of competitive pressure. Such a policy would also permit the identification of areas where the use of competition and competition surrogates would be most effective and areas where it might be damaging. The preparation of even partial competitive input-output matrices or the identification of the most competitive parts of the system would greatly help in the design of such a policy.

Wages and Salaries

The World Bank's experience suggests that distortions in wages and salaries are probably among the most costly obstacles to institutional performance. A strong argument can be made in many developing countries that high unemployment among unskilled workers is caused by keeping wages at inflated levels for political or social reasons. But with skilled workers and some professional and especially managerial workers the issue is exactly the opposite: political and other social factors have kept their salaries lower than their equilibrium price. This situation might be observed sometimes throughout an economic system, but is nowhere more pervasive than in the public sector, where attempts to reduce the difference between the highest and the lowest remunerations are more intense. Such wage distortions help explain one of the most intractable problems in developing countries, that of attracting and retaining high-quality staff in the low-specificity, noncompetitive activities. Many of these activities, such as the delivery of agricultural and social services, require a large number of staff, which few countries can afford to remunerate adequately. Any strategy to improve the performance of these activities will have to deal with the issue of how to remunerate their staff.

In the present world of instant communications and close contacts among all countries, certain skills, especially at professional levels, can be considered an internationally tradable commodity. The tradability of labor is far more complex than that of goods and services, most of which have a fairly high degree of homogeneity and are influenced by purely economic considerations. With labor, however, the degree of tradability will be determined by cultural factors: in some societies skilled workers, professionals, or managers are more willing to emigrate than in others. Cultural factors and language barriers may somewhat protect developing countries from the loss of skills, but by and large a proportion of skilled workers or managers will emigrate if their potential earnings outside the country are much larger than they can earn by staying. The depletion of all types of skills when workers and managers were attracted to OPEC countries may prove in the long run to have been more damaging for the development of some countries than the increase in oil prices, even when remittances are taken into account.

At first sight, it might appear that the most tradable skills are those related to high technology, because they are more universal (engineers, doctors, skilled workers), but this is not necessarily the case. In line with the arguments presented elsewhere in this book, it may be that in several countries the difference between internal and external remuneration is less for the high-technology or managerial expertise than for skills related to people-oriented activities. Thus the most significant effect of the brain drain might be its depletion of the small supply of skilled workers and managers trained for low-specificity occupations in the country. Unfortunately, there is no available analysis of brain drain along these lines to corroborate this hypothesis.

To achieve performance levels that are high by international standards it will be necessary for tradable skills to be remunerated at fairly close to international levels.[8] In practice, there is a spectrum of activities from the more tradable to the less tradable. If the equilibrium prices for different types of labor prevail in a developing society, there is a considerable difference between the remunerations for different skills. If this difference is reduced, the effect of remunerations as an incentive declines. In other words, there is a tradeoff between performance and equality. This hypothesis is reflected in figure 2.

If the degree of inequality (measured by a simple index such as the absolute difference between the highest and the lowest salary or wage) is zero, meaning that all remunerations are the same, a minimum level of performance will be achieved. As remuneration differs, performance levels will increase until a degree I_1 of inequality is reached, beyond

**Figure 2.   Institutional Performance at Different Degrees
of Inequality, with and without Political and Cultural Constraints**

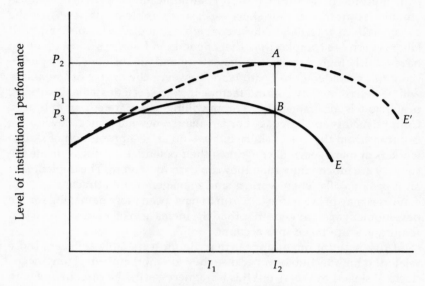

Degree of inequality in pecuniary and
nonpecuniary remuneration

which additional increases in inequality will not result in higher performance and might in fact begin to reduce it. The function might have a fairly wide area in which significant variations in inequality will induce no noticeable change in performance.

The level of I_1 and the corresponding level of performance P_1 will vary considerably for each society (and for groups within a society, a hypothesis that merits further exploration). The variations will depend on political and cultural factors, the internal level of wages for the tradable skills, the proportion of those tradable skills in the labor force, and whether there are important differences in wages, for example, between the public and private sectors. More important, variations will depend on the relative weight of pecuniary remuneration in the total incentive package. Other factors, such as status or the possibility of doing professional work in a pleasant environment, with freedom from political influences, might be significant. In fact, remuneration might be defined for this analysis as including all other factors.

Function E indicates how other factors, particularly the cultural and political constraints, define the relationship between degree of inequality in remunerations and the level of institutional performance. One can conceive of a "shadow" function E' drawn under the assumptions that many of those cultural and political constraints do not exist or have been lifted. Under these conditions, a higher level of performance P_2 is achieved with a level of inequality I_2. Given the actual constraints, however, such a level of inequality will push performance to P_3. Those constraints thus reduce institutional performance by AB.

This relationship also can be analyzed at different levels of GNP per capita (as a proxy for levels of development) to study the differences among countries that are closer to and farther away from the international levels of remuneration. The hypothesis here is that the higher the average income, the less inequality will be necessary to achieve the highest level of operational performance. The functions in figure 2 will move and change shape over time or in a cross-sectoral comparison of countries at different income levels. The hypothesis is that the maximum point for the higher functions will move to the left, from situation D_1 to D_4 (figure 3). These different points can be joined to form a function EE, which could be labeled "equality function" because it illustrates how the degree of equality increases without loss of operational performance as income levels rise. It is assumed that the performance level with zero in-

Figure 3.   Institutional Performance at Different Degrees of Inequality and Rising Income Levels

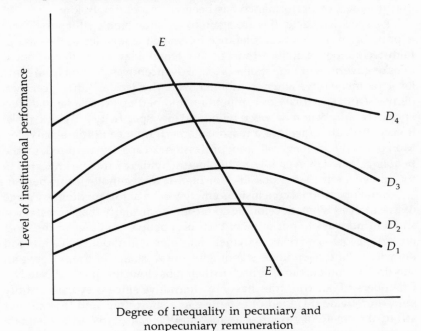

Degree of inequality in pecuniary and
nonpecuniary remuneration

D = GNP per capita as proxy for level of development

equality increases at higher income levels: only rich countries can afford socialism.

In some cultures, salary differences would cease to be a significant incentive to performance at a lower level of inequality than in others: at any given time some societies can accept more inequality than others before negative social consequences begin to appear. The acceptable amount of inequality will vary according to the political orientation of the group in power, but some societies are capable of accepting important differences while others have developed fairly egalitarian trends. Some traditional societies should take advantage of their cultural acceptance of income differences and offer international levels of remuneration for some activities.

Negative effects on performance could occur before or after reaching the maximum degree of inequality that is politically feasible. In some cases, the political environment will accept more inequality than is necessary for maximum performance; in others, the achievable performance will be constrained by the political environment. The lower the level of development of a country, the higher will be the level of inequality that is optimal as an incentive for performance, and the more important will be the political determinants of the amount of inequality that the society is willing to accept. In many cases, so little inequality has been acceptable that the level of performance has been correspondingly low.

Low-specificity activities are again in an unfavorable situation. There is probably more political tolerance for wage inequalities in the case of high-technology activities than in low-technology or people-oriented ones or government monopolies. Actual disincentives derived from a low level of inequality, when combined with the lack of any incentives derived from specificity or competition and perhaps with a large difference in remuneration between high- and low-specificity activities, make it very difficult to achieve a reasonable performance in these activities. Moreover, the managerial and professional capacity required in the people-oriented or even low-technology activities cannot be imported to the same extent that is possible for high-level technological expertise.

Several operational conclusions emerge, even at this preliminary stage of the analysis. First, developing countries, particularly the poorest ones, should find ways to put some of their best people in charge of the most important low-specificity activities. These people should have a broad knowledge and deep understanding of the workings of the society and should reformulate the approach to their jobs along the lines indicated by Chambers.[9] Poor countries have no alternative since they cannot fully import or create this kind of expertise in a short time, and they cannot afford the waste of resources that would be caused by an inadequate operation of these activities.

Second, policymakers should be aware of the tradeoff between institutional performance and equality and assess the significance of such a tradeoff in their country. A mainly qualitative assessment might determine the political resistance to inequality. Some information is generally available, such as actual differences between wages in the public and the private sector and between remunerations at the local and the international level. This information may give a reasonable estimate of the position of groups within the country with regard to this issue.

Third, if the degree of politically accepted inequality is much lower than is desirable for effective operations, ways should be found to reduce the gap. A more explicit discussion of this tradeoff, together with some notion of the magnitudes involved, may in itself be a help by increasing awareness of the problem. Studies could concentrate on the low-technology and people-oriented activities, where the wage differences should generally be much larger than they are now. Which solutions to adopt will depend on each case. A massive increase in remuneration to rural primary and secondary teachers might be impractical, for example, because of the large numbers involved and financial limitations. But less costly alternatives could be found to tackle at least part of the problem, such as skewing salary scales to remunerate managers, senior personnel, and high performers considerably above the average. One principle that could be explored is to set salaries for the top management, or elite, in all activities throughout the economy at approximately the same level and provide the same package of nonmonetary incentives.

Fourth, in most cases, pecuniary rewards will not be the solution to the problem of retaining staff in the country or of attracting and retaining staff in the low-specificity activities. Other types of incentives—status, perks, long-term security, improved work environment, promotions, and the like—will have to be explored. Governments may have specific policies in this respect for the public sector, but much more needs to be done. Countries in general and institutions in particular will have to develop alternative incentives. Here, Etzioni's distinction between utilitarian (pecuniary) and normative (nonpecuniary) types of incentives is relevant.[10] The issue is the extent to which a broad set of normative incentives can be developed, particularly at the lower levels in an institution. Professionalization—the development of values, standards, and institutions that are inherent in each profession or skilled work—is the classic example of this normative type of incentive. In line with the previous chapters, professionals try to control production when some of the attributes of specificity are missing in an organization's core technology or when the discipline of any form of competition is missing. In these cases, it is important to have the actors internalize their commitment to the organization. Professionalization does precisely this.[11]

Professionalization is discussed in the next chapter at the level of the individual institution. At the macro level, however, it is a potentially vital tool for achieving higher levels of institutional performance, particularly in countries with meager financial and human resources, which cannot afford to offer pecuniary incentives. Moreover, imaginative innovations are required to achieve some form of professionalization not only at the upper levels of the hierarchy but also at the bottom—especially for staff delivering services directly to clients and beneficiaries. These innovations will be culture and country specific but, again, governments could lead the way with policy efforts to promote professionalization and encourage private steps in this direction. They could, for example, encourage national associations at all professional levels, sponsor contests, or organize local groups similar to guilds. Such approaches could, of course, degenerate into a caste system, but if economic progress is fast and excesses and ossification are carefully avoided, they could serve a useful purpose during a long transition period. In any case, what are the alternatives?

Commitment

Perhaps the strongest conclusion derived in chapter 4 from the evaluation of World Bank experience is that the firm commitment of a country is an essential ingredient in the success of an institutional development program.[12] Conversely, lack of commitment is the main cause of failure. This conclusion applies not only to institutional development programs, but also to development programs in general. Commitment is usually discussed from the perspective of an international lending agency such as the World Bank, but it is of equal concern within a country, when programs initiated or promoted by central or sectoral agencies require the participation of other agencies and actors.

In the course of this analysis the issue of commitment was found to be closely related to the concept of specificity. Different degrees of agreement among members of an organization on objectives and methods define different degrees of specificity, and the potential for agreement declines at lower levels of specificity. In the evaluations of World Bank projects commitment was viewed mainly in the context of possible disagreements between country officials and the Bank, and occasionally of disagreements among country officials. But the nature of the problem is the same and can be analyzed in a way that is useful in all contexts.

It is seldom clear what is meant by adequate commitment or the lack of it or what can be done to increase and sustain commitment. This section reviews the concept and discusses ways of assessing and sustaining commitment in general—that is, not from the perspective of a development agency or of a central government agency. The question of commitment has previously been treated, directly or indirectly, by political economists and writers on development, perhaps most notably Albert Hirschman, and by economists and organization theorists, particularly Herbert Simon. In the following pages some of these earlier writings are pulled together and reviewed from an operational perspective. Thus, for example, the model of human behavior implicit in this discussion is that of interest groups—bargaining and conflict (political theory)—but in an environment of great uncertainty and bounded rationality, so that organizations maintain considerable slack (Leibenstein) and individuals satisfice rather than maximize (Simon). Similarly, the strategies for influencing commitment discussed here could be reinterpreted in Hirschman's terms as ways of increasing the voice of the interest groups, building loyalty, or threatening exit.[13]

Characteristics

Lack of commitment occurs when one or more of the main actors—whether an institution or individual—fails to support the agreed goals of a program, the agreed priority attached to meeting the various goals, or the agreed means of achieving them. Commitment may be formal or informal. Typically, the main agency responsible for a program formally declares its commitment, but significant individuals remain informally uncommitted.

When there is commitment to a program, there is agreement about the objectives and the methods for achieving them and the main actors will form a coalition to support those objectives. According to one view, organizational goals are set by a negotiation process that takes place among members of dominant coalitions. Each coalition attempts to impose its goals on the larger system, but typically no coalition completely determines what goals will be pursued. In certain cases, however, new interests or a new consensus might emerge—for example, through leadership.[14] Although in organization theory a "dominant coalition" is internal to an organization, the concept can be extended to encompass all those outside the organization who have a stake in an institutional development program.

VARIATION AMONG ACTORS.   Commitment is often discussed as if the country, the implementing agency, or even a development agency were monolithic. In practice, this is never the case. Individuals will have varying degrees of commitment to different program objectives according to whether the objectives support or conflict with their particular interests and priorities. It is necessary to distinguish between institutional, group, and individual commitment. There may be formal commitment from the executing agency of the program, but covert opposition or lack of interest on the part of individuals or groups within the agency. Frequently, there are differences in commitment between levels of the hierarchy, as when policymakers agree on a reform, but implementing staff are not committed to change; in the reverse situation, there is agreement on a course of action with officials at the technical level, but change is unacceptable at the political level.

The commitment of actors who are external to the program's implementing agency or agencies may differ from that of internal staff. External actors may include individuals (for example, politicians), groups (for example, landlord and tenant groups among beneficiaries; in people-oriented activities the commitment of beneficiaries is as important as that of program officials), or institutions (for example, central government agencies that contribute or deny resources to the program). Internal staff will by definition have a great deal of influence over the outcome of the project, just as a development agency will have considerable influence over internal staff because of its contribution of resources and imposition of conditions. Commitment to the program within an international development agency is also important and suffers from the same strengths and weaknesses as commitment within the country agencies.

VARIATION OVER TIME.   Commitment may increase or decrease during the preparation and implementation of the program as the situation evolves. The actors themselves may be replaced by changes of government, ministerial shuffles, creation or reorganization of agencies, political appointments of state-owned enterprise managers, or transfers of civil servants. Incentives and pressures affecting actors may also change; for example, there may be shifts in government policy or priorities, in the availability and cost of financial or other resources, or in personnel regulations affecting pay, promotions, or postings. Inasmuch as a typical institutional development program lasts several years, some change is inevitable. Some events—such as a change in government— may lead to a change in formal commitment and cancellation or renegotiation of the program. More likely, however, is the loss of informal rather than formal commitment, as evidenced by vacancies or inappropriate staffing of key posts, by failure to release funds for certain activities, or by a slowdown in program implementation. The variable nature of commitment over time means that the task of building up and then sustaining commitment is essential throughout the whole cycle of a program; it must be seen as a continuing process.

VARIATION ACCORDING TO PROGRAM ACTIVITY.   The degree of commitment varies according to the type of program or activity involved and is at least partially predictable. In general, there will be more commitment to high-specificity activities, especially those related to advanced technology, but there may be less to low-specificity activities, such as institutional development programs. This distinction is particularly important for technical assistance components: countries are more likely to accept technical assistance in high-technology activities than in institutional development.[15] Commitment is also likely to be low in programs or components to benefit the very poor; not only are technologies less specific, but the very powerlessness of the poor gives them little voice in the activities of the bureaucracies supposed to serve them.

Commitment may also vary with the activities undertaken at different stages of the program cycle. For example, program preparation activities often unite a variety of people with a common interest in securing external or internal resources, but they may or may not share an interest in the efficient use of resources once secured. This is particularly true of programs that use investment funds first and then launch activities that require the use of some recurrent funds. It is not that commitment is lost at a certain point in time, but that effective commitment to the secondary activities was never present and the divergence between formal and informal commitment manifests itself only at certain points of the program cycle.

Complex programs that are implemented by many agencies or financed by many institutions are likely to elicit weaker or less uniform commitment because of the large number of people involved. Integrated rural development projects that have complex institutional development objectives and multiple implementing agencies and beneficiaries are an example.

Thus, to be operationally relevant, commitment has to be defined and assessed by type of activity, by the actors and groups within the implementing agency or agencies, by the actors external to the implementing agency, and by the stages of the program cycle.

Assessing Commitment

A reasonably systematic approach to assessing commitment is possible, although it often requires specialized skills in political and institutional analysis. I focus first on assessing internal commitment, then on the external commitment of other government agencies, program beneficiaries, and interest groups in the society that will be affected by a program.

INFLUENTIAL ACTORS. Not everyone's commitment is equally intense or equally important to the success of an institutional development program. An assessment of commitment should therefore concentrate first on identifying the individuals and groups who share common interests and who have the power to influence program performance.[16] At the upper levels of implementing organizations, individual officials may be important; at lower levels, groups of people are likely to share influence and interests—for example, all the first-line supervisors in an extension service. Interest groups may be defined around levels in the hierarchy (managers and foremen), departmental loyalties (marketing and production), professional loyalties (irrigation engineers and rural development specialists), cultural loyalties (religious, ethnic, or tribal origin), or age (which may determine attitudes to or possibilities for career advancement). Intersecting with such interest groups within the implementing agency will be patron-client groups, which may or may not coincide with the formal departmental organization of the agency.

Most organizations will be made up of large numbers of intersecting and often shifting coalitions of interest. Once the coalitions are identified, a few key groups and individuals can be pinpointed whose strategic placing gives them significant influence. Given the hierarchical structure of bureaucracies and public enterprises, the interests of more senior individuals and groups tend to determine the incentives and actions of those below. An assessment of commitment can therefore start with influential figures at or near the head of the organization. If they effectively share the objectives of the program, attention can be turned to those one step down in the hierarchy to determine where conflicts in motivation occur; it will be at these points that the chain of common interest is broken and commitment is lost.

The process of identifying significant actors and groups should not be restricted to the formal hierarchy but should also include those whose influence may be more informal or indirect but nonetheless real. Among the individuals and interest groups that may wield enough power to merit attention are: (1) those who control, formally or informally, agendas of important meetings and committees; (2) those who control the budget process and hence the distribution of financial resources; (3) those who control the procurement of physical resources that may be directed to favored goals or activities; (4) those who control the quality of staff assigned to different activities and the informal application of formal personnel policies (both of which can affect performance); (5) those who get the most or best resources and may therefore hold informal power; (6) those who are irreplaceable and hence influential (possibly those with scarce technical expertise, knowledge of complex bureaucratic procedures, or special contacts); and (7) those who control information, another source of informal power. Contingency theory has generated a number of propositions regarding the development and distribution of power in organizations. The most accepted one is that units or groups that are able to cope more effectively with uncertainty inside and outside the organization acquire the most power, followed by those whose skills are difficult to replace, and those that are central to the objectives of the organization.[17]

THE OBJECTIVES.   Incentives and pressures, which together determine the objectives and hence the commitment of the participants, can be divided into three categories: official, informal, and personal. These categories may vary in strength and may complement or conflict with each other. The official goals and pressures influencing commitment are the government policies and procedures and the agreed goals and methods of the program. Although these may be clear to senior managers, they may not be communicated equally well to junior officials. Middle-level staff who are unclear about their role and goals cannot be committed in any real sense of the word to a program. Informal objectives and pressures on staff reflect the often unstated goals of those in authority who are not in agreement with official goals. If, for example, in a state-owned enterprise the manager's informal goal is personal profit, his subordinates are unlikely to be committed to maximizing corporate profit. In practice, informal goals will often be more important than formal ones. Commitment may also be influenced by the personal values of individuals and their ambitions for themselves, their families, or special groups to which they belong. Personal goals and allegiances will often determine attitudes toward work and career and hence influence the pattern of informal pressures affecting subordinates.

The strength of a person's commitment to a program will therefore be determined by the extent to which his personal and informal objectives conflict or agree with the formal objectives, or by the extent to which the program supports whichever objectives are dominant. It follows that a program should be designed so as to create a situation in which influential actors cannot ignore the formal objectives during implementation (that is, formal goals are made the dominant objectives) or in which there is a minimum of conflict between formal and other objectives.[18] Identifying important interest groups and individuals and assessing the incentives and pressure affecting them are the first steps in creating such a situation.

At a more general level, identifying the key actors in an institution and analyzing their motivations should permit an assessment of the commitment of the institution as a whole to the program. In some cases, there might be a consensus and the success of the program would appear to be assured. In others, internal divisions and the potential for conflict would suggest that a program should not be pursued or that it would run a very high risk of failure.

EXTERNAL INTEREST GROUPS.   The previous analysis has referred to the factors determining commitment within an implementing agency. A similar analysis can be made of the commitment of individuals and interest groups who are outside the implementing agency but who can influence the outcome of a program. The identity of relevant public agencies will often be obvious; for example, the ministry of finance, the planning office, or the parent ministry of an independent agency or public enterprise. But the pattern of influence will vary widely among countries; for instance, the planning office may or may not have much actual power, and the influence of the ministry of finance will depend on whether the implementing agency requires budgetary resources. The commitment of external agencies can often be more easily assessed if it is determined by the top management or a particular group within the other agency and does not require the full participation of actors at all levels. For example, the support of the planning agency for a sectoral institutional development program will be determined by the head of the agency and the person in charge of the particular sector. Since interagency power relationships work both ways, account should also be taken of the extent to which the implementing agency will be able to influence other relevant agencies and thus affect their commitment.

Commitment may be less easily assessed in operations in which external actors other than government agencies have an important role. In people-oriented programs, for example, it may be difficult to predict slum dwellers' willingness to pay for certain services or farmers' readiness to adopt a new technology. Finding out about commitment can be easier if the interested groups are organized, which is the case when corporations and trade unions are affected. In the absence of organized groups, as is the case in people-oriented programs whose beneficiaries are distant, scattered, and inarticulate, assessing commitment—that is, the likelihood of participation—may require a deeper analysis.

THE OPERATIONAL CONTEXT.   Whether a program is to be financed by a development agency or by the country itself, an early assessment of commitment is important because it should affect the basic design of the program—the choice of goals, methods, components, and implementing and coordinating agencies. During preparation and appraisal—or their equivalents—a more thorough assessment of commitment should be made by examining the network of activities involved in implementation, stopping at each critical activity or assumption (for example, about coordination), and determining whether the incentives exist for implementing officials and external actors to behave as planned. Given the volatile nature of commitment and the turbulent circumstances in which most organizations operate in developing countries, a continuing watch must be kept during implementation. This sequence might not be strictly applied everywhere, but the basic elements of the assessment should be followed as closely as feasible.

Assessing the commitment of implementing organizations is complicated when officials disguise their own personal and informal goals or are only partially conscious of the effects on their behavior of others' informal goals. One way to assess their motives, incentives, and pressures is through informal discussions, although this method raises the danger that the subjective judgment of the evaluator and his own beliefs and assumptions will be projected onto the conclusions. Nevertheless, such discussions, particularly with more junior staff, often reveal a view of organizational resources, goals, and priorities that is very different from that of senior managers, and it may offer a good clue to informal priorities. But sometimes, when it is necessary to assess the commitment of groups rather than individuals in an organization, a more structured approach is useful. Guided interviews of groups of peers in the absence of their supervisors can be particularly valuable, especially when presented in a nonthreatening way as a discussion of operational problems and solutions.

A second, more objective way to test the commitment of an implementing agency is to compare the performance of officials with their statements about priorities. If, for example, they have taken no action in certain areas that were declared to be a priority, and their inactivity cannot be explained by insurmountable gaps in resources or skills, then the amount of time spent on other activities will reflect their real priorities. The actions taken and the tasks performed provide objective evidence of whether there is genuine commitment to program activities and complement the findings of interviews. Assessing performance poses obvious problems at the stage of program identification, but it is often possible to find similar programs and to draw inferences from them about potential commitment to the proposed activities.

Assessing the commitment of people who do not belong to a government agency or an organized group presents great practical problems, especially in the case of people-oriented programs. The beneficiaries are not only physically and culturally distant but also often separated by a language barrier from the staff of development agencies and of the central government agencies. Greater use could be made of locally recruited sociologists and anthropologists to conduct structured interviews and participant observation of groups affected by the project.[19] These approaches may often be more productive than the commonly used questionnaire survey for discovering social relationships and attitudes.

Strategies for Influencing Commitment

When an assessment of commitment has been made, international development agencies and core government entities can respond to the situation in at least four ways. First, they may accept the pattern of commitment as it stands and advocate adopting the programs, components, or policy changes in areas where commitment is high and avoiding those where it is weak. Second, they may use their dialogue with the implementing agency or agencies to build commitment through education and persuasion. Third, they may attempt to influence commitment by negotiating changes in the structures and processes of implementing organizations so that officials who are committed have greater influence on those who are not. Fourth, they may make use of financial leverage. These approaches are on a continuum from least to most reactive. They can most profitably be used in combination, with the central government agencies and the development agencies both adapting to and attempting to change the political environment. In designing an institutional development program, for example, the development agency might first launch a major effort to improve financial management, for which there is full support, and postpone for a later stage the improvement of maintenance, which appears to be controversial. If the first phase succeeds, it will be easy to move to the second. Demonstrating the success of a program is probably the most effective way of strengthening commitment.

THE CHOICE OF PROGRAM ACTIVITIES.   Although certain components may be essential for a given program, there may be considerable discretion over the inclusion of others. In such circumstances, the program designers can avoid components to which the implementing agency is likely to be uncommitted, and thus they can sidestep the problems of poor performance or of conflict between the implementing and the financing agencies. This principle, although something of a truism, may be difficult to apply. Program components that are apparently technical and therefore uncontroversial in nature may have important bureaucratic and political consequences for influential actors and may thus raise issues of commitment; an example might be a technical assistance component for improving accounting and financial reporting.

The corollary of this principle is that, at least in the early stages, institutional development programs should focus on areas for which there is a consensus among the implementing and financing agencies. If an urban development authority's main problems are in resource mobilization and efficient resource allocation, for example, the thrust of an initial program might be in improving the efficiency of revenue collection, an activity which will often be of interest to implementing officials. A subsequent operation might then successfully tackle the more sensitive issue of investment programming.

In practice, there are difficult tradeoffs to be made. If commitment can decline over time, it can also be built up over time. The financing agencies must decide how far they are prepared to sacrifice immediate objectives which are developmentally desirable but politically sensitive, in the hope of building the commitment needed to tackle the sensitive issues over a longer term. At the same time, they must show flexibility during implementation to modify or sometimes even eliminate components if it becomes clear that commitment has disappeared.

DIALOGUE.   As a means of building understanding and commitment, there is no substitute for dialogue between financing and implementing agencies in the process of joint identification and preparation of programs, when this process is seen as an exercise in which both sides learn and modify their approaches. Given the existence of multiple interest groups, the dialogue cannot be confined to a small number of senior policymakers if it is to be effective. Examples of widespread consultation and education include the joint formulation of policy; structured workshops, at which officials with varying interests and from different levels and agencies can air their differences and develop consensus on programs; and "program launch" workshops to disseminate the concept and strategy of the program to all those involved in its implementation and to enlist their public commitment. These techniques can also be used during implementation to review progress and strategies and to help sustain commitment.[20]

The time spent in reaching a joint understanding with influential officials is warranted when commitment is expected to be weak or changes proposed under the program are likely to be particularly controversial. As noted above, weak commitment can be expected when achievement is hard to measure and hence poor performance is not easily detected and when achievements will not be apparent for a long time and hence offer little immediate political or bureaucratic gain. These conditions are precisely the ones found in low-specificity, noncompetitive activities, as previously discussed.

CHANGES IN ORGANIZATIONAL PROCESSES AND STRUCTURES.   Most institutional development programs include activities that can be designed so as to influence the implementing agency's commitment. By increasing or decreasing the motivation and power of the various participants, four complementary management development activities can powerfully affect commitment at the middle and lower levels of an implementing organization, given the commitment of top management. First, setting clear and attainable official goals increases control, and hence commitment, by reducing subordinates' scope for pursuing informal goals and giving superiors norms by which to judge their subordinates' performance. Second, developing monitoring systems increases accountability and hence also commitment.[21] Third, developing systems for the supervision of activities simultaneously increases both the managers' control over the operation and the accountability of the participants. Fourth, commitment can also be increased by rewarding staff for good performance—whether rewards are material, as when managers' bonuses are linked to public enterprise performance, or nonmaterial, as when badges of merit increase the prestige of successful field staff in some delivery programs. The training and visit system of agricultural extension, discussed in chapter 10, illustrates how all of the above approaches can increase commitment and effectiveness in an activity—increasing the responsiveness of a bureaucracy to small farmers—for which low commitment is the norm.

In projects where the commitment of external actors is important, at least three additional approaches can be used across organizational boundaries. First, influence over other organizations can be built by using a variety of coordinating mechanisms, from weak links such as ad hoc meetings, through regular planning meetings and the appointment of liaison officers, to strong links such as written working agreements, full-time committees, and participation in interdepartmental structures.[22] Second, budgeting systems can be developed so as to increase leverage over other organizations. In a Colombia rural development program, for example, the annual budget given to implementing agencies depends on their performance in the previous year.[23] Third, new organizations can be developed to influence existing institutions; for example, a state enterprise board can be established to set prices or a tariff reform department can be introduced into a prime minister's office to provide a focus for policy reform. Organizing local communities to have effective influence over service delivery agencies can also increase bureaucratic commitment in people-oriented programs.[24]

Each of these strategies is a means of increasing the influence of a committed individual or institution over others less committed. Obviously, the success of such approaches depends on the existence of a strategically placed, committed individual or core group. And there is no substitute for the process of education and persuasion that builds this initial commitment among senior managers of the implementing agency. The reform of organizational processes and structures, like the use of leverage and conditionality, must therefore complement the education process. When this process fails to win the commitment of the core group, new organizational systems and structures may be installed, but they are likely to be no more than symbolic responses to the influence of the financing agencies.

Notes

1. Robert E. Lucas, "On the Size Distribution of Business Firms," *Bell Journal of Economics*, vol. 9, no. 2 (Autumn 1978), pp. 508–23.

2. New York: Oxford University Press, 1983.

3. For example, David K. Leonard and Dale Rogers Marshall, eds., *Institutions of Rural Development for the Poor: Decentralization and Organizational Linkages*, Research Series 49 (Berkeley: Institute of International Studies, University of California, 1982); David C. Korten and Rudi Klauss, eds., *People Centered Development: Contributions Toward Theory and Planning Frameworks* (West Hartford, Conn.: Kumarian Press, 1984); David K. Leonard, *Reaching the Peasant Farmer: Organization Theory and Practice in Kenya* (Chicago, Ill.: University of Chicago Press, 1977); and Jon Moris, *Managing Induced Rural Development* (Bloomington, Ind.: International Development Institute, Indiana University, 1981).

4. This point is made much more forcefully by Robert Chambers in his paper, "Normal Professionalism, New Paradigms, and Development," Institute of Development Studies, University of Sussex, December 1985.

5. See Gustav Ranis, "Industrial Sector Labor Absorption," *Economic Development and Cultural Change* (April 1973), pp. 387–408.

6. Mary M. Shirley, *Managing State-Owned Enterprises*, World Bank Staff Working Paper 577 (Washington, D.C., July 1983).

7. See Lawrence F. Salmen, *Listen to the People: Participant-Observer Evaluation of Development Projects* (New York: Oxford University Press, 1987).

8. As in many other instances, India might be the exception that proves the rule. The country has such a large supply of highly skilled workers and professionals who meet world standards that it can afford to pay much lower remunerations without a major reduction in performance.

9. Chambers, "Normal Professionalism."

10. Amitai Etzioni, *A Comparative Analysis of Complex Organizations*, rev. ed. (New York: Free Press, Macmillan, 1975), chaps. 2 and 3.

11. Professionalization is a form of socialization, whereby the members of an organization acquire common beliefs, attitudes, and behavior in support of common goals.

12. This section is adapted from Richard Heaver and Arturo Israel, *Country Commitment to Development Projects*, World Bank Discussion Paper 4 (Washington, D.C., November 1986).

13. Albert O. Hirschman, *Exit, Voice, and Loyalty* (Cambridge, Mass.: Harvard University Press, 1970); Harvey Leibenstein, *Beyond Economic Man: A New Foundation for Micro-Economics* (Cambridge, Mass.: Harvard University Press, 1976); and Herbert A. Simon, *The New Science of Management Decision* (New York: Harper, 1960).

14. See Richard W. Cyert and James G. March, *A Behavioral Theory of the Firm* (Englewood Cliffs, N.J.: Prentice-Hall, 1963).

15. Francis Lethem and Lauren Cooper, *Managing Project-Related Technical Assistance: The Lessons of Success*, World Bank Staff Working Paper 586 (Washington, D.C., 1983).

16. This process is more formally known in organization theory as environmental scanning and stakeholder analysis. See, for example, William E. Smith, Francis J. Lethem, and Ben A. Thoolen, *The Design of Organizations for Rural Development Projects: A Progress Report*, World Bank Staff Working Paper 375 (Washington, D.C., 1980).

17. See David J. Hickson and others, "A Strategic Contingency Theory of Intraorganizational Power," *Administrative Science Quarterly,* vol. 16 (June 1971), pp. 216–19.

18. In organizational analysis, commitment is seen as occurring when individuals identify with and extend their efforts toward organizational goals and values. See Yoash Wiener, "Commitment in Organizations: A Normative View," *Academy of Management Review,* vol. 7, no. 3 (1982), pp. 418–28.

19. See Salmen, *Listen to the People.*

20. More details about these techniques are given in Heaver and Israel, *Country Commitment to Development Projects.*

21. The use of planning and feedback systems to influence motivation is discussed in greater detail in Richard Heaver, *Bureaucratic Politics and Incentives in the Management of Rural Development,* World Bank Staff Working Paper 537 (Washington, D.C., 1982), pp. 39–49.

22. These options are explored in greater detail in Smith, Lethem, and Thoolen, *The Design of Organizations for Rural Development Projects: A Progress Report.*

23. See the World Bank, *World Development Report 1983* (New York: Oxford University Press, 1983), box 9-9.

24. See Samuel Paul, *Community Participation in Development Projects: The World Bank Experience,* World Bank Discussion Paper 6 (Washington, D.C., 1987).

9 : *The Performance of*
Individual Institutions

This chapter deals with the determinants of performance of individual institutions or groups of them. Incentives continue to be the central focus. It has been postulated that specificity and competition provide two central sets of incentives determining institutional performance. In addition, there is a third set of incentives derived from "management"—a concept used as shorthand to embody the organizational structure and management of an institution, including personnel policy, management techniques and style, training, and so on. But depending on their activities, institutions differ in the extent to which they are exposed to each of these incentives. This issue is presented graphically in figure 4.

Figure 4. Incentives to Institutional Performance by Type of Activity

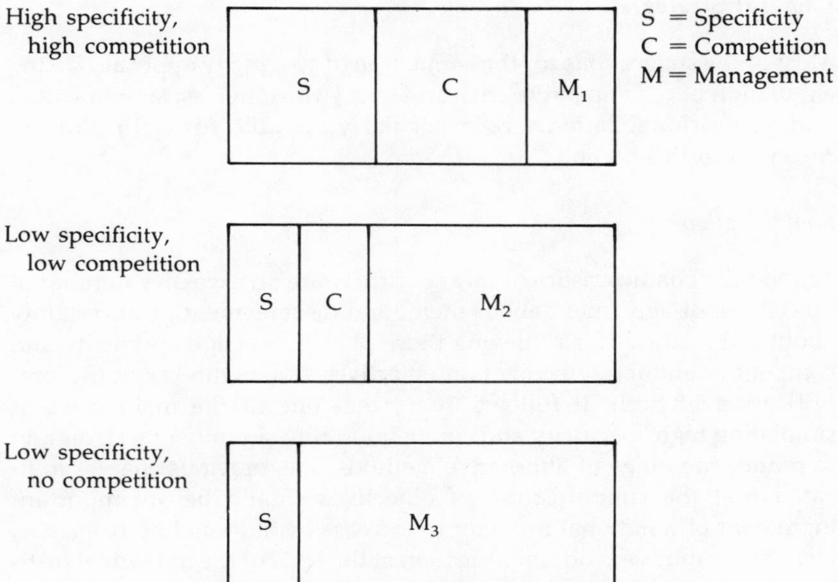

High specificity, high competition

| S | C | M_1 |

S = Specificity
C = Competition
M = Management

Low specificity, low competition

| S | C | M_2 |

Low specificity, no competition

| S | M_3 |

Each rectangle represents the total amount of incentives to performance that an institution is exposed to at any one time. The hypothesis is that for high-specificity and highly competitive activities a large portion of the rectangle will be filled by the incentives emanating from those characteristics, and those derived from management will be relatively minor. At the other extreme, the performance of a low-specificity, noncompetitive activity will be determined largely by the management incentives.

The question is, what is the difference in the characteristics of M_1, M_2, and M_3? The essence of the so-called contingency theory in organizational analysis is precisely that administrative and managerial solutions cannot be transposed from one situation to another.[1] The conceptual framework presented here provides a way of analyzing more systematically the concerns of contingency theory. The remainder of this chapter explores the possible differences between M_1, M_2, and M_3 and looks at organizational and managerial ways to simulate the incentives derived from specificity and competition when these factors are not present and to amplify those incentives when they are weak.

The tentative nature of the operational conclusions discussed in this book is nowhere more evident than in this chapter. Many require further elaboration and practical testing. The discussion does not pretend to be comprehensive but concentrates on solutions that depart somewhat from the conventional.

General Strategies

Most of the suggestions for the simulation of specificity apply also to the simulation of a competitive environment. Two strategies, simplification and professionalization, are particularly suitable for both and are reviewed in this section.

Simplification

Among the characteristics of low specificity are an excessive number of objectives, disagreement about them, and disagreement or uncertainty about the methods for achieving those objectives. High specificity and competition induce agreement on objectives and methods and the simplification of both. It follows, then, that one of the main ways of simulating high specificity and competition is to simplify objectives and to reduce the range of alternative methods. The previous chapter indicated that the simplification of objectives should be an important ingredient of a national program to increase institutional performance. Here the emphasis is on simplification at the level of the individual institution.

Perhaps one of the best ways of illustrating the overall difficulties of management and decisionmaking along the specificity-competition spectrum and the advantages of simplification is to refer to the Thompson-Tuden matrix, shown in figure 5. Typically, low-specificity, noncompetitive activities will belong in box 4, where there is virtually no systematic decisionmaking and maximum potential for disagreement. Thompson and Tuden cite the need for "inspiration." It is important, then, to get these activities out of that box and into box 2; that is, to achieve agreement at least about objectives, since in this type of activity it is very difficult to achieve agreement, or eliminate the uncertainty, about methods or technologies. In practice, the best and perhaps only way to agree on objectives is to simplify them drastically. The failure to do so has thwarted the success of such complex undertakings as integrated rural development programs and many other poverty-oriented programs, and it might still thwart many of the structural or sectoral adjustment programs now under way. As shown in chapter 10, the genius of the training and visit system was to have transformed the management of agricultural extension, which has always been seen and treated as a box 4 activity, into box 1 by drastically simplifying and streamlining objectives and methods. This might not always be possible, but some form of simplification is essential for that type of activity if it is to have a good chance of success. Indeed, the difference in management complexity between boxes 4 and 1 in this matrix is another indication that an arithmetic simplification of goals will bring a geometric increase in the chance of success and in the possibility of managing the program.

Although a lack of clear goals can sap an institution's vitality, there is a

Figure 5. Matrix of Decisionmaking

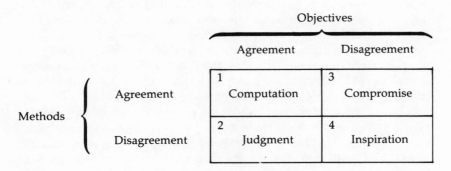

Source: Based on James D. Thompson and Arthur Tuden, "Strategies, Structures, and Processes in Organizational Decision," in *Comparative Studies in Administration,* James D. Thompson and others, eds. (Pittsburgh, Penn.: University of Pittsburgh Press, 1959), pp. 195–216. Used by permission of the publisher.

limit to how much a multiplicity of conflicting objectives and methods can be simplified. If charismatic leadership or astute political bargaining is able to produce a clear and viable set of objectives there is no doubt that the institution will benefit. But if clarity of objectives is achieved artificially, by simply driving underground real and serious differences, the problems will eventually come back to haunt the institution. In fact, one of the objectives of the so-called learning process is precisely to set in motion within an institution the process of clarifying its objectives and methods.[2] Artificial attempts to impose simplified objectives and methods by using a blueprint have been particularly unsuccessful in box 4 situations where that approach is not warranted. The advantage of the training and visit approach is that it contains a built-in learning process, which permits the redefinition and simplification of objectives and methods as the program progresses.

Crises have traditionally been an occasion for reassessment and the simplification of objectives. Again, high-specificity activities have an advantage. For them, institutional failure is clear and visible, becomes evident fairly quickly, and has serious consequences. Management and governmental attention quickly focuses on problems related to the core technology. And the crisis causes decisionmakers to narrow the institution's objectives, agree on them, and provide the necessary resources. With low-specificity activities, it takes longer for decisionmakers to focus on the crisis, and the inherent disagreements might induce political rather than professional decisions about simplification.

Professionalization and Socialization

The lack of specific incentives, combined with the lack of financial resources to remunerate staff adequately in highly labor-intensive, people-oriented activities, strongly suggests that nonpecuniary incentives should play a crucial role in those activities and that innovative solutions should be found to provide them. In figure 4, not only is M_3 larger than M_1, but also it should be composed of a much larger portion of nonpecuniary elements; the poorer the country the higher that portion should be. Professionalization and socialization are two solutions that can help compensate for the lack of monetary incentives.

Although professionalization is a term generally used only in regard to highly skilled professions, the concept can be extended to most skills, even at low levels. It has a technical and normative basis: a professional person has "systematic knowledge or doctrine acquired only through long prescribed training and . . . adheres to a set of norms relating to the service ideal and its supporting norms of professional conduct."[3] The challenge for a country, a region, or a group is how to inculcate such values in, for example, extension and health workers, primary teachers, and low-level functionaries in district offices. And, not the least important, how to inculcate them in actual professionals and middle- and higher-level managers.

The solutions will have to be tailor-made to the general and institutional culture of a country. Each country will have to find its own ways of developing strong, well-defined norms of conduct for various skills and of inculcating new sets of values and nonpecuniary incentives. Avenues such as the formation of local and national professional associations and guilds and the encouragement of informal groups within institutions will have to be explored. If the analysis presented here is correct, it suggests that progress in the less developed countries, for example, in Sub-Saharan Africa, will depend to a large extent on the success of such efforts. There is some risk that professionalization will excessively stratify the society, but many of the less developed countries have no alternative but to take this risk and to reduce the danger through careful planning. There is a surprising lack of research on how professionalization can be introduced and how it affects a society. With a stretch of the imagination, however, one can see a parallel between professionalization and the increased use of paraprofessionals and nongovernmental organizations to help strengthen the institutional structures of developing countries: they are extreme solutions to very extreme situations.

Scott has an additional argument in favor of professionalization. He says that using professionals "is particularly effective when the work is also uncertain, a condition which mitigates against pre-planning and subdivision: and . . . the work does not involve high levels of interdependence among workers . . . the work of professionals takes place within a structure of general rules and of hierarchical supervision, but individual performers are given considerable discretion over task decisions."[4]

Organizational socialization is defined as "the processes by which the beliefs, norms and perspectives of the participants are brought into line with those of the organization."[5] Socialization can be formal, as when it takes place in training programs, or informal, as when certain patterns of behavior evolve in an institution because some actions are accepted and rewarded while others are rejected. In low-specificity, noncompetitive activities, socialization could play a crucial role in getting staff to internalize the institutional values and to identify with the institution's objectives and ways of doing things.

The process of socialization is determined by the nature of the institution and the culture of the society, and the subject has hardly been explored in the context of promoting the effectiveness of institutions in poor countries. Training programs have been geared primarily to imparting technical and professional knowledge, and it requires a special effort to make them promote socialization. Each institution needs to design its own program internally to suit its own needs. In Sub-Saharan Africa, the

proliferation of training programs designed mainly by expatriate technical assistance, without much local participation, has probably prevented
these programs from becoming a vehicle for socialization.

Mechanisms to Compensate for Lack of Specificity

The lack of specificity is such a serious deterrent to institutional effectiveness that many of the commonly accepted management and organizational principles need to be modified, sometimes drastically, when
applied to low-specificity activities. This section explores managerial and
organizational solutions that could simulate a higher degree of specificity
in low-specificity activities. In other words, "specificity surrogates" are
discussed that could bring the level of performance of these activities
closer to that of the high-specificity activities. It will not ever be possible
to achieve the same level, but the gap could be narrowed through a judicious use of management and organization theory.

Paradoxically, the characteristics of low-specificity activities make it
extremely difficult to arrive at clear operational guidelines for them—
which is presumably why management science has neglected them. As
indicated, people-oriented activities need strong incentives, but their low
specificity makes the design and implementation of strong incentives
almost impossible. Similarly, low-specificity activities need flexibility to
operate effectively, which means that their objectives and incentives
should not be specified in too much detail.

In table 4 the techniques and approaches for simulating specificity
have been divided into several categories: general strategies, recruitment,
staff incentives, training, management, managerial techniques, and
organizational structures. Undoubtedly, other classifications are possible, but the main interest here is in the general thrust of the analysis.

Recruitment

One real dilemma is that many of the characteristics that make individuals especially effective in people-oriented activities are innate and cannot
be taught. To attract a capable staff it is therefore essential to have a
recruitment system that can identify and select people with these traits.
Stating this need is relatively easy; the difficulty comes in actually
attempting to hire hundreds or thousands of poorly educated individuals
to expand rural primary education or health services. Is it feasible to
worry about recruitment techniques under those circumstances?

The problem may be less severe than it first appears. There is evidence
that effectiveness in low-specificity activities is also heavily linked to
motivation, particularly at low levels. Harrison indicates that "there is no
evidence to suggest that unusual abilities deriving from intellectual
capacity are required for village level extension work; on the contrary, it

would seem that the abilities required are possessed by many people and are brought out by the greater professionalization and motivation which manifests itself in better work behaviour."[6] In addition, socialization through training could somewhat mitigate the problems of recruiting staff with the necessary qualifications. But there still remains a need to select personnel who are more likely to internalize the values and norms that the institution wishes to.

In view of these problems, special efforts should be made to improve the recruitment process. The main difficulty is that the state of the art is not sufficiently advanced. Recruitment methods are neither objective nor broadly applicable and do not ensure the hiring of staff with a comparative advantage for working in people-oriented activities. Recruiting is an art which only a few people have; they in turn have to be located. Still, a heavier emphasis on this function would surely yield positive benefits. Better recruitment officers and better training for them would be a good investment even in the context of political pressures in hiring. Similarly, more research on recruitment techniques to develop methods suitable for the conditions in developing countries may also yield important benefits.

The recruitment of managers is of central importance because of the role of outstanding individuals in explaining institutional performance and the "artistic" nature of management, particularly in people-oriented activities. Perhaps the biggest contribution to performance in this area would be made by a more careful recruitment system for managers. Their experience and proven success should be more valuable than the right educational background.

Unfortunately, focusing on the recruitment of managers with better potential for success in low-specificity activities goes against the norms of many civil service systems in developing countries. Many hire generalists across the board, on the assumption that each assignment will build on special strengths. The career path is often exactly the opposite from the one suggested here, because the newest and least qualified recruits are sent to the rural areas—to precisely the assignments this analysis has shown to be the most difficult—while assignments in the capital city are handed out as premiums. Also, high-specificity and low-specificity activities require such different management skills that transfers and rotations of managers should be handled with extreme care. A few selected transfers of the "best and the brightest" may, however, make managers more aware of the differences among activities and contribute to the testing of new approaches.

Staff Incentives

Personnel policies in the low-specificity activities have to contend with the handicap of weak incentives that cannot be made too precise. As already discussed, professionalization and socialization can help to com-

Table 4. Managerial and Administrative Approaches for Simulating Specificity

General strategies	Recruitment	Staff incentives	Training	Management	Managerial techniques	Organizational structures
Drastic simplification of objectives and methods, and the establishment of internal processes to do so	Identification of the innate characteristics needed by workers in low-specificity activities	General incentives that are stronger and more persistent (such as professionalization and socialization)	Much higher proportion of on-the-job training and of professional support from managers and staff	Greater involvement of upper and middle management in political and cultural issues in the institutional environment	Cautious and moderate use of quantitative techniques; avoidance of spurious quantification	Flexible for activities with a large proportion of higher-level staff
More intensive use of nonpecuniary incentives	Recruitment methods designed to attract staff with those innate characteristics	Greater differentiation in remuneration and nonpecuniary incentives (such as increased status) in favor of low-specificity activities	Training that continues for the duration of assignments	Stronger and more sustained incentives (pecuniary and nonpecuniary) for middle management	Minimal amount of written reporting and data processing	Fairly rigid (but with operational flexibility) for activities with large numbers of lower-level, geographically scattered staff
Emphasis on professionalization (professional values and doctrines) at all levels		As much specification of objectives as possible, but without spurious quantification	Training in human relations, pedagogy, and the development of flexible approaches	More central role of supervision combined with operational support; possible creation of parallel staff line	Special efforts to identify, measure, and judge effects of staff actions; cautious use of monitoring and evaluation	More complex; more supervisory levels
Emphasis on socialization (values, beliefs, and perspectives of each institution)					A strong set of internalized norms and values as a basis for socialization and professionalization	Stronger "staff" structure, parallel to the line structure
						Designed so higher-specificity activities exercise pressure on low-specificity ones

Research to develop
incentives, training
programs, manage-
ment approaches
and techniques,
and organizational
structures that will
have the effects of
specificity

Especially designed
evaluation systems
that trace effects of
staff actions and
magnify them
through internal
methods

Feedback from clients,
beneficiaries, and
suppliers

Work environment
especially attuned
to low specificity;
greater importance
of teams

More intensive use of
previous records of
performance as a
basis for providing
incentives

Middle management
more attuned to
pressures and sig-
nals from field-
workers, clients,
beneficiaries, etc.

Few precise rules com-
bined with a flex-
ible management
style

pensate for this deficiency. In addition, stronger incentives can be introduced by management (see figure 4). A worker in an industrial plant could have as part of his incentive system a production bonus. Managers can easily assess the quality and level of production, as well as the exogenous factors that affect the worker's productivity. The use of a production bonus is more problematic with a rural extension worker; although an increase in yields can be measured, it is impossible to isolate the role of the extensionist from the many factors that determine agricultural production. And what kind of production bonus could be invented for a personnel officer? Probably none, and if one were offered it would probably be spurious, input-oriented, and providing the wrong incentives. The effectiveness of personnel officers will have to be induced through other means.

Incentives in low-specificity activities can be made more specific, however. One way is to specify the objectives and methods for separate functions of the organization, but without determining them so rigidly and mechanically that they violate the nature of the activity. The other extreme would be to leave objectives and methods underspecified and hope that they would somehow be clarified during implementation, which is impractical. Not enough experience has been analyzed and not enough experiments have been undertaken to determine the optimal levels of specificity of objectives and methods for different types of low-specificity activities. The experience is indeed available, but it needs to be analyzed more carefully to enable the fine-tuning of such specification.

Another way to strengthen incentives is to identify and trace the effects of actions of individual agents or groups. Without progress in this area, low-specificity activities will remain condemned to the use of general incentives. The ability to measure effects is the basis for being able to magnify them through specific incentives. How can one improve the measurement of effects? Among several possibilities, the easiest in most cases is for the supervisors to focus on the results of their subordinates' work. After all, the ones best qualified to judge the effects of an extension worker or of a primary school teacher are their immediate supervisors. In principle, supervisors should be doing this assessment all the time, but in practice it is seldom done. Even if it is, few supervisors link their assessment to the reward system, and even fewer are trained to perform this task.

Often, however, it will be the client or beneficiary, not the supervisor, who will have a better notion of the effectiveness of a person's work. This will be the case with personnel officers, counselors, and many agents in social services. The feedback from clients and beneficiaries is potentially of great significance in achieving institutional performance. There is also evidence that peer rankings of the competence of agents correlate more closely with objective measures of performance than do the rankings of supervisors.

Of course, the whole thrust of this book underscores the risks of introducing incentives that are based on quantitative indicators of inputs or outputs—of measuring the performance of health workers, doctors, or counselors by the number of persons attended or seen. Such measures easily become dysfunctional since they lead to contacts that are more numerous but superficial. In fact, a system of incentives heavily dependent on output or input measures has been considered dysfunctional in almost all cases.[7] This applies in particular to low-specificity activities.

Other methods for tracing and measuring effects include better monitoring and evaluation of operations. Monitoring systems could be designed to keep track of a number of key effects and would be valuable even if they measure the effects of teams or large groups rather than of individuals. Special evaluation studies could be performed periodically to assess effects in greater depth. Again, there is a need to develop methodologies for making these monitoring and evaluation exercises possible in the context of developing countries, not only for ongoing programs but also for the assessment of completed ones so as to define standards for future activities.

Even if major advances are made, it will never be possible to trace and measure the effects of low-specificity activities as precisely as those of high-specificity activities. In practice, there will be few substitutes for better supervision and training and for less specific incentives, such as professionalization and socialization.

Postulating that incentives in the low-specificity activities should be stronger and more persistent has more profound operational implications than is at first apparent. First, ways should be found to increase the status of the low-technology and people-oriented activities so that they will attract the best minds and the relevant talents. A provincial head of education should have at least as much status and remuneration as the heads of the provincial power or telecommunications system or of a private industrial plant. Chapter 8 discussed the tradeoff between performance and equality and highlighted the need for greater differences among remunerations for different skills. This differentiation should be extended to the high- to low-specificity dichotomy. At present, many people-oriented activities have such low status and remuneration that they do not attract the necessary talent. Thus, even if all the necessary changes in incentives were to be made, real improvement would not materialize for a long time.

Second, many people-oriented activities occupy large numbers of agents and those in the public sector represent a large proportion of the national budget. The high-technology sector is relatively small and occupies fewer people who are paid higher salaries, whereas important programs in education, agriculture, and health employ vast numbers of teachers, extension workers, and health workers. According to the principles discussed here, these agents should receive remunerations at least similar to those in the high-technology sectors. But this is often financially impossible. The fact that the formal training of staff in low-specificity activities is of shorter duration also conspires to maintain the salary differentials. Some judicious differentiation in salary scales along the lines described in chapter 8, together with a package of nonfinancial incentives, is indispensable for improving performance.

Even within the same organization there is often a differentiation in monetary and nonmonetary incentives that tends to favor the higher-specificity activities. As discussed previously, the central technical group acquires considerable internal political power. These differences should be eliminated as much as possible and in some cases reversed. The impact of a first-class personnel officer may not be as obvious as that of a first-class engineer, but their real productivity would be apparent if it could be fully measured and compared.

Third, incentives in low-specificity activities should be not only stronger but also longer lasting because progress in these activities should be expected to take more time. This calls for persistence and steadiness to keep the incentive system in place for the many years required to achieve results.

Another issue is related to the kind of work environment that is best for people-oriented activities. Several studies claim to have defined the optimal working conditions, although they do not distinguish among different types of activities. The most favorable conditions are found when work is done in small groups, among friends, under general rather than close supervision, and with adequate information about the functioning of the entity and what is being done. Other studies stress the importance of informal groups.[8] In general, work conditions in people-oriented activities may be more favorable than in many of the technology-oriented ones. The dehumanizing aspects of the factory, about which so much has been written, do not apply here. Many people-oriented activities will be operated by small groups or lonely agents scattered over large areas.[9] Supervision will inevitably be general rather than specific, and the information about what is being done might be scarce. Not much seems to be known at this point about whether people-oriented activities are more likely to induce the formation of groups of friends or other types of informal groups.

Because of these characteristics, low-specificity activities will be subject to wider fluctuations in performance. First, small groups and individuals working on their own are likely to perform at a much higher or a much lower level than large groups. Second, broad incentives, as opposed to specific ones, also result in wide fluctuations in performance. A very specific set of incentives and of the corresponding control mechanisms ensures a minimum level of performance, but at the same time it acts as a disincentive to the achievement of higher levels.

Training

Since work in many low-specificity activities is more of an art than a science, innate talent and successful practical experience should be valued more than educational background. This applies to the highest levels of management as well as to agents dealing with farmers and villagers. Experience in building primary health care systems strongly confirms this point.[10] Moreover, in some cases education beyond the primary level was found to be detrimental to performance because staff with secondary education had expectations about compensation and advancement which the institution could not meet.[11] This anomaly has implications for training.

Training personnel for technical operations is a straightforward task, but what about the training of health workers? The standard approach is to give them a few weeks of essentially technical training in basic health care, and occasionally there may be brief sessions later to update information. But the training should also include some pedagogical or promotional techniques to enable workers to educate different groups of people and introduce better nutritional and hygienic practices. Training should also promote professionalization and socialization. Teaching such skills to low-level workers is difficult.[12] One crucial element that is absent from traditional approaches is training to make workers more flexible. The particular health care methods advocated will differ slightly among localities, and the techniques used to convince villagers to adopt them will also need to be modified. Even the technical solutions required might differ in each case, and workers will have to make minor adaptations to them. To be flexible, workers need a deeper knowledge than for the blind promotion of a particular solution. They also need the ability to elicit questions from their clients and to demonstrate empathy with their plight—difficult traits to acquire.

Two main differences in the training strategies for high- and low-specificity activities are a matter of degree, but so important that they might be differences in kind. The first is that training has to be much more continuous in low-specificity activities because it is a matter of repeated adaptation to new situations. How continuous depends on the circumstances. The knowledge imparted is only partially cumulative and, especially in the case of staff with relatively little education, it is not realistic to expect low-level personnel to adapt their skills and solutions to the changing realities. Second, training for low-specificity activities should concentrate less on teaching specific techniques and more on offering a mixture of traditional formal training in techniques, on-the-job training, and professional support to help the agents deal with operational problems. This structure of training is adapted to low-specificity activities and applies to all levels of staff. The principles can perhaps be more readily accepted for lower-level agents, but an in-depth analysis of the circumstances would indicate that they apply to higher levels as well, and perhaps especially to managers.

Management

This section addresses the special characteristics of the role of management in low-specificity activities and the management styles that are more appropriate in these activities.

Management of low-specificity and especially people-oriented activities is distinguished, first, by a relatively greater need to deal with the political, economic, and cultural environment because it can affect a people-oriented activity in many ways. High- and middle-level managers need constantly to assess which external pressures are under their control and which are not and adapt their operations to changes in the external environment. In some instances, these external influences are such that the chief executive should be someone particularly capable of managing the political dimension, which should be his main concern, and someone else should be delegated to be in charge of operations. This pattern is usually found in a line ministry, but it should be applicable to a wide range of entities, including autonomous or parastatal agencies and even provincial or regional ones, in this category of people-oriented activities. Whether a similar conclusion might apply to a high-specificity activity will depend on the type of environment it faces.

In the case of an autonomous agency in charge of rural development in a district, for example, it might appear that what is required is a professional manager who is an expert in rural development. However, the solution is not that obvious. The manager will have to deal with many units in the district, provincial, and central governments, since several components of the rural development effort may be undertaken by other agencies not under his direct control. He also will have to contend with political pressures at the three levels and is likely to spend a large portion of his time on them. He may thus neglect the actual operations of his own agency, or, in an attempt to be a good technician, he may concentrate on operations but lose political support and bring about the eventual demise of the program. A clearer separation between the political and technical leadership of the program is required.

The second characteristic of the management role in people-oriented activities is the more extreme need to adapt managerial techniques and approaches to the local culture. Many managers are not aware of these issues or do not concentrate on them, but this adaptation is essential for a successful program. It requires a thorough knowledge of the locality and a sensitivity to local needs, which means that in most cases the managers should be local people.

Third, middle management has a more important role in people-oriented activities than in high-specificity activities, particularly in the rural areas. Although higher-level managers will be primarily responsible for dealing with agencies and politics that are external to the organization, middle managers might also participate intensively in political negotiations in addition to supervising technical operations. In contrast, a middle-level manager in a high-specificity activity, such as the head of a provincial power plant, has largely technical responsibilities. Middle-level managers in people-oriented activities also spend a higher proportion of their time training, coaching, and providing operational support, and probably less time directly controlling operations, than do managers in technological activities.

For these reasons, middle management requires stronger and more sustained incentives than are generally provided. The set of incentives will depend on the characteristics of each society, but some possibilities are a special status, direct comparability in remuneration with similar work in high-specificity activities, and salaries that are closer to those of high-level managers and considerably above those at the nonmanagerial level. Again, professionalization and socialization have potential importance for middle managers.

Fourth, in low-specificity activities managers—especially at the middle level—need to cultivate a management style that is open to pressures, or "incentives," from lower-level staff and from clients and beneficiaries. This will require important changes in the way most people-oriented activities are now managed and changes in the managerial culture in many countries. Managers will need to improve communications with workers in the field and become much more oriented toward field operations: they will have to get used to leaving their offices in the capital or provincial city more often for direct contact with their subordinates in the small towns and villages.

In many people-oriented activities, particularly those delivering a service, agents work by themselves in the field. Although their task may appear to be simple—such as persuading villagers to adopt a particular program of preventive health—the issues they face are extremely complex. Managers may provide the necessary administrative supervision, but they are not always able to give the necessary professional support.

This point is at the heart of the differences between technology-oriented and people-oriented activities. Each decision made by an agent will have an element of uniqueness—whether advising a farmer on methods of production, persuading a villager to boil water, or solving a problem for a client of a ministry. The agent decides alone, on the spot. It is therefore essential that he get professional support, in addition to continuous training and opportunities to compare his experience with other agents. Most agents have little education or experience and should not be left to make difficult decisions in isolation. The issues they confront might seem minor in a global context, but could be matters of life and death for the people involved.

Managers in these cases should have as much feedback from their agents as possible, so as to monitor progress and change approaches; they should take part in a continuous dialogue with each agent. The question is, which managers? Often, and particularly at the lower level, the immediate supervisors or lower-level managers might be able to fill this role at least in part. In other cases, the supervisors would not be prepared to do so, or it would not be their "style." One suggestion is to establish a functional line parallel to line management to provide training and professional and operational support to the field agents and to focus on the dialogue between agents and the institution. Basically, this would extend the functional (staff) line that exists in most large organizations to make it more directly related to operations. In addition, the supervisory function should focus more on support than on control. The literature and, more important, experience point out the danger of having excessive managerial control over the judgments that are typically made in the field in low-specificity activities.[13]

Managers in low-specificity activities should also put special emphasis on tracing and measuring the effects of the actions performed by their staff, either individually or in groups. The difficulties of doing this and the lack of methodologies have prevented or discouraged managers from making use of this potentially important management tool.

The best management styles for high- and low-specificity activities might overlap a great deal, but the style for people-oriented activities might have to be somewhat looser or more democratic than is desirable for technology-oriented ones—that is, it should not rely excessively on quantitative objectives and specific controls. A loose style does not preclude great precision and tightness in certain aspects of the operation, however. In rural extension work, for example, management can ensure that visits to farmers are made on a strict schedule, but it cannot define too rigidly what the extensionist should do on each visit. It might be argued that a tight management style is as feasible in education as in industry. A closer look, however, suggests that in education management can be tighter with respect to the "inputs" (the number of classes, the teaching material distributed, and so on) than to the form in which education is imparted.

Creating a work environment that enables individuals to perform as well as possible is probably more important in the people-oriented activities than in the technology-oriented ones. Optimal conditions are provided by a minimum organizational skeleton that leaves sufficient flexibility to adapt behavior and decisions to the special characteristics of the activities. A closely related issue in low-specificity activities is the need for an internal learning process that will allow the institution, at all levels, to clarify and agree on its objectives and the methods to achieve those objectives. The impossibility of a blueprint approach in these cases has already been discussed.

Managerial Techniques

Managerial and administrative techniques can help a great deal to compensate for low specificity. As indicated in chapter 4, these techniques range from the highly mathematical to others based on the social sciences. In this respect, a word of caution is needed since the use of quantitative techniques in low-specificity activities is often unwarranted. Mathematical techniques, such as systems analysis, critical path methods, and financial analysis, have evolved very rapidly in recent years. Their traditional application in planning and financial analysis has been extended into new fields, many of them low-specificity activities. Often the result has been spurious quantification of operational aspects that cannot or should not be quantified. Management's attention has been diverted from a general overview of the activity and from qualitative considerations to operations and effects that can be quantified, with negative effects on institutional performance.

What is the most practical degree of precision that can be simulated in a low-specificity activity? In principle, even the most vaguely defined activities have some quantifiable aspects, but they are usually the inputs and not the outputs or effects. It is much easier to monitor the number of interviews made by a counselor, the length and content of those interviews, or the number of persons counseled than to evaluate the actual effects of the counseling. Witness the major methodological difficulties of tracer studies in education. In health care systems, there is a tendency to quantify visits, medicines distributed, or courses given rather than to monitor the actual impact on health conditions. And little effort has been made to improve the techniques and methodologies for identifying and measuring the impacts. If some quantification of impact is deemed to be useful, however, it should be tied to a system of rewards; otherwise it will not have a positive effect on performance. Similarly, if quantitative indicators are tied to rewards but the measures of performance are incomplete, the system will give distorted incentives.[14]

Many other examples of excessive emphasis on quantification can be given. Since the mid-1970s, the increased interest in monitoring and evaluation has pushed managers toward greater concentration on measurable aspects—but again they have focused on inputs rather than on effects. Perhaps the best illustration is the rather poor impact of the monitoring and evaluation systems that have been established in agriculture and rural development projects.[15] Their effects on management or on operations are unclear, as is the extent to which they have diverted management's attention to inputs, to the neglect of basic objectives. A detailed evaluation of monitoring and evaluation systems would probably find they have done little to improve the quality of decisionmaking by management. In fact, in recent years there has been a sort of "qualitative backlash"—attempts to go beyond the purely quantitative indicators to get a broader picture of program implementation and impact.[16]

Another example of excessive use of mathematical approaches is related to the use of computers. Although their potential benefits are well known, some applications greatly increase their potential negative effects. Consider, for example, the not uncommon situation in which managers do not know and are not interested in learning how to use their monitoring and evaluation system or any other management information system available. The systems, then, generate no benefit. The availability of computers, however, generates a demand for information. Scarce, skilled personnel devote their time to gathering data and writing reports instead of working directly in operations. Data gathering is a bottomless pit which, if unchecked, can absorb an inordinate amount of scarce resources for no useful purpose.

It is difficult to fight the overwhelming progress of the quantitative techniques which, in many of the low-specificity activities, may deliver more and more information about less and less. Some drastic steps will have to be taken to avoid waste and distortion. Particularly in countries with acute scarcities of skilled or literate staff, an all-out effort should be made to reduce to a minimum the requirements for data and written reports and to increase reliance on oral reporting, especially at the lower levels. With the exception of accounting and auditing, most activities, especially the low-specificity ones, could do with less data. This is a risky course of action, but even a cursory analysis of reality would suggest that the damage caused by fewer data and less reporting would be less than the waste and distortion caused by excessive reporting and partial information.

The dilemma is that quantitative techniques are the most direct and obvious method of simulating, at least partially, the discipline of specificity, but they are not automatically useful, and there is a good chance that they might have a negative effect. The introduction of these techniques should proceed with extreme caution. The actual demand from management is essential in determining their application; there is no point in introducing techniques that are not going to be used. Managers should be encouraged to define as early as possible the information that they are most likely to use, and the institution should adapt the choice of techniques to those requirements. Managers or professional staff should periodically review the use being made of the techniques and assess whether their continuing application is beneficial to the organization. A reorientation in their application may well be needed so that the techniques are used to measure effects instead of inputs.

Beyond this initial point, the analysis becomes increasingly complex because a judgment about which techniques to use is contingent on many variables. One is the distinction between programmed and unprogrammed decisions. Programmed decisions typically rely on quantitative techniques, but unprogrammed decisionmaking requires judgments for which only a limited amount of quantitative data is actually useful. How does one give this quantitative input only the proper weight and not more? To go back to an old example, many aspects of educational counseling could be subject to standard quantitative techniques. An agency specializing in this activity could introduce normal accounting and financial procedures, organize the procurement of supplies, and establish some sort of planning. But the proportion of unprogrammed decisions in educational counseling is very high at the lower levels of the hierarchy and the use of quantitative techniques very limited. One reasonable hypothesis is that in high-specificity activities the relationship between programmed and unprogrammed decisions is like an inverse pyramid, in which the highest proportion of unprogrammed decisions is at the top and the lowest at the bottom. In people-oriented activities, the shape changes into a rectangle, because the proportion of unprogrammed decisions *should* increase at the lower levels.

In low-specificity activities that provide services, are very decentralized, and have low-level staff scattered over wide geographical areas, it is necessary for the management system to include a strong set of internalized norms because of the latitude that field staff have in making day-to-day decisions. Every day, field-workers face complex situations with little managerial supervision or control and few mechanisms for communication. The quality of their performance will depend on their having internalized the "right" values and learned how their discretionary powers should be applied. In this respect, internalized norms are a surrogate for specificity and can ensure an adequate institutional performance.[17] In order for staff to internalize the institutional norms, there need to be standardized rules that have been tailor-made for the activity, good oral or written communication, and an effective system of social-ization and, if applicable, professionalization.

Organizational Structures

Organizational structures and processes can help simulate the character-istics of high specificity, but the dilemma is similar to that described for management techniques. In principle, the organizational structures that fit well with people-oriented activities are closer to the "community" model. Weber's rational-legal structure is perhaps the least useful if mechanically applied.[18] But the need for a solid organizational structure and process to improve decisionmaking is especially acute in people-oriented activities. A mechanic can operate a piece of equipment by himself, for example, because the task is well defined and routine; the organization is needed only for supervision and emergencies. In contrast, a personnel officer makes decisions every day that are not routine, and institutional support in reviewing and discussing those decisions could improve their quality.

Does it really follow from the characteristics of the people-oriented sectors that their organizational structure should be flexible? It is true that more flexibility is required, but mainly with regard to the decisions being made and their supervision. For a number of people-oriented activities it is possible to conceive of fairly rigid organizational structures as instruments for simulating the discipline of specificity. In large, widely scattered activities involving numerous agents, some basic structure is indispensable; it would act as a skeleton or framework to support the institution and provide a minimum of coherence. In a way, this is the purely organizational counterpart to strong, internalized norms. In a small personnel department or in a small school, more flexible structures might be more effective.

Paradoxically, many people-oriented activities require both a rigid structure and considerable operational flexibility. This becomes clearer with regard to supervisory levels. Research has found that the greater the complexity of the work performed, the fewer the number of workers a supervisor is able to manage.[19] The complexity of nonprogrammed deci-sions thus requires a great deal of supervision and, consequently, more hierarchical levels. The organizational structures of low-specificity activ-ities are therefore bound to be more complex. If the tasks are difficult to define, the agents have more freedom to determine them, and the careful supervision of lower-level staff—those close to the clients—will pay off in improved performance.

The uncertainty and complexity of low-specificity activities also mean that staff need to process a larger than average amount of information in the performance of their tasks. Given the constraints already mentioned, the result will be considerable pressure either to reduce performance standards, or to reduce the need to process information, or to increase the agency's capacity to process it.[20] The evidence from developing countries indicates that a lower standard of performance is too often the solution to the dilemma. A better one would be to increase the effectiveness of oral communication, since this is the most affordable way to process information in poor countries. This point reinforces what has been said earlier about the need for better communication between middle-level managers and their subordinates and for closer supervision of field-workers.

The paradoxical need for both rigidity and flexibility in organizational structures gives rise to yet another issue. Institutions that plan significant changes or face a changing environment require flexible structures to adapt to the new circumstances. But flexible structures are more difficult to manage. This fact suggests that change is likely to be slower in people-oriented activities, where the need for change is greatest.

A final approach is to promote an organizational structure in which the high-specificity activities put pressure on other parts of the organization that have a lower degree of specificity to induce them to perform better. The technical core could pressure personnel and administrative departments, or one section of the technical activities could exert pressure on another. In practice, the main issue is how to organize this kind of pressure without turning it into a negative force, and managers will have to find the balance that is right for their own organization. This approach is discussed in more detail in the next section.

Mechanisms to Compensate for Lack of Competition

Since competition is an important factor in determining institutional performance, a logical operational implication is to increase the competitive atmosphere faced by an institution or to design managerial or organizational solutions that will simulate competition for entities which are not exposed to it. The challenge is to create competitive, market-like conditions that will increase the output and improve the performance of an institution.[21] In chapter 7 the concept of competition was expanded to include not only external economic competition but also three surrogates: external pressures derived from clients, beneficiaries, or suppliers; external pressures derived from the political establishment and controlling or regulatory agencies; and internal pressures derived from managerial or administrative measures. Mechanisms can be found in all four categories for introducing or simulating competitive conditions. Several are discussed below. As elsewhere in this book, the treatment of the operational implications is not meant to be exhaustive, but merely indicative.

External Economic Competition

A powerful stimulus to institutional performance comes from external economic competition. Exposing public agencies to this stimulus is always difficult, and the solution falls in the realm not of management or administration, but of politics. It has two main components. One is to change the operating rules of public entities so that they are able to compete with similar activities in the private sector; this is feasible for many state-owned enterprises. The other is to encourage private entrepreneurs and community-based organizations to compete with public institutions in the provision of goods and services.

A public monopoly could be eliminated, for example, and private companies allowed to take over the services. The form of direct competition will depend on the type of service; often competition may be effective for only part of an institution's functions and will thus help to define the public sector's comparative advantage. For many mass delivery services, the overhead costs may be much higher and effective access much lower when public institutions try to provide the complete service, and it would be advantageous to turn over much of the high-cost retail distribution to private operators or community groups. Competition in even part of the operation may well have an impact on the behavior of the institution as a whole. This approach, however, involves detailed attention to the procedural apparatus of licenses, permits, regulations, and standards by which bureaucratic monopolies are maintained.

An alternative is to keep public ownership, but to modify its operational rules so that it is exposed to the type of market discipline that private monopolies face. Despite the risks (analyzed in chapter 7), this measure could be acceptable to governments, because it permits the continuation of most forms of political control and at the same time ensures a higher level of performance. Freedom to set prices and production levels is an essential element. Recent attempts at public enterprise reform in Africa and Latin America are based on this approach. The framework under which the enterprises operate is defined as clearly as possible, including the obligations of the enterprises and of the central government agencies that regulate and control them. Performance contracts between the central regulatory agencies and the enterprises could be a significant tool for implementing such reforms, but their use has been limited.[22]

Several countries have already introduced the public sector to private competition. In Argentina allowing the private sector to maintain roads has improved standards and generated entrepreneurial activity; in addition, it has prompted the public agency to conduct its own maintenance operations more like a competitive contractor, although it operates parallel to the private sector. The Bangladesh Agricultural Development Corporation has liberalized domestic marketing arrangements for fertilizer supply so as to increase competition among private dealers and to retrench its own costly and ineffective structure at the local level. In Indonesia a family planning program has used traditional itinerant herb vendors, alongside the public agency, to take contraceptives to remote rural areas. Other examples include the contracting out of railway line maintenance and repair shop work in Yugoslavia and the purchase by state industry of repairs, parts, and other services from worker cooperatives that use the factory plants after hours in Hungary.

The total or partial privatization of public enterprises and services has recently become a hot issue. It is only indirectly related to the question here of improving the performance of activities in the public sector. The privatization of parts of public agencies, leasing contracts, and similar measures are, however, alternative ways to increase competitive pressure on agencies that remain in the public sector and performing functions similar to those of private organizations.[23]

Clients, Beneficiaries, and Suppliers

One competition surrogate that might be harnessed to improve institutional performance is the pressure from clients, beneficiaries, and suppliers. Although the pressure from clients and beneficiaries has been the subject of considerable action and study, the pressure from suppliers has been much less explored. In a way, all are different forms of Hirschman's concept of "voice." Any attempt to increase and channel these pressures needs two starting points: organizing the clients, beneficiaries, and suppliers to exercise pressure on the institution and preparing the institution itself to detect and usefully absorb those pressures.

The mechanisms used to channel the clients' and suppliers' views to the institution are largely determined by the culture. They are similar to the mechanisms of local participation, which need to be introduced with sensitivity to local values and patterns of behavior. This kind of pressure has to be seen as bringing knowledge and information to the institution that will help improve its performance and, more broadly, as giving clients and suppliers a certain degree of power in running the institution.

It is important to distinguish between pressure from individuals and pressure from groups. Effective individual pressure requires a degree of sophistication and a particular cultural environment that can be found in only a few cases. Small farmers and urban slum dwellers need some form of organization to channel their pressure. Local participation does, in fact, assume the existence of such groups.[24] Anyone who has had any field experience can easily visualize the impossibility of a small farmer seriously influencing the performance of a credit agency that is his only source of funds or pressuring an agency that sells him fertilizer. Individuals are usually intimidated by bureaucracies and are barely able to sustain their rights as buyers or sellers.[25]

Clients, beneficiaries, and suppliers should be able to see clearly the potential benefits to them of exerting pressure and experience some tangible improvement in their position as quickly as possible after actions are taken; small farmers should not have to wait a long time for solutions to their problems. The form in which clients or suppliers are organized depends on the type of institution they are attempting to influence. Sometimes clients could actually participate in running the institution or at least in defining its policies. An example is the participation of farmers' organizations in defining the programs of research centers to ensure that their needs are taken into account or in running an irrigation system. This approach can be made much more effective by training clients, beneficiaries, and suppliers in how to deal with public institutions and how to organize themselves so as to maximize their influence. This training should be a central function of local and provincial governments.

Many activities and programs in the developing world fall in this category of competition surrogates. Perhaps the most successful to date is that of the water users' associations in the Philippines that were set up in the 1970s to repay construction costs of the irrigation network. These associations have become closely involved in decisions on design and other issues related to construction and have markedly changed the role and improved the performance of the National Irrigation Administration, the public agency in charge of irrigation development. The NIA experience also illustrates the importance of training users in organizational skills—including how to deal with public institutions.[26] Although these user organizations cooperate with public agencies, many community-based organizations stand somewhat apart—either because the public sector is seen as failing to meet important needs or because bureaucratic agencies are hostile to autonomous groups. The most successful groups have learned what matters to their constituents, a process that enables them to put increased political pressure on the bureaucracy or to bring about some accommodation between the interests of their members and those of the public agency.

The debureaucratization campaign in Brazil (mentioned in chapter 7) focused primarily on the points of contact between the bureaucracy and the public in the provision of services, the issuance of licenses, permits, and documents, and so on. Instead of attempting a comprehensive reform of the system, the campaign attempted to simplify those interactions and make them more expeditious. In this way the reformers gained entry to public services for further attempts to improve their performance. The practical consequence is that this approach created a demand for debureaucratization from the public and encouraged individuals and groups to press for further specific improvements. The idea was also adopted by several large companies in the private sector.[27]

Pressure from suppliers is much less common, and little use has been made of it. The nature of the institutions and of the suppliers determines the form in which this pressure could be exercised. If suppliers are few and large, as in many industrial or transport activities (supplying coal to a steel mill and gasoline or electricity to a railway), individual suppliers can exercise pressure on the enterprise—and the enterprise can influence the supplier. How to make positive use of these interactions depends, among other things, on the monopolistic power of each of the actors. If a public agency has a large number of suppliers of different sizes and importance, there is little chance of organizing them to make use of their potential pressure. Still, in the few cases where it might be practical to organize suppliers, the opportunity should not be lost.

The task becomes relatively easier if the suppliers are small and homogeneous, in which case they can be organized much the same as clients or beneficiaries. The Kenya Tea Development Authority (KTDA) is to a significant degree answerable to its suppliers—the growers. One reason is that individual growers may decide not to pluck tea if KTDA's prices are unsatisfactory (although they cannot sell it elsewhere: KTDA is a monopsonist for peasant growers). In addition, the interests of growers are vocally and effectively represented by District Tea Committees, which have powerful political connections, shareholdings and board representation in individual KTDA tea factories, and representation on the KTDA's board itself. There are also informal group pressures on KTDA local staff—for example, when growers feel that leaf grading or transportation is inefficient. Similar approaches can be developed for farmers and small truck operators in relation to agricultural marketing boards; for suppliers in relation to sugar, oil, or rubber factories; for artisans in relation to government or private distributors; for milk producers in relation to processing plants; and so on.

The other side of the problem is that the institution needs to be able to detect and absorb these external pressures. Since, by definition, the institution is not exposed to a competitive environment, it would have little incentive to seek information, or pressure, that would enable it to improve its performance. The institution therefore needs to change its whole orientation from an inward-looking to an outward-looking stance. This can be done by introducing incentives and changing management style. For example, a special unit could be devoted to collecting the views of clients or suppliers; personnel in contact with clients or suppliers could undertake special activities; the organization could be decentralized with more local branches; special committees could be formed to include the agency staff as well as clients or suppliers; suppliers or clients could be given representation on advisory or executive committees; and special training programs for staff could focus on this issue. This outward-looking posture or greater receptivity will take different forms depending on the specific circumstances. The point is that, if an institution is really interested in having feedback, it has to prepare itself to reach out for comments and to respond to them.

Another innovative approach is co-location and retailing.[28] Services and goods are provided by several agencies at a single location—perhaps even offered through a single official—in a sort of "public supermarket" that simulates as much as possible a retail market operation. Co-location could begin by providing goods or services that are linked to a project—for example, agricultural inputs and marketing—and eventually include other, unrelated services, such as the provision of land titles and pensions by central ministries. Where the scale of operation is small, as in remote areas, this method could be extremely useful. It has already been successful in Australia, Bangladesh, and Papua New Guinea. This approach is particularly appropriate when there is no integrated project to induce interagency coordination at the local level.

The idea is promising, but needs further study. It would require careful planning and negotiation with the relevant agencies and sensitivity to local conditions. Arranging for several institutions to use the same local office or location is merely the beginning. In addition, procedures need to be simplified—for example, the multiple role of mobile agents (who serve as intermediaries, disseminate information, and collect data) should be more narrowly defined—and changes will be necessary in the incentives to staff performance.

Co-location also provides good opportunities for inducing clients to participate directly and perhaps provide a few services themselves. Some of the "supermarkets" could be community initiatives or mixed markets in which both public and private goods and services are provided. Local private markets have always been the center of life in rural communities; why not local mixed markets?

At another level, standardized mass tests of educational achievement are a competition surrogate that has been widely applied and has had significant positive effects on education. The tests have profoundly influenced curriculum content and teaching methods and have motivated teachers and parents to higher productivity in educating their children. It is possible to have standardized assessments of student achievement without in any way inhibiting a custom-made education. In fact, a national exam probably produces more individualized instruction than do some of the old mass education systems with standardized content and methods. Sometimes the effects of national standardized exams are unintended and dysfunctional, but these unwanted results are probably outweighed by the positive effects on low-productivity educational systems.

In this case the exam acts as an external pressure that imposes discipline on the system. The pressure is based on results, and the results can be easily measured. Perhaps other activities could be identified (some types of health services or accounting?) for which a similar competition surrogate could be devised.

Politicians and Regulators

Probably the most complex of the competition surrogates, and the least developed in practice, is the pressure from politicians and regulators. The basic idea is to use in a positive way the pressure exercised by the political establishment and by the regulatory and controlling agencies to ensure that a particular agency achieves its objectives. In other words, politicians and regulators need to be persuaded to act, even if partially, as clients or shareholders rather than as controllers or inspectors. They should be taught to focus more and more consciously on the institution's performance in addition to pursuing their political and regulatory objectives.

This surrogate is not a far-fetched or utopian approach, although it is seldom used. In the case of a national railway enterprise, for example, the central government agencies and the political establishment should define a number of objectives to be achieved by the railway and impose a number of restrictions on its operation. Similarly, objectives and restrictions could in theory be defined for a government agency such as the ministry of agriculture. Aside from purely illegitimate interventions, politicians and regulators can put pressure on the entities to ensure that the original objectives are being achieved. A regulator in a central agency would be able to do so in a general way; a politician might have a more detailed focus, especially if he has regional interests. In a broad sense, both the regulator and the politician are "clients" of public entities.

Use of this surrogate entails, first, a change in the attitudes and in the terms of reference of regulators and politicians so that they act less as controllers and more as clients who focus on performance. Second, the process for changing these attitudes and focus needs to be strengthened. Again, the public enterprise reform programs mentioned earlier, in which the rules of the game and the specific objectives for the enterprises are defined, are one way of moving toward these changes. In this sense, performance contracts are a form of competition surrogate. Other approaches require changes in the organization, management, and staffing of the regulating or central agencies; in a number of countries this will need legislative changes. Similar changes could be made in the entities themselves, much along the lines indicated earlier to prepare institutions to seek and absorb pressure from clients and suppliers. A valuable tool for inducing or forcing politicians to focus more on performance is an effective system of monitoring the performance of government entities, focused as much as possible on results and less on intermediate inputs. Again, low-specificity activities will be at a disadvantage, but considerable progress can be made, as demonstrated by the monitoring system for public enterprises designed by Leroy Jones and applied in Pakistan and Korea.[29]

The Brazilian experiment in debureaucratization suggests another way of changing the attitudes and functions of politicians and regulators. The points of contact between a particular entity and the political and regulatory establishments would provide a focus for an analysis of their roles and allow a better dialogue among these groups.

All of these measures are becoming more possible as attitudes in most countries shift from a purely political interest in public institutions toward a greater concern with their performance and resource allocation. More important, there is a broader understanding that better performance helps rather than hinders the political agenda. Aside from its ideological elements, the trend toward privatization is driven by the need to use existing resources more effectively. Adding explicit criteria for performance now appears to be feasible as politicians are becoming more responsive to this issue.

The ultimate competition surrogate in this respect is, of course, the budget process in the government. A more open and visible method of determining the budget priorities and greater emphasis on performance as a criterion for receiving funds, in addition to the purely political considerations, could make the budget an important instrument for putting pressure on and inducing discipline in the public sector. To incorporate in the budget process a larger commitment to performance by the political establishment, several mechanisms could be explored: for example, performance monitoring systems for individual agencies could be combined into a standardized central system, and monitoring could focus more on performance. But this is a big subject in itself, outside the scope of this book.

Internal Competitive Pressures

External pressures such as those discussed above will be effective only if organizations change internally in response. This is difficult to do: personnel in large organizations (in the private as well as the public sectors) are usually adept at sheltering themselves from the cold winds of any form of competition and external pressure. Large private firms, however, have been forced to adopt competitive styles of management to maintain their efficiency, and it is worth considering how these techniques can be applied to the public sector (without resorting to unrealistic "corporate-style" solutions).

Even if the external pressures are low, several internal competition surrogates could be pursued. The pressures can come from management style, organizational measures, and evaluation.

It is possible to conceive of a management style that would induce better performance by enhancing the internal competitive atmosphere. What constitutes a competitive management style? It uses organizational measures, described below, to induce a competitive atmosphere. It also uses an incentive system that overtly puts some individuals or groups in competition with others for promotion or for the most desirable positions or assignments. It might give similar assignments to different groups within the organization to create internal competition. A flexible organizational structure—for example, one based on task forces rather than on strict functional divisions—will provide a manager with more flexibility for creating a competitive atmosphere. However, flexible task-oriented organizations will usually be more appropriate for high-technology or knowledge-oriented activities. It is much more difficult to implement such an approach in a national entity providing a service with mainly semi-skilled personnel. Task forces have been effective only in exceptional situations, such as those requiring rapid responses. To function, task forces require great latitude—hardly a practical or permanent solution for a large organization.

Another, more subtle way of having a competitive management style is to emphasize results, output, or fieldwork rather than reporting, paper work, or a complex hierarchy. Paper work and hierarchies provide all manner of covert mechanisms for avoiding competition and diluting responsibilities. A prerequisite for generating a competitive atmosphere is the possibility of identifying the effects of actions by individuals or by groups within an organization. If that is very difficult, the outcome of the competitive play and the relative position of the workers will depend essentially on managers' judgments of their capacities. Again, low-specificity activities are at a disadvantage.

Organizational measures to increase the competitive atmosphere in an institution include such classic examples as (until recently) the separate divisions of General Motors and the independent operation of companies that have been bought by a conglomerate. The possibilities are harder to come by in the public sector. In a few instances public entities produce goods or services that are similar but differentiated by price or quality. More common is the conglomerate phenomenon: mail and telecommunications, marketing and credit, transport and distribution. In these cases, creating divisions that operate as independently as possible might be more effective than trying to achieve high levels of coordination.

Although opportunities for competition in the public sector are scarce, with imagination some could be created. Many public entities that provide goods or services nationwide could divide their operations to discriminate among markets: mail services, railways and buses, agricultural marketing and the supply of farm inputs, even some of the central ministries. One effective way of introducing a more competitive atmosphere is through decentralization, especially of those institutions with a national coverage. A wide array of public institutions, from central ministries to highly specialized agencies, could decentralize their operations but remain a single entity, or they could be broken up into regional units.[30] Decentralization increases competitive pressures in several ways, particularly if management reinforces the competitive environment. It brings the institution closer to beneficiaries or clients, making that type of competitive pressure more effective. It also introduces the possibility of generating some form of competition among the decentralized units. In spite of regional differences, mechanisms can be designed to compare performance among units.

Another extension of this concept is to induce competition between teams or sections within an agency. In some circumstances this might be done by holding contests or offering bonuses. A greater challenge is to structure organizations so that units vie with each other in demanding better performance from, and providing better service to, other units within the institution. As indicated before, technical departments can put pressure on other units so that their output does not jeopardize the technical activities (in this case the specificity and competition surrogates coincide). And the units that are directly exposed to the effects of external competition can pressure those that are not. Most of the successful cases of institutional development contain some element of this approach. In the KTDA, staff in various sections—extension, leaf collection, transport, factory operations—have a strong interest in the performance of the section responsible for the preceding step in the tea production process. Leaf collection staff, for example, are expected to deliver quality leaf to factories and therefore put pressure on extension staff. This process is backed up by the management's spot-checking system and by buyer-seller relationships within the KTDA—for example, factories can refuse to buy poor leaf from collection centers, which in turn can refuse to buy poor leaf from growers unless it is sorted before purchase. As shown in the next chapter, similar structural pressures are part of the training and visit system in which farmers' pressures on the agricultural extension staff encourage them to put pressure on subject matter specialists to come up with more relevant solutions.

For these measures to be fully effective, however, several other structural changes are required. Managerial accountability has to be substantially decentralized so that managers are made responsible for performance over which they have direct control. This has implications for the definition of performance criteria and budgeting procedures. Similarly, the general incentives that such changes and competition surrogates would provide to the staff need to be reinforced by personal incentives for better performance. Pay scales and promotions could be based more on criteria of performance and output, so far as that is feasible in public sectors. Such measures need to be complemented by increased personal responsibility, which calls for an emphasis on evaluation and job assessment. Otherwise, the situation would be similar to that of agencies which are exposed to economic competition but have their hands tied by regulations and controls.

The final category of internal competitive pressures is evaluation, which could be internal; external by clients, suppliers, politicians, or regulators; and mixed. Much has been written about internal evaluation, but its effects have been limited. Evaluation from above, by another unit of the central government, is an old technique used with varying degrees of success in developed and developing countries. For the rest, the subject is largely unexplored.

The limited success of monitoring and evaluation is regrettable. Monitoring in particular was designed as a shortcut to bypass ponderous and largely ineffective management information systems. The World Bank has promoted it in many institutions, particularly in agriculture. The main difficulties have been managers' reluctance—often the consequence of lack of understanding—to support and make use of the system, and an excessive emphasis on the purely statistical and data processing aspects of the activity. In principle, monitoring and evaluation could be a valuable tool for inducing better performance, but its use should be selective, more economical, and driven by the interest of the managers.

Clearly something different is required. Some form of performance evaluation undertaken by the clients or users, by themselves or with the institution, holds promise. It could be an integral part of training clients on the best use of the services provided. To be effective, evaluation has to be done by independent evaluators who have adequate access to relevant information, and it has to have a system for feedback to the operations of the agency. One prerequisite for success is the commitment of management to profiting from the evaluation, but the conditions under which such a system will work need further study. If there is too much imbalance between the size and power of the institutions and the clients, joint or partial evaluations might be more appropriate. A tripartite approach, including an independent entity to ensure impartiality, is also feasible.

It is unlikely that a package of external and internal competition and competition surrogates and the structural changes just described could be fully implemented except in a handful of cases. Partial applications would also be useful, however, and should not be discounted. Much more difficult is to determine in which cases competitive pressures will have a positive rather than a negative impact.

Notes

1. W. Richard Scott, *Organizations: Rational, Natural, and Open Systems* (Englewood Cliffs, N.J.: Prentice-Hall, 1981); and James D. Thompson, *Organizations in Action: Social Science Bases of Administrative Theory* (New York: McGraw-Hill, 1967).

2. David C. Korten, "Community Organization and Rural Development: A Learning Process Approach," *Public Administration Review*, vol. 40, no. 5 (September-October 1980), pp. 480–511.

3. Harold Wilensky, "The Professionalization of Everyone?" *American Journal of Sociology*, vol. 70, no. 2 (September 1964), pp. 137–58.

4. Scott, *Organizations*, pp. 222–23.

5. Amitai Etzioni, *A Comparative Analysis of Complex Organizations*, rev. ed. (New York: Free Press, Macmillan, 1975), p. 142.

6. Roland Kenneth Harrison, *Work and Motivation: A Study of Village-Level Agricultural Extension Workers in the Western State of Nigeria* (Ibadan: Nigerian Institute of Economic and Social Research, 1968), p. 258.

7. Peter Blau, *Bureaucracy in Modern Society* (New York: Random House, 1956), pp. 61–66.

8. See David K. Leonard, *Reaching the Peasant Farmer: Organization Theory and Practice in Kenya* (Chicago, Ill.: University of Chicago Press, 1977), chaps. 3 and 4.

9. Many writers claim that conditions are more favorable when the work is performed by several small groups, but little is said about individuals working by themselves. Working in isolation is probably less conducive to good performance than working in a small group.

10. Sven Steinmo, "Linking the Village to Modern Health Systems," in *Institutions of Rural Development for the Poor: Decentralization and Organizational Linkages*, David K. Leonard and Dale R. Marshall, eds. (Berkeley: University of California, Institute of International Studies, 1982), pp. 160–61.

11. Leonard, *Reaching the Peasant Farmer*, chap. 6.

12. See David Werner and William Bauer, "Helping Health Workers Learn" (Palo Alto, Calif.: Hesperian Foundation, 1982; processed).

13. See, for example, Martin Landau and Richard Stout, "To Manage Is Not to Control: The Danger of Type II Errors in Organizations," *Public Administration Review*, vol. 39, no. 2 (March-April 1979), pp. 148–56.

14. See Peter M. Blau and W. Richard Scott, *Formal Organizations* (San Francisco, Calif.: Chandler, 1962).

15. See Dennis J. Casley and Denis A. Lury, *Monitoring and Evaluation of Agriculture and Rural Development Projects* (Baltimore, Md.: Johns Hopkins University Press, 1982).

16. Lawrence F. Salmen, *Listen to the People: Participant-Observer Evaluation of Development Projects* (New York: Oxford University Press, 1987).

17. See, for example, Herbert Kaufman, *The Forest Ranger: A Study in Administrative Behavior* (Baltimore, Md.: Johns Hopkins University Press, 1960).

18. As discussed in chapter 4, and see Max Weber, *The Theory of Social and Economic Organization*, A. M. Henderson and Talcott Parsons, eds. (Glencoe, Ill.: Free Press, 1947).

19. See Gerald D. Bell, "Determinants of Span of Control," *American Journal of Sociology*, vol. 73 (July 1967), pp. 100–03.

20. Scott, *Organizations*, p. 233.

21. Geoffrey Lamb and Bernard Shaeffer, "Market Surrogates," World Bank, Projects Policy Department, Washington, D.C., March 1981, p. 1.

22. John R. Nellis, *Public Enterprises in Sub-Saharan Africa*, World Bank Discussion Paper 1 (Washington, D.C., 1986).

23. For the experience on divestiture in developing countries, including privatization and liquidation of public enterprises, see Elliot Berg and Mary M. Shirley, *Divestiture in Developing Countries*, World Bank Discussion Paper 11 (Washington, D.C., 1987). See also Gabriel Roth, *The Private Provision of Public Services in Developing Countries* (New York: Oxford University Press, 1987).

24. Samuel Paul, *Community Participation in Development Projects: The World Bank Experience*, World Bank Discussion Paper 6 (Washington, D.C., 1987).

25. Robert Chambers, *Rural Development: Putting the Last First* (London: Longman, 1983).

26. Korten, "Community Organization and Rural Development."

27. Helio Beltrão, "Debureaucratization and Freedom," Brazil National Debureaucratization Program, April 1982; processed.

28. Lamb and Shaeffer, "Market Surrogates," p. 13.

29. Leroy P. Jones, "Towards a Performance Evaluation Methodology for Public Enterprises: With Special Reference to Pakistan," paper presented at the International Symposium on Economic Performance of Public Enterprises, sponsored by the U.N. Department of Technical Cooperation, Islamabad, November 1981. See also Young C. Park, *A System for Evaluating the Performance of Government-Invested Enterprises in the Republic of Korea*, World Bank Discussion Paper 3 (Washington, D.C., 1987).

30. These suggestions are made only from the managerial and administrative point of view. Although the political ramifications of decentralization or regional devolution are far-reaching and would be a central element in a decision of this kind, they are not considered here.

10 A Successful Managerial Approach: The Training and Visit System of Agricultural Extension

The training and visit (T&V) system of agricultural extension is a managerial approach that successfully combines many of the operational conclusions described in the previous chapters. The system was designed, promoted, and implemented by an Israeli expert, Daniel Benor, one of the most remarkable and successful men in the development field. It has been applied in many countries in Asia, Africa, and Latin America, but notably in India, Indonesia, and Thailand. In recent years, its application in Africa has expanded rapidly. In particular, the efforts in Burkina Faso, Côte d'Ivoire, and Kenya have shown important successes. Steps have also been taken to apply the principles of T&V to programs in population and health and are under consideration for certain types of education services. The World Bank alone has helped finance more than ninety projects based on this approach.

The T&V system is an organizational and managerial approach which happens to have been applied first to rural extension systems. Its principles are extremely simple. Its purpose is to develop a professional extension service capable of providing farmers in developing countries with technical advice. The emphasis is on communicating to farmers relatively simple technical know-how and improved agricultural management practices so that they can increase production and eventually make more efficient use of available inputs, credit, and research. To achieve this, farm families are aggregated into groups and each group is assigned to a village extension worker (VEW). A VEW usually has eight such groups assigned to him, each of about 100 farmers, although the exact number may vary widely according to local conditions. On a fixed day, generally once every two weeks, the VEW visits each "contact farmer" and any interested members of his group in that farmer's field. The contact farmer is responsible for communicating messages between his group and the VEW. The ratio between farmers and contact farmers also varies but is generally one to ten. Every two weeks VEWs also participate in a training session conducted by subject matter specialists (SMSs), during which field problems arising in the previous two weeks are identified and resolved, and recommendations to be stressed in the coming two weeks are reviewed in depth and practiced in the field. The VEWs devote all their time to these duties and are therefore relieved from all other activities and operate under a single line of command; they report to an agricultural extension officer (AEO) with whom they meet routinely.[1]

The frequent contacts between farmers and VEWs are built into the system to prompt the extension worker to seek improved technical solutions which he discusses during training sessions with SMSs and other VEWs. The SMSs, in turn, work with research centers to respond to farmers' questions and seek solutions to their problems. SMSs are also trained by staff from the research centers. Thus a dynamic link emerges between the farmers, the VEWs and their supervisors, and the SMSs and the research workers.

Basic Principles of Organization and Management

What is so special about this? At first sight, it appears to be just another organization for rural extension. A closer look at it from the perspective of this study, however, suggests that such an organization could (and should) have a profound influence on the effectiveness of many low-specificity, particularly people-oriented, activities and perhaps others as well. It combines many of the operational implications derived from the preceding analysis and applies intelligently a number of basic principles of organization and management that are often forgotten.

First, T&V brings to agriculture, which is probably the most difficult activity to manage, the discipline derived from specificity and competition. It does so by striking the right balance between a tight, simple organizational structure and a flexible operational content. Because an extension service is highly scattered geographically and extension workers operate by themselves over a large territory, there is no factory or office from which to exercise control. Instead, T&V provides clear and simple lines of authority, separating staff (SMSs) and line functions. It also insists on some standards of discipline which appear modest in comparison with other activities, but which are revolutionary in the context of less developed agricultural areas. For example, it ensures that the visits to farmers take place on the same day of the week and, if possible, specifies whether in the morning or the afternoon.

Within that rigid organizational skeleton, which simulates as much as possible the discipline of a factory, a high degree of flexibility is achieved through the continuous interaction between farmers, extension workers, SMSs, and researchers. When working well, the mechanism is extremely responsive to the needs of the clients and permits those clients to exert effective pressure on the institution. In this respect, T&V internalizes a form of competition surrogate. The strength of the clients' pressure comes from their continuous interaction with the extensionist and from his interaction with the higher levels. Whatever farmers' organization is in place will also find a channel through which to exercise pressure. The extension service is not meant to be a cut and dried activity directed entirely from the top.

Second, T&V provides permanent technical support to the main actors in this play: the extension workers. This is an absolutely crucial point. The extension worker has to deal with a most complex situation: large numbers of farmers, large areas, and often an unclear technology that has to be adapted to the specific circumstances of each farmer. And extension workers are left to work alone, with only sporadic training and supervision. They are expected to be not only good technicians, but also good promoters and psychologists—to be sympathetic—so that they can induce farmers to adopt the recommendations and change their behavioral pattern. Extensionists have to be good not only in the technical aspects of agricultural production, but also in its economic implications, to assess whether specific recommendations make sense to each group of farmers. Many extensionists have the additional handicap of being younger than the farmers they are trying to advise.

Upon careful reflection, one realizes that this is an impossible assignment, especially for low-level workers with a relatively poor education and poor pay. It is surprising that similar situations have continued for so long in other services. Like the extension worker, health workers, teachers, and others who provide services and technical assistance to large numbers of people need much more professional and administrative support than they normally get. There is no reason to expect that anyone would be able to deal with such an assignment on his own. The heavy emphasis on continuous training and professional support from subject matter specialists in T&V is a promising way of solving this dilemma. The traditional approach, of assuming that professional support will come largely from the line supervisors, is not feasible in this type of activity. A much heavier and systematic staff function is required.

In fact, the word "training" is too limiting to reflect what should take place in the fortnightly sessions with the SMSs. Training, indeed, but also debriefing of the field experience and advice on how to approach particular situations. The SMS should learn as much as the extensionist, and the exchange of views among extensionists should be as important as the role of the SMS.

In practice, many SMSs have fallen short of this ideal; some have been narrow technicians that have contributed little beyond their specialty. But, as programs are developed following the principles of T&V, the staff function of the SMSs should evolve along the lines described. The origin of staff functions—as distinct from line functions—was the need for persons who have more professional knowledge and experience than the line staff and supervisors and who are free from managerial responsibilities. The hypothesis here is that most people-oriented activities require such a strong degree of professional support that staff functions along the lines proposed by T&V are essential to achieve a high level of performance. In most instances, the field-worker cannot be expected to perform adequately on his own or only with some help from his immediate supervisor; he needs continuous support and training. The organizational form of this highly intensive staff function will depend on the particular circumstances; it does not necessarily have to be the solution arrived at by T&V.

Third, T&V simulates a competitive atmosphere without being competitive in the economic sense. When working well, the direct and continuous contact between farmers and extensionists enables the farmers to pressure the extensionists and improve the quality of their work. Similarly, the extension workers put pressure on the SMSs and researchers by giving them fast feedback on the results of their recommendations and information about the technical requirements of the farmers. T&V can be seen as a moving chain in which each part puts pressure on the others to keep moving in the right direction.

Fourth, the whole operation, including supervision and control, is oriented toward actual results in the field. The salient points are that these are final results, not intermediate steps; and they are found in the farmer's field, not in the extensionist's office. If the extension work has a noticeable effect, little supervision is needed, but if the results are poor, special attempts are made to evaluate the situation. T&V has also cut through the bureaucratic maze to greatly reduce the paperwork and reporting required. Written reports by the VEWs are kept to an absolute minimum; communication is primarily oral, particularly through the training sessions. This combination of emphasis on results in the field and de-emphasis on office work and report writing is probably one of the main explanations of T&V's success. The T&V effort to minimize report writing is a major contribution; it is consistent with "intermediate technology" and modest ambitions and introduces a touch of realism.

It may be argued that de-emphasizing monitoring and evaluation and report writing greatly reduces the chances of learning from experience. Many of the new activities in the development field are experimental and difficult to plan accurately because of the lack of knowledge and the dependence on behavioral factors—they are what Hirschman calls "voyages of discovery." A mechanism for learning from experience is therefore thought to be essential to enable managers to redesign the program and change course whenever necessary. That may be so, and a whole school of thought has emerged around this point. My hypothesis, however, is that above a minimum level, written reports will not serve a useful purpose and will detract from achieving the basic objective of the exercise, in this case an increase in agricultural production. An intermediate "output" such as report writing is an elegant and widely used way to avoid grappling with the real issues. It would be preferable to have fewer records and to learn less, but to increase the chances of achieving the basic objectives of the program. Success is a far more powerful teacher than reporting. Furthermore, the more profound knowledge that contributes to the design of future operations is acquired over the long term and comes mainly from special evaluation studies undertaken outside the institutions in charge. T&V has a built-in learning process for all the participants; it takes place in training and in the planned interaction at all levels. This form of learning is the most effective in an operational context. Whatever simple records are kept in this learning process would certainly be more valuable for the operation than would lengthy reports.

Fifth, T&V gives training a new meaning. Continuous education and training of staff have a long history and a well-deserved reputation for being worthwhile. But in T&V training is continuous in a different way: it is part of the normal activities and enmeshed with actual operations. As such, it is influenced by the activities themselves and becomes much more relevant and an integral part of the staff functions. The broad nature of training is closely linked to the serious attempts in T&V systems to promote socialization and professionalization. Training undertaken in this way inevitably induces an esprit de corps and pride in the activity, which together with success—results in the field—has generated an important sense of professional responsibility among the extensionists and helped reinforce the internal norms and behavioral patterns.

Sixth, T&V defines a small number of "impact points," or areas on which efforts will focus; that is, it pays particular attention to the clarification and simplification of goals. These impact points are carefully selected to ensure that they are important concerns of farmers and offer a good chance of success in a relatively short time. This selectivity of the T&V system contrasts with programs that try to achieve too much on too many fronts at the same time.

Seventh, T&V recommends only feasible improvements that do not require major changes in current practices. This limitation is not only part of the orientation toward goal simplification, but also essential to the success of the program. One reason for the past failures of agricultural extension is that the system promoted complex and drastic changes, which farmers resisted—often with good reason, since they later proved to be the wrong solutions. In addition, those solutions required farmers to take unwarranted risks. T&V first attempts to make marginal improvements on existing production practices, often on a small section of the farmers' land; for example, if farmers are producing maize, the extension worker tries to identify and promote simple but improved methods for maize. Only after the credibility of the technical solution and the system have been established would T&V tackle more complex objectives, such as a change in cropping patterns.

Eight, T&V operates under the premise that not all constraints faced by agricultural production can be tackled simultaneously. The technology promoted by extension therefore tries to take into account the constraints faced by the farmers at a particular time. This is another aspect of goal simplification. If fertilizers were not readily available, for example, technical recommendations would not include the intensive use of fertilizer.

Ninth, the T&V program is postulated as an improvement or reform of the existing extension system rather than as a brand new institution. This approach, with few exceptions, offers less resistance and, again, is part of goal simplification. In many cases, however, the introduction of T&V does imply a radical change in the way extension is carried out—a change that should be seen as an institutional development effort and eventually undertaken at the national level.

The dynamic of the system is well reflected in a World Bank report which discusses the T&V experience in India:

> The most encouraging and, in the long run, the most important result of the introduction of training and visit extension is the development of a dynamic link between farmers, extension staff, and research workers. Frequent and systematic contact between research and extension is built into the training and visit system: direct, frequent, and repeated contact between farmers and VEWs (supplemented from time to time by SMS) forces the extension service to focus on technically and financially feasible recommendations for improving farm production; the VEWs' regular contact with research through the SMS gives them the opportunity to raise immediate production problems; and to respond effectively to such questions, SMS need to work with researchers to resolve field problems. Through this sequence, pressure is placed upon researchers to concentrate on the practical field problems of the average farmer. There are signs that such a linkage is emerging [in India]. Monthly workshops between SMS and research staff of agricultural universities and departments of agriculture are becoming a regular avenue of contact. The workshops provide a continuous forum in which the content of the fortnightly training of VEWs and [agricultural extension officers] is developed and field trials are planned and analyzed, reflecting actual field problems.[2]

Prerequisites of Success

Although T&V has been applied in many countries, the main effort has been in India. To date, twelve states have adopted it through projects which, when fully developed, will cover about 70 percent of India's net cropped area and serve about 64 percent of the country's farm families. Many indicators attest to its positive impact and evaluations are still under way, although, as usual, it is difficult to disentangle the effects of extension from those of many other factors influencing agricultural production. Given the very nature of the strategy followed, many of the most notable achievements are neither obvious nor dramatic; for example, the speedy modification of a technical recommendation in the face of a sudden scarcity of some input such as fertilizer or the amelioration of the damage caused by drought. Specific achievements include promoting the development of oilseeds and pulses in Orissa, expanding the use of a new variety of rice in Assam and of high-yield varieties in West Bengal, and increasing the yields of several crops in Rajasthan.

Among the prerequisites for the success of T&V is that it accept few shortcuts in its structure. The "direct, frequent, and repeated" contacts among all the participants are essential for the functioning of the system as it is originally conceived. Even if an apparently minor detail such as the schedule of visits is made less rigid the nature of the approach will change. If no resources are available for a particular level of operation, it is probably better to reduce the scale and coverage rather than to modify the structure.

T&V also requires that the organization be devoted almost exclusively to agricultural extension. Once T&V begins to be successful there is a danger that political powers and other institutions will try to use it to deliver other services and inputs, to collect information, or to be a political tool. This has proved to be a recipe for failure. Clearly, however, all the development institutions in a country could not simplify their goals so rigorously because the farmers and other beneficiaries would not be able to absorb the many services and goods from myriad agencies; nor will all services be organized with perfect purity. Some compromises will therefore have to be made. Since not all services need to reach farmers at the same time, a sensible solution is to introduce a phased approach.

Another prerequisite, especially for T&V but also for most institutional development efforts, is the need for a constant stimulus for long periods of time. T&V in India is expected to require special attention for many years to come. There has been considerable discussion of whether T&V would have succeeded without the constant impulse and support provided by the World Bank, in particular the leadership of Benor himself. I believe that this is not an issue. It would be unrealistic to expect that any institutional change such as the introduction of T&V could be implemented without considerable effort over a long period. It is an uphill battle that requires continuous encouragement and incentives to maintain progress in an environment with weak institutions. If some of these central prerequisites are not in place or there is little likelihood of a long-term effort, T&V should not be introduced.

The World Bank report just cited summarizes some of these prerequisites:

> It is important to recognize and understand well the nature of the effort involved in the radical organizational reform embodied in the extension projects. The work only begins with the posting of staff—which . . . is difficult in itself. Far more difficult to change are the operating procedures and attitudes of extension staff. Once the reorganization of the extension system takes place, a process of continuous improvement begins through identification of weaknesses and steps to remove them. This process requires intensive supervision and guidance to see that the extension system develops on sound lines . . . The detailed working methods must be checked and corrections made. Usually in each state extension service there are a few officers who understand the approach very well. It is necessary to reinforce and support their understanding and identify more such officers. The only way this can be done is through direct field supervision of extension operations, checking on farmer reactions to the extension service and adoption of recommendations, attending a sample of the widely dispersed training sessions, and discussing with all levels of the extension service what is observed in the field.[3]

Although achieving success in this field is extremely difficult, progress has been enormous. Many of the remaining difficulties have to do with modifying long-cherished attitudes and behavioral patterns: changing from an office orientation to a field orientation, emphasizing results rather than report writing, or abandoning comprehensive approaches in favor of impact points. Many researchers who have always had a more academic orientation still feel it is more important to publish a paper than to be of direct use to farmers. This attitude has changed in India and is beginning to change in other countries.

Criticisms of T&V

T&V has been criticized on many counts, but some of the most important ones stem from misunderstandings. The most common criticism is that no matter how efficient the extension service, it cannot do much to improve agriculture in view of the many other constraints: land tenure problems, inadequate transport, nonexistent marketing and credit systems, unrealistic prices, unavailability of inputs, and so on. It is true that until most of those barriers are overcome a fully developed agriculture sector is not possible. But it is false to say that progress cannot be made through better extension. On the contrary, the larger the number of constraints, the more useful a good extension system is in helping farmers adapt to the more difficult circumstances.

Perhaps this misconception regarding the importance of extension derives from the notion that a specific technical package has to be promoted among farmers. Usually those packages require several inputs and services, and the lack of some of them makes it difficult if not impossible to use the package. But the main role of extension is precisely to help farmers when conditions are not perfect. Technical packages usually have to be adapted to local environments, and this is what a well-conceived extension is supposed to do. The continuous dialogue between farmers, extension workers, and researchers is what permits that adaptation. In practice, the extension service seldom has to deal with the intricacies of promoting a specific technical package, but rather with what to do when the quality of seeds is poor, the fertilizer does not arrive on time, prices decline, a plague attacks the crops, or the rains are late. The more abnormal or unexpected the situation, the more the extension service is required. If all farmers were willing to apply the technical package, all inputs were available on time, and pricing and marketing arrangements were right, it might be possible to dispense with the extension system. It is the complexity, heterogeneity, and unpredictability of agriculture that make an extension service essential; industrial activities generally do not need that kind of support.

A related criticism is that often there are no technical packages and, as a consequence, an extension service has nothing to extend. It may be true that airtight, comprehensive technical packages are lacking. But wherever there are farmers, their production methods can always be improved. It might not be a spectacular improvement, but it probably represents considerable progress over the existing method. Often there is no obvious technical package or recommendation to begin with. On the first visits the extensionists concentrate on learning about the farmers' methods and problems; this information is brought to the SMSs, who propose some improvements themselves or relay the problems to research. The wheel begins to turn in this way, propelled by farmers' problems rather than by technical packages promoted by research.

Another criticism is that although T&V might be of some use with low-technology agriculture, it would not function well with more sophisticated techniques. This argument is hard to understand, unless one assumes that farmers will stagnate at a certain level. New techniques and situations will always arise, and it is highly unlikely that farmers at any level of technology will always be fully conversant with all the developments in the many relevant disciplines. Obviously, the nature of the extension system will change as the technology becomes more highly developed; perhaps fortnightly visits will not be necessary and the extensionists may have Ph.D.'s, but the same management and organizational principles will apply.

A more serious criticism concerns the cost of implementing T&V. Since T&V requires a large staff, especially for supervisory and training activities, the costs are higher than for a more traditional structure. But then it is the benefit-cost relation that is relevant. There is mounting evidence that the positive effects of a well-functioning T&V system will more than compensate for the additional costs incurred.[4] Even under very conservative assumptions, the rates of return have proved to be quite high. As Benor puts it, the poorest countries are precisely those that cannot afford to do without a good extension service. In fact, experience with T&V suggests that the main risk stems from an inadequate or partial application of its principles. Because of the unity of the approach, the absence or variation of a critical element drastically changes the nature of the system. In such cases, there is a high risk of ending up with an expensive and heavy organization and with few benefits.

Application of T&V Principles to Other Activities

To date, the T&V approach has been applied only to agricultural extension and partially to health services. But there is no reason it cannot be applied to other activities, especially those that provide services to geographically scattered populations faced with unclear or changing technologies. Activities that immediately come to mind are health care systems, including family planning, and programs such as nutrition and special education. The principles of T&V are also broadly applicable to less obvious areas, such as primary education, industrial extension, management of large agencies, and even internal auditing.

Health care, family planning, and nutrition programs encounter an environment similar to that of agricultural extension workers. They could benefit from the same discipline and organization that characterize the T&V system. A strict schedule of visits, for example, would ensure that health workers contact their clients regularly at predetermined times and thus would make field supervision possible. Health services sometimes suffer from having the workers perform numerous tasks for several agencies—the same problem that plagues extension. They would benefit from clearer lines of command, and the organizational skeleton of T&V could be applied almost unchanged. The details, such as the frequency of visits or the number of beneficiaries per health worker, would of course differ.[5]

More important differences appear in the definition of impact points, the two or three areas in which the program should concentrate. Health services distinguish between curative and preventive care. To implement a program in preventive health might require a change in attitudes on the part of the beneficiaries that might be alien to their culture and therefore difficult to achieve. In addition, many of the effects of preventive health are less obvious and immediate than those of curative medicine—or, in agriculture, of higher yields. Preventive health belongs in the same category as maintenance, which generates negative effects that require higher incentives to be accomplished and often a different set of cultural values; the outcome of good performance is nothing visible.

This presents a dilemma for the design of health programs because the best way to begin is through curative health. Later, as the positive effects of the program build confidence among the beneficiaries, preventive elements can be introduced which then would have a better chance of being successful. A similar dilemma appears with regard to the types of service to be provided by health workers. In agricultural extension, success has come from clearly separating technical advice from the provision of inputs or other services, such as agricultural credit. This has had the added advantage of freeing the system from having to deal with financial matters. The solution in health is less obvious; perhaps the best approach, particularly if the program begins with curative aspects, would be to combine the technical advice with the provision of a few medicines.

Health care, family planning, and nutrition services do have one advantage over extension programs in that their technologies have a wider application than agricultural technology and do not have to be adapted so much to specific situations. Some health techniques, such as malaria prevention, can be applied under extremely varied conditions. A disadvantage is that many of these techniques require a sustained effort over long periods of time and necessitate changes in habits that are difficult even for people in developed societies. Family planning programs are practically useless if the recommended practices are not followed consistently; boiling the drinking water will fail as a preventive health measure if it is done only some of the time.

What about the role of the SMS equivalent in a health program? As in agricultural extension, SMSs should train the health workers, provide them with professional and pedagogical support, and act as an intermediary between the beneficiaries and the researchers. It would be a mistake to mix the role of SMS with that of regional health centers or clinics to which patients are referred for treatment. Their function should be kept separate, although some individuals might play a double role in sparsely populated areas. The ratio of SMS to health workers could be larger than in agricultural extension, and perhaps the training sessions less frequent, depending on how much uniformity there is among the techniques being propounded and how varied the conditions among beneficiaries.

Similarly, the link with research could take on a different character in a health service. One can conceive of regional health research centers for developing new solutions and adapting others to local conditions. But it is likely that a larger proportion of the research would be undertaken at the national or even international level. Regional centers could act as intermediaries, bringing the results of national and international centers closer to the beneficiaries. "Research" in health could also have another connotation; it could refer to a higher level of expertise, in a regional hospital or in specialized national centers, to which the SMS equivalent could go for advice and training when additional backup was needed. This kind of "research" would probably be more scattered than in agriculture and more national in scope. A more complex organization might therefore be needed to make sure the network includes all the necessary components.

A similar set of circumstances prevails in several types of education, especially primary education. Rural primary school teachers are in somewhat the same situation with regard to their students as the extension and health workers with their constituencies. Because the students are in one place and not geographically scattered the teacher's job is a bit simpler, but one impediment is that the significant results of their teaching will not be apparent until far into the future. A primary education system could profit from following the principles of T&V because of the low level of preparation of the large majority of rural primary teachers and the practical difficulties of ensuring the quality of their performance on a daily basis. Continuous training and support are required not only to help teachers adapt to new circumstances, but also to upgrade their basic skills.

In primary education, the equivalent of the technical messages or recommendations of agricultural extension would be a fairly well-established and quite uniform curriculum, although cultural and regional adaptations might be necessary if, for example, values were to be taught. The role of SMSs would be similar: providing continuous training, helping teachers adapt to their specific circumstances, and advising on individual cases. Although at first sight research would not seem to be necessary, the intrinsic characteristics of this activity suggest that it would indeed be useful in adapting the educational system to the needs of the country and ensuring the quality of its performance. This research could be much more centralized than in agriculture.

It is beyond the scope of this analysis to go into the details of how the principles of T&V should be adapted to the different types of education, but their application could increase the effectiveness of an activity that traditionally has been difficult to manage, especially in the rural areas. In addition to forging links in the student-teacher-SMS-research chain, the approach can create a more disciplined organization—for example, by ensuring that classes take place on time according to a predetermined schedule and that the program of courses is implemented as required for each group of students. If combined with national exams along the lines discussed earlier, such a system could be a very powerful instrument for improving the performance of the educational system.

Instituting T&V principles in education could be an expensive proposition, however, and the logistical implications have to be carefully studied. The establishment of permanent contacts between teachers and SMSs, for example, implies mobility, which may require the purchase of transport vehicles. But if the expected benefits are remotely similar to those that have been achieved with agricultural extension, poor countries just cannot afford to turn down this opportunity. Upgrading their education system is an essential ingredient in the modernization process and worth much more than the expense. It could be an extremely productive use of development assistance.

Other applications of the T&V principles are being actively explored. In the case of internal auditing (and, by extension, accounting) these principles could make the unit more relevant to the organization, provide it with more discipline, and systematize relations between the auditing unit and the rest of the organization. A structure similar to that of T&V could orient internal auditing more toward supporting other activities of the organization rather than trying to control them; for example, the internal auditing system might work to raise the standards of accounting and financial management.

The same set of principles could be applied in different forms to a large national agency or ministry, such as education, health, or public works. In a medium size country, these will be complex operations with hundreds of managers at different levels. In large countries even state or provincial agencies will have those characteristics. Many managers, especially at the middle level, may have little education or experience and little or no training as managers. Like primary teachers, extensionists, or health workers, they require more professional support than is usually provided by the supervisor next in line. The hypothesis is that functional support, specifically for management, is necessary to improve performance. An SMS equivalent, tailored to each case, can provide continuous training and feedback for managers, organize sessions in which they can exchange experiences, and give them advice and support in the handling of operational problems. This role, of course, differs substantially from that of the original subject matter specialist in agricultural extension. The closer we get to "soft" activities such as management, however, the more the SMS job will be not only to provide training and professional support, but also to be a catalyst and to promote an exchange of experiences, which in principle should be more productive than the training itself.

Research could and should have the same characteristics as in the activities discussed earlier. All countries should have at least one management center or institute that will prepare management specialists, provide consulting services, and undertake research. But the nature of this research should change, just as the work of agricultural research stations has changed under the influence of T&V. Most management research should be oriented toward the analysis and resolution of the practical problems raised in the training sessions by managers at all levels. As I have said several times, a pressing problem in institutional development is how to adapt specific managerial and organizational techniques and approaches to the cultural and political realities of each society. And I have also said that inadequate managerial capacity is probably the most important bottleneck in developing countries. A promising way to improve the situation is to adapt the T&V principles to management along the lines just described.

Further Improvements in T&V

The best way to kill a good idea is to popularize it, get everyone to jump on the bandwagon, and then implement it so badly that it fails. At this point, the main concern of those interested in the success of T&V should be to make sure that when it is introduced, particularly in agriculture in Sub-Saharan Africa, it is implemented properly. In countries where a lack of commitment is evident the program should be aborted as quickly as possible to avoid further losses.

The basic structure of the T&V system could surely be further improved and refined, even for its original use in agricultural extension. One concern is the need for more systematic analysis of how to modify the basic structure to suit each application, especially when conditions differ markedly from those in which the system was originally successful (homogeneous, flat, irrigated terrain). If Daniel Benor is around there is no problem because he knows how to do it—for example, in heterogeneous, mountainous, rainfed conditions—but he cannot be around everywhere and forever.

Perhaps the most difficult and crucial period in all development programs is the start-up, when the new system is being introduced and the old one phased out. T&V is no exception. This is when the system is more susceptible to becoming a "top down" approach. An antidote might be to introduce some elements of the learning process approach, as propounded by Korten.[6] The objective is to bring together all those involved in adapting T&V to the particular circumstances and find a systematic way of jointly planning and monitoring the start-up period. If the approach is going to be applied to activities other than agricultural extension, the start-up experience of T&V should be reviewed.

In the case of extension, more could be done to increase farmers' participation at other levels of the system beyond their direct contacts with the extensionists. On a selective basis (perhaps as a reward to the best farmers), they might interact directly with the SMSs and the researchers; selective feedback at higher levels could be very healthy for the system.

Farmers need to be trained so they can make better use of the T&V system and learn to influence it. This training could be done by the organization itself or by another entity. From time to time, for example, a couple of farmers could participate in the fortnightly training sessions of extensionists. The principle behind these suggestions is to use more actively the potential pressure from farmers as a competition surrogate to help improve performance.

More systematic efforts could be made to increase the socialization (building up internal norms and commitment) and eventually the professionalization of the staff. Is it enough in all cases to build up socialization only through technical training? Could training be modified to enhance socialization? What other measures could be taken?

These few suggestions are offered to underscore one point: T&V is one of the few successes in this difficult area of low-specificity, noncompetitive activities, and it should not be allowed to stagnate or to suffer from misguided applications.

Notes

1. See, for example, Daniel Benor and Michael Baxter, *Training and Visit Extension* (Washington, D.C.: The World Bank, 1984); Daniel Benor, James Q. Harrison, and Michael Baxter, *Agricultural Extension: The Training and Visit System* (Washington, D.C.: The World Bank, 1984); Gershon Feder and Roger Slade, *Aspects of the Training and Visit System of Agricultural Extension in India: A Comparative Analysis*, World Bank Staff Working Paper 656 (Washington, D.C., 1984); Gershon Feder, Lawrence J. Lau, and Roger H. Slade, *The Impact of Agricultural Extension: A Case Study of the Training and Visit System in Haryana, India*, World Bank Staff Working Paper 756 (Washington, D.C., 1985); Gershon Feder, Roger H. Slade, and Anant K. Sundaram, *The Training and Visit Extension System: An Analysis of Operations and Effects*, World Bank Staff Working Paper 719 (Washington, D.C., 1985); and Richard Heaver, *Adapting the Training and Visit Extension System for Family Planning, Health, and Nutrition Programs*, World Bank Staff Working Paper 662 (Washington, D.C., 1984).

2. World Bank, Agriculture and Rural Development Department, "Agricultural Extension in India," AGR Technical Note 5 (Washington, D.C., August 1981).

3. Ibid., p. 19.

4. Feder and Slade, *Aspects of the Training and Visit System*; Feder, Lau, and Slade, *The Impact of Agricultural Extension*; and Feder, Slade, and Sundaram, *The Training and Visit Extension System*.

5. Heaver, *Adapting the Training and Visit Extension System for Family Planning, Health, and Nutrition Programs*.

6. David C. Korten, "Community Organization and Rural Development: A Learning Process Approach," *Public Administration Review*, vol. 40, no. 5 (September-October 1980), pp. 480–511.

11 Conclusions for Program and Project Design

Perhaps one of the most important operational conclusions of this analysis is that adequate consideration of managerial and institutional constraints will greatly change the design and complexity of programs and projects. Since the early 1970s, many development programs and projects, particularly those financed by international lending agencies, have included a large number of components. They have dealt with several sectors, subsectors, and geographical areas, involved a number of institutions, and tackled simultaneously multiple development constraints. In contrast, "old-style" programs generally addressed only one subsector, one institution, and one development constraint. As a result, some claim that programs and projects have become too complex and difficult to implement and that their effectiveness has been reduced. Others suggest that the increased complexity is necessary in light of the countries' new development objectives and strategies and that simpler programs would not be as effective.

This evolution of programs and projects stems from four main changes in the development field in the past two or three decades. First, it has been recognized that in any one setting there is a group of interrelated constraints on development, and attacking just one constraint will not be effective. When a road-building project is planned, for example, there may be several constraints that prevent the productive structure in the region from responding adequately to the incentive offered by the new road, and additional measures may be required to stimulate development. For this reason, some or all of the constraints may have to be attacked within one project or program. A program to increase agricultural production, for example, may have to ensure that investment and action programs related to constraints in irrigation, marketing, and roads take place at the proper time, either as part of one program or in some other way.

Second, development objectives themselves are now broader. In the previous example the objective may be not only the growth in agricultural production but also the wide distribution of benefits in order to alleviate poverty. Such broader objectives have come in part from the

193

realization that benefits are not automatically distributed among the population according to the prevailing social values and political objectives. Third, it has been firmly established that services such as education and health, which were traditionally considered to be more a consumption activity, are important influences on the level of production. As such, they are being included as components in development programs. And fourth, many countries, especially in Asia and Latin America, have already completed most of the relatively easy initial stages of the development process; they have built basic infrastructure and used up the resources most readily available. The second generation of programs entails less obvious alternatives and solutions that are technologically and institutionally more difficult.

The complexity of programs and projects has gone through three phases. Until the early 1970s, development projects were relatively simple: highways, irrigation works, school construction, and railway rehabilitation. In the following decade the trend was toward greater complexity: more components, more agencies involved in implementation and supervision, and multiple objectives. This increased complexity was found especially in the so-called new-style projects in integrated rural and urban development and in education, population, and health. In the World Bank's experience there are numerous projects that involved two or three executing agencies in the early 1970s, whereas similar projects in the same country and in broadly the same sector involved thirty, forty, or even more agencies in the late 1970s. In a sample of the new-style projects three-quarters of them had more than one implementing agency, and one-third of them more than four.

Many of these complex operations faced serious implementation difficulties, which were traced mainly to the strain they imposed on very weak institutional structures. Since the early 1980s these difficulties have reversed the trend in complexity. Recent programs are more selective of the components included and have switched from a regional focus to activities at the national level. In general, objectives are becoming less ambitious. In fact, there is concern in some circles that the pendulum has swung too far in the other direction and that programs do not contain the minimum ingredients for success.

Now the development community seems to be entering a fourth phase with the so-called structural and sectoral adjustment programs, which help finance investments and also introduce policy reforms. In these programs, the policy components seem to be increasing in complexity. Several instances of "integrated policy development" can be identified among the more ambitious adjustment programs. And, just as with the investment programs, the first indications of excessive complexity are beginning to appear. Goal simplification does not seem to have been an objective.[1]

These swings are caused by the lack of an adequate conceptual framework for systematically considering the institutional constraints in project design. The notes that follow try to develop such a framework on the basis of the analysis made in the previous chapters. It focuses on investments and institutional development, but it applies equally to policy reform.

The Problem of Complexity

There is no widely accepted definition of program or project complexity. A program is considered complex if it contains a large number of components, deals with several sectors and subsectors, involves many institutions at different levels, or tackles multifaceted technical or sociological issues. The degree of complexity that may be acceptable varies widely. Different environments permit the implementation and subsequent operation of programs with widely different levels of complexity, and a program that is feasible in some environments could be impracticable in others. The challenge to the designer is to establish the proper relationship between the objectives of a proposed project or program and the degree of complexity that is feasible in the particular environment. One of the main purposes of program design is to achieve a balance or fit between the program and its environment.

Although many factors influence that balance, the question of whether a program is unduly complex usually hinges on the need for coordination among components; the greater the need for coordination, the more complex the objectives. Components that are essential to the achievement of the program objectives need to be distinguished from those which, although desirable in their own right, are not essential. A successful rural development program, for example, may require water, seeds, fertilizer, credit, and extension and marketing services, which will inevitably entail the coordination of a number of implementing agencies. Whether other components (water supply or schools) should be added will depend on how much additional coordination will be needed. If the same agencies would be involved in the coordination of these additional components, the administrative burden might be too great; but if the components were separately designed and implemented, no added coordination problems would arise. In the latter case, the costs and benefits of including the components can be considered independently.

In matching program objectives against feasible levels of complexity in a particular environment, four groups of factors should be taken into account: technical, economic, institutional, and political. The technical factors are mainly those derived from the choice of technology. A nuclear power plant is technically complex, while a rural road program is not. In some cases, the appropriate technical solution may involve tradeoffs between elements of different complexity at different stages. To cite an earlier example, a capital-intensive method for building a road will add to the technological complexity of the project, but if skilled personnel are available it will make the management of the construction relatively simpler. A labor-intensive technology may be simple, but it could increase the managerial difficulties of building and subsequently of maintaining the road. If agricultural programs are based on simple technologies, few inputs may be necessary and they could be implemented by one or two agencies. But a higher technology needs more inputs—fertilizers, pesticides, and tractors—which may require the participation of several agencies.

The technical factors also include the scale of the operation—on the assumption that size adds complexity—and geographical dispersion. An education program composed of many schools scattered throughout a country will typically be more complex than a program dealing with schools in one city or just one school. People-oriented activities such as some education or rural extension projects will be inherently more complex than infrastructure projects, for the reasons discussed earlier.

The economic factors that affect the complexity of a project are principally those related to the synergy, or interdependence, of various components. The rate of return of two program components together may be higher than that of each of the components if undertaken separately. A rural road could have a rate of return of 10 percent and an agriculture project in the same region without the road, 11 percent, but the combined return if both investments are undertaken simultaneously may be 18 percent. Even more important are those cases in which each separate component would have an unsatisfactory return, but the combined return will be satisfactory. The amount of synergy varies widely. Some core components will have a strong interaction, while others are fringe components that add little to the total impact of a program. The latter could be eliminated if other factors indicate that coordination would be difficult.

The third group, institutional factors, has to do with the number of agencies in charge and with their capacity for effectively implementing and operating the various components and—a fundamental point—for coordinating among themselves to achieve the program or project objectives. The difficulty of this task is compounded when the components are implemented and operated by agencies that perform unevenly or that are located at different hierarchical levels—for example, when a central agency must coordinate with a provincial or municipal agency or when public and private agencies must work together. Disparities in the power and relative importance of agencies make implementation more arduous.

The absorptive capacity of the individuals (farmers, artisans, middlemen) who are supposed to benefit from a project or program is another institutional consideration. Can they reasonably be expected to utilize, simultaneously, all the different goods and services to be provided? In some cases, a phased approach may ensure better utilization. If institutional constraints are a serious impediment, it may be possible to deal with some of them by using expatriates as managers or advisers or by providing intensive staff training, but these approaches are seldom successful in the short run.

Finally, there are political factors, all of which are based on commitment—the extent to which the government, individual agencies, and key people believe in and support the overall objectives of the program and each of its components. This topic was extensively discussed in chapter 8.

The way the technical, economic, institutional, and political factors interact will affect the program design. From an economic point of view adding more components will probably increase the total rate of return of the program, but institutional constraints may call for reducing the number of components because they involve agencies with different levels of performance or unduly increase the cost of interagency coordination. How the technical and political factors interact depends on specific circumstances. Particularly difficult (and unfortunately very typical) problems arise in the case of components which are interdependent and therefore necessary for the program's success, but which imply a degree of complexity that strains the administrative capacity of the implementing agencies. Credit and extension services may be necessary, for example, to achieve a substantial increase in agricultural production. If such services are not already adequate, it may be very difficult to establish or strengthen them as part of an agricultural development project, and efforts to do so would undoubtedly add to its complexity. A separate program of institutional development would simplify implementation, but it might take years before the services became available. This is a difficult choice, and the best solution can be found only in the context of a specific program.

The basic problem is how to design a program that is complex enough to meet high-priority development objectives and yet is simple enough to be implemented and operated by the available institutions. In practice, the dangers stem not only from overdesign, which makes a program too complex for the country to handle, but also from underdesign. Some of the oversimplified operations now under way in several countries may be contemplating fewer components than are necessary to achieve the objectives.

Recommendations

The previous analysis suggests several ways of dealing with complexity. A good first step is to review carefully the relationship between program objectives and design. Objectives are usually defined in the political arena and are not always realistic in the light of the resource endowment of a country, including its administrative capacity. Previous chapters have already highlighted the crucial importance of goal simplification in exponentially increasing the chances of achieving those goals, particularly for low-specificity and noncompetitive activities.

In the hierarchy of objectives, some are relatively simple, such as basic infrastructure, and others are complex, such as rural development, a change in behavioral patterns of large groups, or policy reform. Although some objectives might appear to be simple (for instance, increasing the production of one crop), their achievement could require many inputs (seeds, fertilizers, roads, marketing) and a project with many components. In a program combining simple and complex objectives, the simple ones are likely to be achieved earlier than the complex ones (see chapter 4).

Program design should distinguish between the principal and the subsidiary objectives. The principal objective could be the opening up of a previously undeveloped region, which requires investments in transport, agriculture, and related training. This is the core of the program, accounting for most of the benefits. A subsidiary objective with limited relevance to the core could be the achievement of a certain enrollment in primary education. The inclusion in the program of a component dealing with this additional objective will depend on whether it is feasible in that institutional environment. In some cases the provision of schools would have a synergistic effect on the achievement of the primary objective of settling families in a new area.

A similar analysis could be made with regard to policy reform programs, which also try to cover all the bases. In each case the principal objectives (trade reform, export promotion, or public enterprise reform) could in theory be enhanced by a series of subsidiary objectives (simplification of import duties, change in some export regulations, or privatization of some public enterprises). But meeting the subsidiary objectives might generate resistance to the program and increase its complexity to the point of endangering the attainment of the principal objectives.

When a potentially desirable project or program does not appear feasible after the political, economic, institutional, and technical aspects have been considered, the solution is to reduce its complexity.

- ○ Divide the program into separate components or subprojects that can be implemented and operated independently so as to minimize the need for coordination.
- ○ Phase in the program over time, an approach that raises the issue of the optimal sequencing of the various components.
- ○ Use pilot programs or projects when the best approach is not clear at the outset.
- ○ Use minimum packages; this solution implies lower targets and

requires a special effort to determine which components are central and should be kept, and which are subsidiary and can be left out.

o Take advantage of existing strength—a leading sector or a strong institution—and cluster a limited number of additional components so they can be implemented either directly by the lead agency or with the resources controlled by it.

The issue of program complexity often boils down to a tradeoff between comprehensiveness and institutional constraints. In the haste to achieve results, many people in the development field commit the sin of comprehensiveness. If the diagnosis is that there are twelve major constraints to development, a program is put together that tries to deal with all twelve, with the predictable consequences of institutional complexity and problems in coordination. Moreover, to make up for the acknowledged lack of implementation capacity technical assistance is imported and, in view of the poor record of such services, in all probability it adds to the difficulties. Seldom is a conscious effort made to identify the few constraints that are the most important and that are likely to be successfully overcome in the short run: goal simplification again. Success itself will permit further action on the other constraints at a later date.

Adopting some of the principles of T&V would make it easier to strike a balance between complexity and feasibility in program design. Select a small number of impact points with high visibility and a good chance of success. Concentrate on those points until the program has generated sufficient goodwill and enjoyed enough success to make further actions much easier. If a rather large degree of complexity is inevitable, there is even more reason not to load the program with components that are unessential for meeting the principal objectives. The excessive complexity of many policy reform programs should be a cause of anxiety in this respect.

Sometimes a choice must be made between regional multicomponent projects and national programs in fields such as agricultural extension, marketing, health, or education services. It seems unlikely that the result of several regional projects would be an effective national service. Would the health components in six regional development programs be a better vehicle for improving the national health organization than a series of six programs dealing directly with that health organization? There is no one answer to that question, however. Sometimes regional programs might help to reinforce a national system that is already strong, but they are less likely to succeed if the national institutions are weak. The only sensible approach is to design a strategy so that national and regional programs are mutually reinforcing.

Pilot projects and programs have a potentially important role to play in design. They are used to test technical and operational aspects on a smaller scale than in a full-size project. A different form of pilot project can be designed to test the tradeoff between economic objectives and institutional constraints—for example, to demonstrate the type of inter-agency coordination that would be necessary. Pilot projects and programs have the advantage of operating at the regional and local levels, where practice has shown that it is easiest to achieve coordination. The usefulness of trying alternative institutional solutions on a pilot basis has been questioned on the grounds that these solutions cannot be expanded to a broader scale. In spite of these doubts, a pilot project could lay the foundation for important institutional changes at the regional or national level. At the design stage there needs to be a fairly clear idea of the nature of the expanded operation and of the process by which the pilot project would lead into that operation.

Institutional development programs themselves are designed with a great sense of totality, which makes it easy to commit the sin of comprehensiveness. Programs begin with a complete analysis of the institutions involved, and the solutions proposed represent a package of actions which, if successful, would create "strong" institutions. But such an approach does not work. The principles of selectivity just discussed should be applied in particular to institutional development, by definition a low-specificity activity. A comprehensive attack on all the problems faced by an institution cannot hope to achieve "final" results in a specified time. Instead, a few aspects can be identified on which progress is feasible given the general operational level of the institution, and the program can concentrate on those aspects for a reasonable period, say, three years. After that, the progress that has been made will have ripple effects on other parts of the institution. At that point a new program can be designed that takes account of the new realities—including changes in personnel—but that focuses on another limited number of objectives. In sum, comprehensiveness in scope and in time should be abandoned in institutional development efforts, and a partial, cumulative, and highly focused approach pursued.

One last concluding remark. If there is one message that emerges from the analysis in this book, it is that the development process for most countries will continue to be a slow, painstaking process, perhaps slower and more painstaking than is generally acknowledged. The analysis confirms that financial resources are a necessary but certainly not a sufficient condition for inducing development.

Recently there has been much talk of a new Marshall Plan for developing countries. This is a good idea, but the shape of such a plan would have to be quite different from the original one. It would have to be for a much longer term, with no expectation of immediate and spectacular results, and it should focus, with patience and persistence, on the limited number of initiatives that most developing countries can hope to undertake successfully at the same time. In other words, a Marshall Plan for developing countries should include an institutional development component—otherwise, the financial resources could be badly utilized. The current emphasis on the adequacy and consistency of macroeconomic policies has been a much needed improvement over previous development strategies, but it should not divert attention from the slow and painstaking efforts needed to improve the countries' capacity to design and implement development programs in the public and private sectors.

Note

1. See Geoffrey B. Lamb, *Managing Economic Policy Change: Institutional Dimensions*, World Bank Discussion Paper 14 (Washington, D.C., 1987).

Appendix

The analysis of the World Bank's experience with institutional development, which triggered the development of the concepts of specificity and competition in this book, was of necessity largely qualitative. It was based on a central core of information from 175 ex post evaluations of World Bank–financed projects. This appendix gives more details about the way in which the material from those evaluations was processed; table 5 shows the regions and sectors represented in the sample.

The Bank prepares performance audits of all projects, generally within one year of their completion. "Completion" is, of course, an elusive concept, which is easier to define for infrastructure than for the provision of services, institutional development, or policy reform. Not only do the investment and operating stages coincide in institutional development programs, but also they generally constitute one phase of a long-term effort. Cases in which there was a series of operations with the same institution were therefore particularly useful for this study.

The performance audits are fairly thorough reviews, based on most of the available documentation about the project, interviews with Bank officers responsible for the operation, and, more often than not in this sample, visits to the project and to the country officials dealing with it.[1] Nevertheless, as indicated in chapter 2, their quality is uneven and the treatment of institutional issues varies considerably, depending on their importance in the project and the emphasis given to them by the evaluators. The methodology and approach followed by the evaluators also vary considerably.

The performance audits included in the sample were carefully reviewed for the purposes of this study, and in a few cases additional documentation was consulted and Bank officials were interviewed about institutional issues. I had done or supervised a considerable proportion of these audits. In addition to drawing qualitative patterns, illustrations, and general conclusions from the audits, I attempted a more systematic exploration of the information on institutional issues and institutional development programs. The method followed was to specify a number of explanatory or independent variables, which were drawn from the reasons given explicitly or implicitly by the evaluators for the success or failure of institutional development programs. Since these variables are

Table 5. The Sample of Evaluations of World Bank–Financed Projects, by Region and Sector

Sector	East Africa	West Africa	East Asia and Pacific	South Asia	EMENA[a]	Latin America	Total
Agriculture							
Livestock	4	0	0	0	0	5	9
Irrigation	2	0	1	0	0	3	6
Plantation	4	4	0	0	0	0	8
Rural development	5	2	2	1	3	3	16
Subtotal	15	6	3	1	3	11	39
Education	4	1	2	1	1	6	15
Development finance companies	1	1	2	2	7	4	17
Industry and pipelines	0	1	0	4	0	2	7
Public utilities							
Power	3	3	4	0	2	13	25
Water supply	2	2	2	1	0	1	8
Subtotal	5	5	6	1	2	14	33
Telecommunications	1	1	4	1	1	2	10
Transport							
Highways	10	8	4	1	4	8	35
Railways	1	4	1	1	2	1	10
Ports	0	4	0	3	0	2	9
Subtotal	11	16	5	5	6	11	54
Total	37	31	22	15	20	50	175

a. Europe, Middle East, and North Africa.

not quantifiable, I ranked them, some from 1 to 5, a few from 1 to 3, and others were used as dummy variables. These variables and their rankings were useful in finding patterns—the discriminant analysis was particularly important—and in guiding the analysis. Part of the exploration included a variety of regression analysis, including sensitivity analysis of the rankings, since it was doubtful how to rank many of the cases. Together, these explorations led to the identification of the sectoral and subsectoral patterns reported in chapter 3 and pointed to the need to develop the concepts of specificity and competition. Given the exploratory nature of this regression analysis, it is not reported here, although the raw data on the rankings are available on request.

The original analysis included one dependent and twelve independent variables. *The degree of institutional performance*, the only dependent variable, attempts to reflect a basic assessment of the performance of the institution being analyzed—that is, the agency that is the object of the institutional development program. In each case only the principal agency was analyzed, even though more than one could have been involved in the project or program. (Ranked 1 to 5.)

The twelve independent variables are:

1. *The degree of specificity of activity* ranks the activities performed by the institutions as a whole, based on the analysis in chapter 5, especially the specificity index. (Ranked 1 to 5.)

2. *The degree of competition* ranks the exposure of the agency to some form of economic competition as discussed in chapter 7. (Ranked 1 to 3.)

3. *The degree of geographical dispersion* refers to the extent to which the agency has its activities concentrated in one place or scattered geographically in operational units of different sizes. (Ranked 1 to 3.)

4. *The degree of political support (or commitment)* ranks whether the agency and the institutional development programs have support from the relevant power holders inside and outside the agency. (Ranked 1 to 3.)

5. *The degree of overt political intervention* ranks the degree to which the agency in general and the institutional development program in particular were subject to different types and levels of political intervention. (Ranked 1 to 5.)

6. *The presence of outstanding managers* was treated as a dummy variable, to indicate whether the evaluations recorded the presence of outstanding managers in charge of the agency.

7. *The effectiveness of management techniques* refers to whether the planning of the institutional development program and the application of management techniques were important factors in the success or failure, as indicated explicitly or implicitly in the evaluations. (Ranked 1 to 3.)

8. *Exogenous factors* were treated as a dummy variable and include acts of God and political and economic upheavals as discussed in chapter 4.

Figure 6.   Correlation between Level of Institutional Performance and Independent Variables Ranked 1 to 5

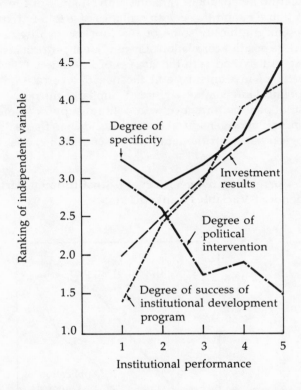

9. *Results of the investment* refers to the degree of success of the investment component associated with the institutional development program as part of the same World Bank–financed operation. The ex post internal rate of return as calculated in the audit (when available, otherwise a qualitative judgment was taken) was used as indicator. (Ranked 1 to 5.)

10. *The degree of success of the institutional development program* attempts to reflect a basic judgment about the success or failure of the program, as opposed to the performance of the institution itself. (Ranked 1 to 5.)

11. *Deficit or surplus* was a dummy variable to indicate whether revenue-earning agencies had a financial deficit or a surplus. For some calculations, nonrevenue agencies were treated as having a deficit.

12. *Low salary levels* were used as a dummy variable because several evaluations attributed low institutional performance and slow progress in institutional development programs to inadequate remuneration, especially of managers and key personnel.

The relevant results of this analysis are discussed in the text. The simple correlations found between the estimated level of institutional performance and independent variables with rankings of 1 to 5 are summarized in figure 6, and those with rankings of 1 to 3 in figure 7. The figures present graphically some of the conclusions discussed in the study: the close positive correlation of institutional performance with the degree of specificity and with the success of institutional development programs and of investments; and the negative correlation with the degree of political intervention (figure 6). Similarly, the positive correlation of institutional performance with political support (commitment), competition, and management techniques is shown in figure 7, although the tautological nature of the latter was discussed in chapter 4.

Figure 7.   Correlation between Level of Institutional Performance and Independent Variables Ranked 1 to 3

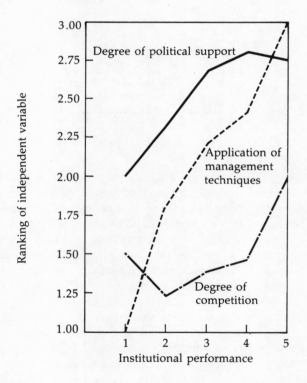

Note

1. In more recent years, the preparation of these performance audits at the Bank has changed considerably. In many cases, the implementation agencies in the countries prepare their own project completion reports, which are then used as the basis for the Bank's report. This, in turn, is vetted by the Operations Evaluation Department of the Bank and used as background for an independent performance audit, which is generally shorter than the previous reports and focuses on only a few issues.

Index

Accountability, 141, 142, 174–75
Accounting systems, 13, 36, 72 n4, 102–03, 162, 171, 190
Administration. *See* Business administration; Management; Public administration
Africa, projects in: effect of exogenous factors in, 33, 34, 166; effect of management factors in, 34, 35, 36, 38, 117, 178; success in, 20–21, 23, 24–25, 86, 87
Agricultural credit, 20, 33, 34, 40, 57, 95, 185, 188, 197
Agricultural extension, 26, 142, 147, 171, 178–87, 191–92, 197, 199
Agricultural marketing, 167, 170, 174, 185, 186, 193
Agricultural mechanization, 26, 49–50, 53, 96
Agricultural projects, 87, 102, 103, 122; effect of exogenous factors in, 33–34, 39, 40, 74, 82, 90, 96, 104, 167–71, 193; effect of internal factors in, 47–48, 51, 59, 69; effect of management factors in, 34–35, 82–83, 119; objectives of, 18, 116, 198; performance of, 19–21, 22, 23, 24–25, 26, 37, 86
Air traffic controllers, 63, 66, 68
Airlines, 81, 86, 122
Appropriate technology, 120–21, 122, 196–97
Argentina, 21, 39, 166–67
Arrow, Kenneth J., 80
Asia, 178, 194; effect of exogenous factors in projects in, 33–34, 167; success of projects in, 21, 22, 24, 87, 170
Australia, 170

Bangladesh, 167, 170
Bankruptcy, 100, 102, 103
Bauer, P. T., 3
Behavior. *See* Individual behavior; Organizational behavior
Beneficiaries, 134, 154, 184, 196–97; and institutions, 31, 89, 90, 95, 125, 135, 159, 167–71
Benor, Daniel, 178, 184, 187, 191
Bolivia, 21, 26, 87
Botswana, 86
Brazil, 23, 33, 38, 39, 104, 168–69, 172
Budget, 105, 136, 138, 142, 155, 172, 175
Bureaucracy, 37, 63, 119, 136, 142, 168–69. *See also* Public administration
Burundi, 33
Burkina Faso, 21, 36–37, 86, 178
Business administration, 28, 30

Cameroon, 23, 25
Central America, 87
Centralization, 117–18, 123, 171, 194. *See also* Decentralization
Chambers, Robert, 130
Civil works, 20, 25–26. *See also* Transport projects
Clients, 154, 164; and institutions, 31, 89, 90, 91, 95, 96, 101, 103–04, 125, 159, 167–72, 175
Colombia, 23, 24, 26, 39, 102, 142
Commitment: assessment of, 138–39; external, 135, 137–41, 142; internal, 131, 135–37, 141–42; political, 15, 32, 35, 40–41, 86–87, 105–06, 115, 132–42, 158, 203, 204; specificity and, 132, 134–35, 151–57

Community participation, 98, 103, 166, 167–70

Comparative advantage, 105, 117, 151, 166

Competition, 81, 82, 130; cultural factors and, 96–101, 123; definition of, 5, 89–92; degrees of, 15, 93, 203; external, 48, 89, 90–91, 93–98, 102–04, 165, 166–72, 173, 175; internal, 48, 89–90, 91, 96, 98, 99–100, 104, 165, 172–76; operational effectiveness and, 123–26, 165; public enterprises and, 37, 89, 90–91, 123–26, 166–67; specificity and, 104–06, 112, 146, 147

Competition surrogates, 89–92, 93–95, 98, 101, 112, 165–76, 179–80

Complexity, 13, 77; of projects, 23, 101, 116, 135, 186, 193, 194, 195–97, 198–99

Computers, effect of, 79, 162

Consultants, 38–39, 139, 141

Contingency theory, 136–37

Coordination, 23, 138, 174; interagency, 20, 118, 141–42, 170, 197

Costa Rica, 21

Costs, 62, 93, 102–03, 187, 195

Côte d'Ivoire, 21, 25, 178

Cultural factors, 29–30, 32, 121, 191; and competition, 96–101, 123; and performance, 50, 63–64, 104, 106, 167, 187–88; and staff, 60, 62, 127–29, 136

Decentralization, 96, 117, 118, 169, 174, 175, 194, 196, 198, 199–200. *See also* Centralization; Community participation

Decisionmakers, 114, 148. *See also* Managers

Decisionmaking, 29, 65–67, 72 n2, 78–79, 118, 147, 162–63, 164; political factors and, 101, 105. *See also* Management

Deficits, 16, 33, 85, 99, 102, 105, 119, 204

Development agencies, 1, 34, 114, 115, 132, 140–42, 193, 194. *See also* U.S. Agency for International Development; World Bank

Development banks, 23, 24, 36, 37, 40

Development finance companies, 19, 21, 22, 23, 33, 140–41

Development Projects Observed (Hirschman), 87

Dill, William R., 92

Discriminant analysis, 16, 203

Drought, 33, 34, 184

Economic factors, 195, 196, 197

Economic policies, 19, 32–34, 114–15, 125, 126, 131, 198. *See also* Tariffs

Education agencies, 22, 33, 57, 59–60, 142

Educational counseling, 49, 50, 53, 54, 55, 59, 62, 161

Educational services, 86, 100, 194, 196, 199; effect of exogenous factors on, 26, 56, 96, 105, 119, 170–71, 189–90; effect of management factors on, 131, 141, 155, 156, 160–61; effects of, 51, 63, 76, 80, 82, 157, 180; objectives of, 83–84, 148; performance in, 12, 22, 25, 31, 111–12. *See also* Primary education; Training

Efficiency: economic, 92; of institutions, 12–14, 85, 96, 119; operational, 13, 39–40, 95, 123

Environmental policies, 58, 64

Equality function, 127–30, 131, 155

Ergonomics. *See* Mechanistic approach

Ethiopia, 21, 23, 38, 86, 87

Etzioni, Amitai, 131

Exit (market action), 98–100, 133

Exogenous factors, 16, 31, 32–34, 78, 204. *See also* Africa, projects in; Agricultural projects; Asia; Educational services; Health services; Latin America, projects in; Low-specificity activities; Power projects; Railway projects

Experience, 76, 79–80, 157. *See also*

Skilled workers; Training
Extension services, 20, 113, 119,
  156. *See also* Agricultural extension; Rural extension services

Fertilizer projects, 12, 26, 33, 34,
  167, 183
Fiji, 21
Financial activities, 12, 23–24, 51,
  55–56, 140. *See also* Accounting
  systems
Financial aspects, 20, 22, 29, 34, 85,
  102–03, 119, 134
Financial institutions, 25, 59, 81, 90,
  140, 142. *See also* Development
  banks; Development finance companies
Financial resources, 111, 132, 136, 138
Ford Foundation, 1, 42 n3

Geographical dispersion, 15, 16, 96,
  179, 187
Ghana, 33
Goals. *See* Objectives
Guyana, 24

Harrison, Roland Kenneth, 150–51
Health services, 2, 100, 112, 187–89,
  194, 199; effect of exogenous factors on, 119, 167, 171; effect of
  management factors on, 84, 150,
  156, 157, 159, 190
High-specificity activities, 49, 76,
  105, 111; effectiveness of, 14,
  51–52, 58–61, 80–81, 84–85, 86,
  112–13, 148; management of,
  61–62, 63, 66, 67, 146, 156; and
  project objectives, 53, 56–57
Highway agencies, 18, 21, 22, 25, 38
Highway projects, 1, 39, 99, 195–96;
  effect of management factors in,
  22, 38, 117, 118–19; performance
  of, 21, 25, 193. *See also* Road
  maintenance
Hirschman, Albert, 3, 26, 87, 98,
  123, 133, 167, 181
Human resources, 111, 134

Implementation of strategies, 21, 78,
  114, 166, 187, 191, 195; effectiveness of, 3, 32, 134, 193, 199
Incentives: external, 48, 49, 93;
  internal, 40, 48, 49, 69, 106; and
  performance, 60–61, 62–64, 90,
  102–03, 104, 145–46. *See also*
  Competition; Management; Speci-
  ficity
India, 21, 22, 23, 33–34, 87, 143 n8,
  178, 183–85
Individual behavior, 51, 63, 64–67,
  75–76, 78–79, 82–83, 93, 133–34.
  See also Managers
Indonesia, 21, 167, 178
Industrialization, 14, 75, 76, 114
Industrial projects, 19, 21, 87, 90,
  102, 103, 121–22
Industrial Revolution, 13, 74, 75, 76
Informal groups, 106, 136, 139, 149,
  156
Information systems, 36, 136, 162,
  175, 181–82
Infrastructure, 26, 36, 87, 103, 116,
  194, 198
Inkeles, Alex, 75–76
Input-output matrix, 39–40, 77, 78,
  91–92, 126; and performance, 12,
  81, 122, 124, 155, 162, 163
Institutional capacity, 119–20, 121,
  198
Institutional development, 195–97;
  definition of, 1, 11–12; state of
  the art of, 28–31, 116
Institutional factors, 2–3, 4–5, 7, 29,
  31–32, 76, 112, 120–21, 195, 196.
  See also Exogenous factors; Internal factors
Institutional variables, 15–16, 201,
  204
Institutions, 134, 136, 137–40; effectiveness of, 2, 4, 12–14, 29, 31,
  37, 49, 79, 97–98, 103; flexibility
  of, 37, 62, 141, 164–65, 173, 179;
  intensity of, 118–19, 121; weakness of, 2–3, 22, 119–20, 184–85
Intensity of effects, 48–49, 51,
  59–60, 68, 93, 95

Interest groups, 99, 133–34, 135–36, 137–38, 141
Internal factors, 19, 21, 48, 49; in agricultural projects, 47–48, 51, 59, 69
Investments, 1, 2, 3, 15, 86, 112, 140, 198; results of, 12, 16, 24–26, 116, 135, 193, 204
Iran, 34
Irrigation projects, 20, 26, 34, 37, 103, 168, 193
Ivory Coast. *See* Côte d'Ivoire

Jamaica, 38
Jet engine maintenance, 49, 50, 52, 53, 55, 58, 61–62, 63
Job characteristics, 63, 66
Jones, Leroy, 172
Jordan, 33

Kaldor, Nicholas, 80
Kenya, 20, 21, 26, 178
Kenya Tea Development Authority (KTDA), 90, 169, 174
Kerr, Clark, 76
Korea, Republic of, 22, 23, 33, 36, 172
Korten, David C., 191
KTDA. *See* Kenya Tea Development Authority

Latin America, projects in: effect of exogenous factors in, 33, 34, 166; effect of management factors in, 34, 38–39, 178; success in, 21, 23, 87
Leadership, 31, 34, 36, 148, 158. *See also* Individual behavior; Managers
Leibenstein, Harvey, 3, 64–67, 77, 100, 123, 133
Liberia, 33
Livestock projects: objectives of, 35, 39, 57, 86; performance of, 20, 21, 23, 24–25, 26, 40
Low-specificity activities, 14, 49, 51, 54–55, 76, 115–17, 154, 155; effectiveness of, 57, 59–60, 63–64, 99, 111–13, 156–58, 164–65, 179; effect of exogenous factors on, 62,

105, 106, 138; management of, 66, 67, 78–79, 80, 121, 130, 158–61, 196; and project objectives, 53, 86–87, 96, 146–47

Macroeconomic policies, 19, 58, 120, 123–24, 132
Madagascar, 21, 25, 33, 34, 35
Maintenance organization, 4, 20, 55, 61, 105, 140. *See also* Jet engine maintenance; Road maintenance
Malawi, 23, 25, 36
Malaysia, 22, 24, 37
Mali, 13, 24
Management, 11, 24, 58, 61, 120, 141–42, 158–61, 171. *See also* Personnel management; Strategic management
Management science, 3, 28, 31, 150
Management techniques, 16, 32, 37–39, 96, 101, 116, 145–46, 161–64, 173–74, 203, 204. *See also* Training and visit (T&V) system
Managers, 15, 34–36, 38, 67, 79, 111, 154–55, 159–60, 164–65, 174–75, 203
Market economy, 92–93, 93–100, 104, 124, 125, 174
Marketing, 56, 60, 119, 173, 199. *See also* Agricultural marketing
Market surrogates. *See* Competition surrogates
Mechanistic approaches, 29, 30, 32, 75, 156, 164
Mexico, 33
Microeconomic theory, 64–65
Middle East, 33
Mining, 39, 86, 103
Modernization, 14, 64, 75–76, 83, 112–13, 120–22
Monopoly, 40, 85, 98, 99, 100, 102, 111, 124, 125, 169
Morocco, 24
Motivational factors, 41, 52, 66, 82, 151

Nash, Manning, 75
Needs-based approach, 31, 64,

117–20, 171
Nigeria, 21, 33
Noncompetitive activities. *See* Low-specificity activities
Nuclear power plants, 50–51, 58, 61, 63, 195

Objectives, 12, 92, 100, 126, 136, 137, 140–41, 162, 193–94; agreement about, 18–19, 40–41, 56–57, 87, 132, 133, 139; of agricultural projects, 8, 116, 198; defining, 48, 51, 52, 53, 56, 62, 95, 116, 171; of educational services, 83–84, 148; of livestock projects, 35, 39, 57, 86; and program design, 119, 197–200; of railway projects, 18–19, 57; simplification of, 101, 119–20, 146–48, 182, 183, 194, 199
Oil palm, 21, 23, 25, 86, 184
Oil prices, 33, 34, 127
Organicistic approaches. *See* Cultural factors
Organizational behavior, 48, 64, 93, 139, 149, 166–67, 185
Organizational reforms, 20, 34, 100, 116, 134, 141–42, 166, 171, 173–76, 185
Organizational structure, 51–52, 66, 141–42, 155–57, 161, 164–65, 173, 179
Organizational theory, 28–31, 65, 76–77, 133, 136–37, 143 n16, 150

Pakistan, 21, 33, 87, 172
Papua New Guinea, 23, 170
Paul, Samuel, 32, 47
People-oriented activities. *See* Low-specificity activities
Performance, 5–6, 11, 27 n7, 55, 75, 87; correlation with project success, 24; effects of, 57, 58, 59–60, 82, 92; effects of specificity on, 51–52, 57–64, 69; influences on, 48, 50, 85–86, 99, 100–01, 104–06, 126–32; input-output matrix and, 12, 81, 122, 124, 155, 162, 163; measurement of, 14–16,

62, 67, 115, 141, 154–55, 161–64, 175; regulatory agencies and, 101, 102–04, 166. *See also* Cultural factors; Incentives; Political factors; *and under specific kinds of projects*
Perrow, Charles, 77
Personnel management, 20, 31, 62, 78, 79, 145, 151, 156, 164. *See also* Staff
Peru, 21
Philippines, 24, 168
Piaget, Jean, 84
Pipelines, 21, 87
Planning, 3, 48, 119, 161, 163; effectiveness of, 11–12, 20, 23, 32, 36–37
Political corruption, 97, 118, 119, 171
Political factors, 31, 86, 95, 99, 134, 140–41, 171–72, 191, 195, 197; and decisionmaking, 101, 105; and performance, 21, 32, 33, 34, 37, 89, 93, 104–06, 128–31; and staff, 38–39, 62, 156, 159
Political intervention, 15, 39, 49, 50, 96, 99, 171, 203, 204. *See also* Regulatory agencies
Poverty, 96, 135, 167; alleviation of, 2, 47, 116, 147, 193
Power agencies, 21–22, 24, 33, 39, 86, 87
Power projects, 57; effect of exogenous factors in, 33, 34, 90, 102, 103; effect of management factors in, 18, 35, 36, 39, 155; performance of, 19, 21–22, 24, 26, 81, 87, 122. *See also* Nuclear power plants
Prices, 39–40, 119, 127, 142, 173; agricultural, 34, 39, 185, 186; energy, 22, 33, 34, 127
Primary education, 2, 37, 68, 69, 150, 157, 189, 198
Private sector, 3, 30, 31, 90, 98, 111–12, 119, 166, 170, 172–73
Privatization, 100, 167, 172, 198
Producer cooperatives, 95
Professionalism, 131–32, 148–50, 151, 155, 157, 159, 164, 182
Professionals, 65, 86, 115, 117, 136, 163, 178–92

Projects, 140–41, 194–200; success
    of, 19–26, 37, 132, 182, 197, 204.
    See also World Bank projects; *and
    specific kinds of projects*
Public administration, 3–4, 25,
    30–31, 42 n3, 56, 100
Public enterprises, 102–03, 120, 123,
    124–25; and competition, 37, 89,
    90–91, 123–26, 166–67; manage-
    ment of, 19, 91, 136
Public sector, 30–31, 56, 90, 111–12,
    119, 173–74

Qualitative approaches, 14, 98, 136,
    162, 173, 201
Quantification, 14, 15, 27 n8, 29, 31,
    36, 66, 155, 161–63, 203

Railway projects, 99, 100, 101–02;
    effect of exogenous factors in, 33,
    34, 103, 167; effect of manage-
    ment factors in, 36, 39, 81, 117;
    objectives of, 18–19, 57; perform-
    ance of, 20, 22, 23, 24, 25–26, 37,
    61, 81, 84–85, 87
Rationalistic approaches. *See* Mecha-
    nistic approaches
Regulatory agencies, 41, 56, 89, 113,
    120, 125–26, 142, 165, 171–72;
    and institutional performance,
    101, 102–04, 166
Resource allocation, 3, 13, 105–06,
    136, 140, 194, 197–98
Resource dependence approach, 92,
    96–101, 117–20
Reward for achievement, 51, 63,
    111, 142. *See also* Salaries
Risk aversion, 67, 83, 101
Road maintenance, 18, 22, 26, 63,
    69, 103, 118–19, 166–67
Rural development, 18, 33, 47, 83,
    86, 167, 194, 196; effectiveness of,
    20, 25, 142, 147; effect of man-
    agement factors on, 117, 158–60;
    objectives of, 116, 135. *See also*
    Agricultural projects
Rural extension services, 39, 105,
    150–51. *See also* Agricultural
extension

Salaries, 16, 39, 62, 99, 113, 117,
    126–32, 155–56, 159, 180, 204
Schumpeter, Joseph A., 3
Scott, W. Richard, 149
Sectoral adjustment programs, 2,
    147, 194
Sectoral patterns, 20–22, 23, 26, 86
Senegal, 24, 34, 102
Services, 1–2, 56, 81, 83, 111–12,
    194; delivery of, 126, 142, 159,
    170; effect of exogenous factors
    on, 78, 98–99, 104; performance
    in, 20, 25, 26, 86, 168–69. *See also*
    Educational services; Extension
    services; Health services
Simon, Herbert A., 64–67, 79, 133
Skilled workers, 39, 78, 80, 117,
    118, 127–28, 136–37, 149, 162, 196
Smith, David H., 75–76
SMSs. *See* Subject matter specialists
Socialization, 143 n11, 148–50, 151,
    155, 157, 159, 163–64
Social science techniques, 29, 30, 78
Spain, 22, 23, 25–26, 34, 36, 37
Specificity, 15–16, 52, 130, 145–46;
    and commitment, 132, 134–35,
    151–57; and competition, 104–06,
    112, 146, 147; definition of, 4–5;
    degree of, 13–14, 48–49, 74, 157,
    203, 240; and technology, 76–77,
    79–85, 86, 120–22. *See also* High-
    specificity activities; Low-
    specificity activities
Specificity index, 68–71
Specificity surrogates, 150–65, 174
Spread effects, 57, 59, 80–81
Staff, 40, 134, 137, 149, 160,
    169–70, 171; cultural factors and,
    60, 62, 127–29, 136; incentives
    for, 151–57; political factors and,
    38–39, 62, 156, 159; recruitment
    of, 150–51; seniority of, 50, 62
Standards, 13–14, 81, 96, 163–64, 165
Strategic management, 32, 113–20
Structural adjustment programs, 2,
    147, 194

Subject matter specialists (SMSs),
178–79, 180–81, 183, 188, 191
Sub-Saharan Africa, 23, 25, 86, 92,
100, 119, 149–50, 191
Sudan, 21, 35
Suppliers and institutions, 89, 90,
95, 125, 167–71, 172, 175
Syria, 33
Systems techniques, 29, 30, 161

T&V system. See Training and visit
system
Taiwan, 22, 34, 36
Tanzania, 21, 86
Tariffs, 22, 39, 93, 142, 198
Task environment, 92–96
Tea, 20, 24, 86, 90, 169, 174
Technical aspects, 20, 22, 23, 24, 25,
174, 195–97
Technical assistance, 1, 18, 19, 40,
86, 120, 135, 140, 180, 186, 199
Technical core, 77, 81, 86, 87, 165
Technical factors, 195–97
Technology, 47, 50–51, 54–55,
77–81, 101, 105, 114, 117; speci-
ficity and, 76–77, 79–85, 86,
120–22. See also Appropriate tech-
nology
Telecommunications agencies,
36–37, 80, 86, 90
Telecommunications projects, 57, 86,
87, 100, 155, 173; performance of,
13, 19, 21, 22, 23, 26, 36–37, 122
Textile production, 54, 55, 58–59, 62
Thailand, 33, 178
Thompson, James D., 72 n2, 77, 147
Time factors, 48, 52, 53, 54–55, 61,
77, 87, 134, 186, 199
Timmer, Peter, 39
Traceable effects, 58, 69, 83, 161
Tractors, 26, 49–50, 53
Training, 48, 49, 117, 149–50,
157–58, 197, 198; and institutional
effectiveness, 13, 20, 24, 31, 125,
145, 168
Training and visit (T&V) system, 142,

147, 148, 178–92, 199
Transport projects, 78, 119, 123,
173, 174, 198; performance of, 19,
185. See also Highway projects;
Railway projects
Trinidad and Tobago, 34
Tuden, Arthur, 72 n2, 147
Turkey, 21, 24, 35, 102

Uganda, 87
Uncertainty, 33, 77, 78, 101, 133,
136, 146, 147, 164
United Nations, 42 n3
Urban development, 18, 20, 21, 33,
100, 103, 140, 194
U.S. Agency for International Devel-
opment (USAID), 1, 16, 42 n3

Viet Nam, 33
Village extension worker (VEW),
178–79, 181, 183
Voice (market action), 99–100, 133

Wages. See Salaries
Water supply projects, 100, 102,
195; effect of management factors
in, 38; performance of, 21, 22, 24, 25
Weber, Max, 164
West Africa, 33, 86
Wheat, 54, 55, 82
Woodward, Joan, 77
Work environment, 156–57, 161
World Bank, 1, 115
World Bank projects, 2, 18–19,
40–41, 85–87, 132, 175; evalua-
tion of, 4, 14–16, 19–20, 23,
102–04, 105, 183, 185, 201–04
World Development Report 1983, 2, 17
n6, 114, 115

X efficiency, 3, 77

Yugoslavia, 24, 34, 167

Zaire, 33, 86
Zambia, 21, 25, 33, 35